OUR RUNAWAY RIGHTS

HOW TO RESTORE BALANCE IN FREEDOM

THE RESCUE OF CORE VALUES AND OUR COMMITMENT TO PROSPERITY

Author:
Rafael Augusto Carreras

1st Edition -   June 2017 / Revised April 2018
Editorial: Dr. John McAllister
Cover Design & Illustration: Kristian Lehner
Author Photo: Cornelia Bujara

Issued in print, electronic and digital formats.
Paperback: ISBN 978-1547155996

For reference visit: http://www.collectionscanada.gc.ca/ciss-
ssci/app/index.php?lang=eng

Publisher:
Carreras, Rafael Augusto. "Our Runaway Globe. Self-Published via
Createspace, Charleston, 2018
www.createspace.com

Printed and bound in the United States
First printing: June 2017
10 9 8 7 6 5 4 3 2 1

DEDICATION

I dedicate this book to every human being in search of equality, respect, and, above all, social reciprocity.

QUOTE on HUMAN RIGHTS

"All human beings are born free and equal in dignity and rights. They are endowed with reason and conscience, and should act towards one another in a spirit of brotherhood."

— United Nations, Charter, 1945

IMPORTANT MESSAGES

Peace and harmony is not in the taking, but in the sharing.

— Rafael Augusto Carreras

Fleeting reciprocity invites prosperity to slowly vanish into no man's land.

— Rafael Augusto Carreras

THE RUNAWAY TRILOGY

Our Runaway Society

Our Runaway Globe

Our Runaway Rights

===

Note

This book is a work of non-fiction. Not a single word or name used in this book is to convey, infer, imply, denote or transmit any kind of intolerance, animosity, hostility, hatred, or discrimination. It is merely to describe what in my personal point of view I see as our reality and with the best of intentions at heart. In some examples, the names used are not real to protect the identity of the people.

Without Prejudice

This book has been written without prejudice and represents solely the points of view and personal opinions of the author. These opinions are written and expressed with respect and autonomy in every concept, idea, and word used in this book, which are formed from decisions based on personal experience and facts from various sources. The research and book were based and written without abandonment of any claim, privilege, or right, and without implying an admission of liability.

TABLE OF CONTENTS

INTRODUCTION

Humans evolve slowly, always with hopes of improvement, but also with continually repeated mistakes. The stunning speed of technological advances over the past two centuries illustrates our strengths but also our weaknesses. These advances are our Achilles heel. To safeguard our privacy, security, and freedom, we have to capitalize on them logically and coherently. Equality, respect, and reciprocity are critical for a peaceful and prosperous society, but increasing numbers of us seem to repudiate these values. In a tolerant, multicultural society shouldn't these values be a common goal?

Oppression that is clearly inexorable and invincible does not give rise to revolt but to submission. – Simone Weil (1909-1943)

Weil's view made sense at the time, but now such oppression would clearly provoke a rebellion. If governments fail to perceive this, it will be their demise. The Democratic Party in the USA failed to see people's needs ahead of time, and a bold and visionary Republican candidate brought them to their knees. He went against the deeply engrained and conventional establishment that had lost the ability to protect and enforce the country's values, so he focused his attention on the majority's real needs. Yes, in favour of all those "silent-screaming" voices, which were only heard by a businessman, who has been trying to prove himself as the chief commander of one of the greatest nation ever established to date.

Equality, respect, and reciprocity are paramount for a peaceful and prosperous society. Unfortunately, many people think like David Lubar, who once wrote that "reciprocity is not mandatory." In a tolerant and multicultural society, shouldn't reciprocity be a moral and ethical requirement, and a goal for all? Or is the lack of reciprocity a justification for injustice and for some people's aggressive backlash? Europe has failed profoundly to integrate or assimilate immigrants, refugees, and asylum seekers because many are simply the wrong type of people. Europeans have focused on pleasing the values and identity of the newcomers, without paying attention to the identity, interests and real needs of the local people that greet them with open arms and good faith. Multiculturalism and diversity have failed to promote integration and assimilation, which ultimately bonds a country tightly together. This is now starting to happen in Canada with open liberalism, placing the country, to the eyes of many Canadians, at serious risk. Integration or assimilation is the ultimate goal, because immigrants adopt the ways and values of their new culture and become part of that new society, without forgetting their past. Without integration or assimilation into their new society, their different values will end up causing problems in the future.

My goal in writing *The Runaway Trilogy* is to promote a better understanding of the nature and importance of basic values and motivate readers to make the necessary positive changes to incorporate these values in their personal lives and social networks. We all ought to understand where we are standing at present and where we are heading, whether we like it or not. All the information in this book was collected from solid, reliable, and proven sources in the hope of bringing issues to light that many people think and worry about but that few understand well or are ready to confront or do something about. All my observations and suggestions are brought to the table in good faith to promote a peaceful, proactive, free society seeking equality and security.

The Runaway Trilogy focuses on three areas of our lives that cannot survive without each other. Part one, *Our Runaway Society*, deals with issues of personal growth. Part two, *Our Runaway Globe*, looks at the health of our planet. The third book, *Our Runaway Rights*, focuses on the underlying issues of our basic human rights, which are taken for granted by some, but are just an illusion to others. This Trilogy focuses mainly on North America, but the issues it raises resonate in every society on planet Earth. The trilogy shows how our personal standards and lifestyles, our relationships with our environment and ecosystems, and our attitudes towards human rights and freedoms have drastically changed in recent years, and not necessarily for the better in some instances. Some problems are under our direct control and can be solved. Others are out of our control and require us to adapt.

Although this book touches on subjects very different from those of the first two books, all three ultimately blend and hold hands around common ethical and moral principles that sustain us as human beings. To achieve a balance in our personal lives, in nurturing our planet, and in a fair and deserved realization of all our human rights and freedoms, we need to understand these issues first and then develop a devoted, relentless, and courageous determination to do what is necessary to rescue our human values.

Our societies have been losing their ability to practice logical and critical thinking along with common sense. Millions of people are aware of this, but unfortunately the great majority remain quiet and do very little, if anything, about it. They are afraid of being called biased, exaggerated, negative, racist, anti-patriotic, or obtuse. Their attitude is similar to that of Louis XV when he famously declared, "après moi le deluge" (after me the deluge). In other words, I couldn't care less what happens after I am gone. Is that an ethical, moral, or healthy thought? Absolutely not!

That attitude needs to stop now. The time has come to take the bull by the horns, dress ourselves with valor, pride, and courage, and do something concrete to ensure a positive and productive future for those who will come after us.

CHAPTER ONE: REASON, INTELLIGENCE, AND HAPPINESS

Reason

Reason is the ability to make sense of things and logically analyze their causes and purposes. Appropriate and balanced reasoning allows us to decipher reality and organize our perceptions into concepts and systems of thought that are structured in an orderly manner through a combination of sound critical thinking, logic and common sense. Reasoning allows us to understand and explain facts, which are the foundation of our conclusions. Thus, the Farlex Free Dictionary defines reason simply as "the basis or motive for an action, decision or conviction [and] the capacity for a logical, rational, and analytical thought; intelligence."

Critical thinking concerns the validity of our evaluation and conclusions. Common sense relates to acquired experience and the ability to successfully apply information learned through time. In reasoning, logic and common sense work closely together. An intelligent person is one who uses both logic and common sense, but above all, critical thinking to arrive at strong and dependable conclusions. Critical thinking objectively analyses and evaluates issues prior to a judgment.

Intelligence

Intelligence is simply the ability to understand, interpret, and apply concepts to deal with challenging situations. It involves the capacity to understand, learn and reason about relationships, facts, events, specific information, problems, and so on. Thus, it is measured by the ability to understand and apply knowledge using critical and logical thinking.

According to Albert Einstein, however, the true sign of intelligence is not the accumulation of knowledge or the efficiency with which it is applied, but rather the level of a person's imagination, together with the ability and skills to put what is imagined into effect. He warned that technology, although very important for human progress, could end up producing future generations of "idiots." Why? Einstein feared that technology would impair the human interaction required to achieve higher levels of intelligence, reasoning, critical thinking, and common sense. Steve Jobs (founder of Apple) had a similar view. For Jobs, imagination and creativity were the key to satisfy people's need for new products and services that they did not even know they needed.

In my personal understanding, intelligence is the ability to accumulate knowledge and apply it efficiently and wisely, in parallel with a great sense of imagination and the skills to combine all of these together for proactive goals and positive outcomes. An intelligent person is one who has strong insights and the ingenuity to achieve new alternatives and solutions based both on past experience and an open attitude towards change. But do intelligent people always have sound critical thinking and common sense? Absolutely not! Unfortunately, intelligent people cannot always have everything, and they sometimes utterly lack good common sense and logic. In many cases, this is their Achilles heel.

Not every intelligent person is reliable in making decisions, but intelligence nevertheless provides the basis for properly understanding problems. As such, it can enable good decision-making by others who may not be as intelligent, but who have good logical thinking, better common sense, and above all, a strong critical thinking process to achieve a balanced objective analysis and evaluation. Einstein was right when he said, "If you can't explain it simply, you don't understand it well enough." A person with a high IQ can solve complex problems faster, but may not necessarily provide answers that are applicable to concrete situations, unlike a person with a lower IQ who possesses good critical and logical thinking, common sense, and the ability to merge these to achieve a practical solution. Therefore, intelligence alone is not the solution for complex problems. Sound critical thinking, logic, and balanced common sense are also required. Solving problems creatively also requires the ability to access different levels of our brain's potential, something highly intelligent people cannot always achieve. In an article in The Telegraph (Nov 14, 2014) entitled "Why do geniuses lack common sense?" Helena Kealey proves this point with three examples:

1. Dr. Michael Woodley of Menie, from the Free University of Brussels believes that individuals who can be classified as geniuses have brains that are wired differently and are programmed to be unable to deal with small details. They are incapable of managing normal day-to-day affairs.

2. Dr. Woodley believes geniuses are "literally not hardwired to be able to learn those kinds of tasks. Every time they attempt to allocate the effort into dealing with the mundanities in life they're constitutionally resisted; their brains are not capable of processing things at that low level." Furthermore, they are, he says, often asexual, as their brains use the space allocated to urges such as sexual desire for additional cognitive ability: "you have a trade-off between what Freud would have referred to as libido and, on the other hand, pure abstraction: a Platonist world of ideas."

3. Dr. Matt Taylor accomplished one of the greatest achievements in space history as part of the team that landed a probe on a speeding comet, yet Dr. Taylor fits the mold of the highly intelligent and absent-minded scientist whose brain is too busy working on the challenges of his research to deal with the minutiae of daily life.

Happiness

Happiness is a feeling of satisfaction, contentment, cheerfulness, and pleasure, a state of delight and comfort without stress and worries, a feeling of well-being that surrounds a person's existence, a sense of gratitude, joy, and happiness enjoyed deeply by the individual. The website *Greater Good - The Science of a Meaningful Life* defines happiness as "the experience of joy, contentment, or positive well-being, combined with a sense that one's life is good, meaningful, and worthwhile."

But what determines happiness, and why is it achieved more by some than others? The best answer I have found was summarized in Bio-Medicine News (March 4, 2008) in an article entitled "Genes hold the key to how happy we are, scientists say":

> Happiness in life is as much down to having the right genetic mix as it is to personal circumstances, according to a recent study. Psychologists at the University of Edinburgh working with researchers at Queensland Institute for Medical Research in Australia found that happiness is partly determined by personality traits and that both personality and happiness are largely hereditary.
>
> Using a framework which psychologists use to rate personalities, called the Five-Factor Model, the researchers found that people who do not excessively worry and who are sociable and conscientious tend to be happier. They suggested that this personality mix could act as a buffer when bad things happen, according to the study published in the March issue of Psychological Science, a journal of the Association for Psychological Science.

Dr. Laurie Santos, from Yale University, teaches a course of how to be happy (April of 2018). She says that happiness is mainly achieved when people show gratitude to others, they procrastinate less, and they focus in increasing positive and productive social connections. Santos insists that by people improving their overall human behavior and characteristics, it will help them succeed more in life, and therefore, enjoy a happier living.

At greatergood.berkeley.edu - The Science of a Meaningful Life, happiness is defined as "the experience of joy, contentment, or positive well-being, combined with a sense that one's life is good, meaningful, and worthwhile." Happiness therefore comes from the disposition everybody has to handle their reality. The better you manage your reality, the happier you are. Thus, when life provides a negative person with a basket full of lemons, that person can become bitter and sad, but if a positive person is given the same basket, they accept it graciously, because if there is nothing you can do about it, why worry? The positive person sees it as an opportunity to make a lemon meringue pie or a margarita (with salt and Tequila) or a syrup of honey and lemon to sooth their throat. They adapt and make the best of their situation.

Here are some interesting quotes about happiness:

- The pessimist sees difficulty in every opportunity. The optimist sees an opportunity in every difficulty. - Winston Churchill

- Success is getting and achieving what you want. Happiness is wanting and being content with what you get. - Meltzer Bernard

- The grand essentials to happiness are: something to do, something to love, and something to hope for. - Allan K. Chalmers

- Real happiness is having good health, something worth doing, proper focus, a feeling of well-being, close friends, a small mansion, a small yacht, and a small fortune. - Anonymous

As odd as it may sound, higher levels of intelligence tend to be obstacles to happiness. There is no correlation between intelligence and happiness, as a study of intelligence and emotional health at the University of Edinburgh (Edelson, Ed. "Nothing Smart About Happiness," *HealthDay Consumer News Service*. Aug. 14, 2005) found:

> According to the results, greater intelligence acts as a double-edged sword when it comes to happiness. On the one hand, smarter people are better equipped to provide for themselves; on the other, those same people may strive continually to achieve more and be less satisfied with the status quo. At low-income levels, the issue of resource acquisition may make a greater impact on personal happiness, but the effects aren't long-lasting. Just like the fading bliss of new romance, at some point, the happiness honeymoon ends. Rather than intelligence, the most salient factor contributing to self-reported happiness in the University of Edinburgh study was quality of life. A bed-ridden genius probably won't have the same amount of life satisfaction as someone of average intelligence that can still get around. Yet, since quality of life is comprised of many external dynamics, such as geography, education, and socioeconomic background, that leaves an important question lingering. If happiness is an internal emotion, what type of internal, innate qualities contribute to it?

Critical and Logical Thinking

Critical thinking is the action of making a reasoned judgement based on objective findings with well-supported information. It tolerates uncertainty by keeping an open mind until all the evidence has been collected. Then, proper reasoned judgement will follow. With critical thinking, we conceptualize, analyze, synthesize, and evaluate the collected information without jumping to conclusions. Critical thinking analyses the what, when, how, who, where, and why objectively, prior to reaching an answer or a conclusion.

Critical thinking also needs logical thinking, which is defined as the fluent movement between thoughts and reason, between perceptions and judgment. A logical person has the ability to discern issues in an orderly, rational, and coherent manner and use reasoning in a consistent and valid fashion.

Common Sense

Common sense is based on the knowledge people gather through experience. It becomes part of their background information about their everyday world and surroundings. The ability to understand and integrate all this knowledge in a consistent, logical, and coherent manner is known as common sense. The most accepted definitions of common sense are:

- The ability to think and behave in a reasonable way and to make good decisions. - Merriam-Webster Dictionary

- The basic level of practical knowledge and judgment that we all need to help us live in a reasonable and safe way. - Cambridge Dictionary

What is striking nowadays is how inadequate the ability is of the younger generation to achieve good levels of logic and common sense. In the view of some people, this is mainly due to their overprotected upbringing, which has limited their exposure to the risks and challenges the world confronts on a daily basis. The increasing use of technological gadgets (cell phones, tablets, computers, game boards, etc.) shares the blame. Many young people have been brought up in a cocoon, a self-absorbed "style system" that makes them sometimes selfish and insensitive due to their technical isolation and need for immediate gratification. The resulting lack of patience and sense of entitlement further inhibit critical and logical thinking along with common sense. Of course, they do not tend to acknowledge it, but it is a given fact of life.

Throughout human history – not just in today's younger generation – our actions have proven that we humans do not easily master logic and common sense. Young or old, we are too strongly influenced by forces that affect us all on a daily basis. These come mainly in the shape of greed, selfishness, and the uncontrollable pursuit of self-interest, often disguised as "progress" or "development."

Some time ago, I received a forwarded e-mail from a friend that really got my attention. I usually do not read these types of messages for lack of time or interest, but I decided to read this one because the source of that message was from a friend I considered smart, witty, and interesting. I am very glad I took the time to read this message, whose intriguing title was "The Death of Common Sense." Before quoting the message, however, I want to acknowledge two other thinkers who are considered to be the first to discuss this idea of the "death" of common sense.

In 1994, Philip K. Howard, a US lawyer, published his *The Death of Common Sense: How Law is Suffocating America*, in which he critiques the US government's regulatory systems. Howard argues that "democracy has become a passive caretaker to a huge legal monument," that buries common sense in a rigid, costly, ineffective, and ever-expanding bureaucratic system. In 1998, Lorie Borgman, a newspaper columnist and speaker, published *The Death of Common Sense and Profiles of Those Who Knew Him*. A summary of her arguments can be found in Appendix 1, and a full version at the following websites:

loriborgman.com/books/

goodreads.com/book/show/17836655-the-death-of-common-sense

Neither Borgman nor Howard mention the death of common sense's sibling, logical thinking, which, in my view, has also passed away. Indeed, it is clear to me that there is a general lack of both critical thinking and common sense in many of our laws as well as in the daily behavior of average citizens around the world. This is so important that I decided to bring to the reader's attention the essence of the independent thoughts of Mr Howard and Ms. Borgman along with my personal thoughts and interpretations. I consider these are added values and ideas that hold hands with what I am trying to portray and achieve in this book. My personal thoughts are expressed after the following requiem to critical thinking and common sense.

Critical Thinking and Common Sense: A Requiem

They both passed away in their sleep while holding hands.

We are here to celebrate their lives and memories for being such an important and integral part of our society, above and beyond what the average person could really envision and appreciate. They were dear friends of ours, and they will certainly be missed.

They were among us for many years. We were very lucky to have them living close, and fortunate for all the lessons we learned from them. Mr Critical Thinking was 86 years old, but nobody really knew how old Ms. Common Sense was. She never wanted to enlighten us with her real age, but she was so lovable that nobody really cared. They both came from a faraway land called Wishful World (wishfulworld.com). They were the pillars of their community. They were both very affable and reasonable, and they always knew the right path to follow in life. With beautiful manners and highly educated, they always seem to be the real leaders that everybody wanted to emulate and follow. They were full of life, with an amazing positive and accurate perspective in anything they were involved in. They always had in their eyes that spark of wisdom, patience, and absolute trustworthiness. Both were very intelligent and always willing and able to extend a helping hand.

Through their experience and wisdom, we learned valuable lessons. Among the most important lessons that helped change many lives, we can list the following:

- Life is unfair and you need to accept it as it is. Adapt to it and always walk forward with your head high (but not with wrong or even silly pride). Walk secure and happy with yourself.
- Respect, truth, and honesty are the main doors to strength and peace of mind, but are ignored by the great majority, especially in business.
- In life, nothing is free, so, yes, you do need to work hard to survive. There is nothing wrong with that.
- We all need to learn and master how to love and respect ourselves and feel proud of this. True self-esteem is a real treasure that provides strength and enhances dignity.
- It is crucial to understand that it is utterly wrong to steal and to cheat. Unfortunately, those actions have been practiced by humans since the beginning of time, and persist up to now, with no hope of stopping. These actions seem to be ingrained in the human DNA and are the main reasons for the infinite number of conflicts and criminal acts in our societies.
- To succeed and advance, you need courage, compassion, and perseverance. Nothing worthwhile comes easily, nothing!

- You need to learn how to distinguish the difference between short-term failure and long-term success. As they say, you may lose a battle but still win the war.
- If you fail, never feel shy or afraid. You need to stand up, re-group your ideas and goals, learn your lesson, lift your chin up, and try again.
- The more you work, the luckier you get.
- Learn how to keep your integrity and your honor as a human being. This is very important for personal growth.
- Develop and treasure respect for oneself. If you achieve it, then respect for others comes easily.
- Learn to be gentle and courteous with yourself and altruistic towards others. Be strict with yourself but honest and kind too. This will fortify your soul and your spirit, and help you position yourself at a higher level in your own and others' eyes.
- Learn to love deeply, to be sincere, and to focus on being loyal. Learn to mean what you say, and learn how to do this on a daily basis.
- You need to understand that whatever you do will either come back to help you or to haunt you. Shouldn't we always, without exception, therefore, make a serious effort not to lie or deceive either ourselves or others?
- Always remember that taking a healthy pride in yourself and honoring yourself are the pillars of a strong, fruitful future full of satisfaction.
- You are the only person responsible for your decisions and actions. You and only you sculpt your future. Nobody does it for you.

Some other valuable messages that Critical Thinking and Common Sense taught everybody, with a kind of comical and serious flair at the same time, have circulated around the world. These are some for the reader to enjoy:

- If you need a helping hand, go get it; it is at the end of your arm.

- The fish swimming against the current might end up electrocuted.
- They who laugh last think slowly.
- Some people are alive only because murder is illegal.
- Those who are born ugly and without charisma, the chances are that in the future they will just get worse.
- If you cannot convince them, confuse them.
- There is always a better world out there, but it is very expensive.
- If the mountain comes to you, run! It is a mudslide.
- If you sense a feeling of great emptiness, eat; you are hungry.
- If you have a clean conscience, it is because you have a bad memory.

Critical Thinking and Common Sense were very practical, with simple and reasonable rules that regulated their daily lives and kept them the right path:

- Saying NO to a child is a sign of character and wisdom.
- Do as you preach, not only as you say.
- Adults are in control, not children.
- "Please" and "thank you" are magic words.
- A big smile liberates the genie.
- Avoid depending on a single income.
- Never place all your investments in one project.
- Save first and then purchase only what you really need with what is left after saving. Cover your needs and learn to save the rest.
- Respect and honesty are costly gifts that require reciprocity. Do not expect them from stingy people.

We all miss Critical Thinking and Common Sense, not just because of their affable personalities, but mainly because of their vast experience and knowledge, which they knew how to incorporate into everyday life in any part of the world.

Before they passed away, they were both struggling with some personal physical and psychological health issues due to external social pressures imposed upon them. Their souls were intertwined in a synchronized perfection; the worse Critical Thinking felt, the worse Common Sense felt as well, and vice versa. They had been each other's soul mates since they first laid eyes on the other, and their health started deteriorating at exactly the same time and speed. Slowly but surely, with the passage of time, they felt weaker and weaker. Modern society has been implementing new rules and regulations that increasingly confined and frustrated Critical Thinking and Common Sense. Little by little, the lack of discipline and the deterioration of the education system caused their ailments to increase. As schoolchildren got more and more say in how they were treated and their teachers and professors less and less, the health of Critical Thinking and Common Sense really started taking a downturn. They saw that the younger generation had been given too much power at too early a stage of life, without having the experience to exercise it properly, and that this had caused adults to lose ground and confidence. As some of their close friends used to say, "It is not the hunters shooting the ducks, it is now the ducks shooting the hunters." Unfortunately, for the younger generation, this applies to both arenas, at home and at school.

To make matters worse, one day the parents decided to take charge and put serious pressure on all the schools, blaming the teachers and the school system for what, in reality, the parents failed to do at home. Those failing parents started what in this trilogy is known as "The Runaway Society." Yes, a great number of parents let their children down – and failed themselves profoundly – by not being firm and strict in educating their children on the basics, such as knowing when to obey and when the word "no" means no! They did not train them in how to show gratitude, be responsible, respectful, forgiving, caring, or unselfish. They forgot to be guides and mentors during the early stages of the children's lives.

Critical Thinking and Common Sense could not bear seeing the young relentlessly change from being human children to cybernetic ones focused on screens and electronic games, with almost no connection to nature. Then, as the years went by, both Critical Thinking and Common Sense started to lose interest in life, especially when the Ten Commandments lost value and fell far back in the list of human traits and priorities. When Critical Thinking and Common Sense realized that humans had completely lost interest in protecting the environment, they were deeply wounded. When they saw, that people had become complacent about privacy, freedom, and reciprocity and were only interested in their own well-being and bottom line, they went into a further decline. In this deep abyss, they lost all interest in living.

The drop that overflowed the glass, that finally pushed Critical Thinking and Common Sense over the cliff was when they concluded that there was no longer any hope on certain important issues. They decided that:

- Justice has and will continue (in a high number of cases) to reward the guilty and punish the innocent.
- Excess tolerance to some immigrants is putting the security and financial stability of citizens at risk in many countries.
- Political correctness is imposing its interests above and beyond the truth.
- Words such as "racist", "anti-Semite", or "Islamophobia", are being exaggerated out of all proportion.
- The abuse of women has not been stopped and mostly goes unpunished or earns very light penalties.

- Lesbian, gay, bisexual, transgender, queer, and 2-spirited (LGBTQ2Q2) people are still not considered fully equal under the law.
- In many countries, the military and police are growing more and more corrupt and abusive against those whom they are morally and legally obliged to protect.

Both Critical Thinking and Common Sense saw how the real perpetrators tended to get off with only a slap on the wrist while the victims got no real restitution. In many countries, and in diverse scenarios within almost every society, unfair, incongruent, or weak legal systems tended to either punish the innocent or allow the perpetrators to get off scot-free. The innocent are the ones needing protection and justice, but the great majority tend to go through their lives without that valuable human right, unless they either have the right contacts or enough money to pay their way out. Throughout the centuries, bullies have gotten away with harming the weaker, in countless cases pushing them to commit suicide, with no solution in sight. To the frustrated and tired eyes of Critical Thinking and Common Sense, some perpetrators behind bars should have lost their so-called human rights, but instead were being helped by lawyers and the legal system to demand their rights like normal and peaceful, law-abiding citizens.

The fact of being born in Europe or North America instead of some places in Africa, South-East Asia, Latin America or Asia can make a world of difference. The latter places have generally done worst in relation to human rights, freedom, and justice. But Critical Thinking and Common Sense realized that these values had also been losing ground in North America and Europe. They could not bear thinking about what it would be like in the future.

One Friday night, they both went to bed exactly at the same time. They kissed each other good night and held hands as they fell asleep, as they always had. And, indeed, they did fall asleep, but never to open their eyes again. Neither could take it anymore, and their hope that the situation could improve had disappeared. I guess they were too weak to fight any longer at their advanced age. Nobody knows who suffered the first cardiac arrest that night, but as soul mates, the other must have instinctively followed its partner immediately. Tragically, both ceased to exist that Friday night. They passed away only with each other's company on a dark winter night without a star in the skies. Next day, nobody really noticed they were gone. It was not until a few days later that the absence of their beautiful spirits started to be felt.

Critical Thinking and Common Sense left a big family behind them. Truth and Trust were Critical Thinking's brothers. His two sisters were Discretion and Reciprocity. Common Sense came from a large family with five brothers named Justice, Responsibility, Honesty, Privacy, and Respect, and four sisters named Freedom, Optimism, Discipline, and Love. They also left behind their own children who, by the way, were triplets, along with eight grandchildren. The triplets were Self-Respect, Self-Esteem, and Self-Control. The grandchildren were Moderation, Manners, Ethics, Integrity, Loyalty, Honesty, Attitude, and Responsibility. They were a very nice and cohesive family. But now the two most valuable, integral, and cohesive members of the family are gone, and only time will tell if the rest can survive.

Moral of the Story

Humans are having a very difficult time applying critical thinking and basic common sense to the challenges of their daily lives. An amazingly large majority cannot fully understand the basic concepts of what critical thinking and common sense really mean, much less apply these concepts in their daily actions. The average person seems to fail in all their efforts to capitalize on what Critical Thinking and

Common Sense offered to the world when they were alive. They were taken for granted and not properly appreciated.

Here are just a few examples of some expressions and ideas that Critical Thinking and Common Sense loved to adhere to and that have been circulating around the world for centuries. With their passing away, these words of wisdom are rapidly being forgotten, and "progress" and "evolution" used as excuses. Some of my favourite quotes that Critical Thinking and Common Sense tried to instill in humans are:

- The heart has reasons of which reason knows nothing. - Blaise Pascal
- It was a man so poor that the only thing he had was money. - Anonymous
- Technology brings us closer to people living far away and distances us from people close to us. - Michele Norsa
- Dress me slowly, I'm in a hurry. - Napoleon Bonaparte
- The richest man is not he who has the most, but he who needs the least. - Anonymous
- We suffer for what we do not have, and we do not enjoy what we have. - William Shakespeare
- The tragedy of this world is that no one is happy, whether stuck in time of pain or joy. - Alan Lightman
- There are no shortcuts to any place worth going. - Anonymous
- I do not know the key to success, but the key to failure is to try to please everybody. - Herbert Bayard
- The more sand that escapes from the hourglass of our life, the clearer we should see through it. - Jean-Paul Sartre
- Most folks are about as happy as they make up their minds to be. - Abraham Lincoln
- Time is the most valuable thing a man can spend. - Diogenes Laertius
- To ensure good health, eat lightly, breathe deeply, live moderately, cultivate cheerfulness, and maintain an interest in life. -William Londen

- Happiness is not a possession to be prized, it is a quality of thought, a state of mind. - Daphne du Maurier
- Remember that happiness is a way of travel, not a destination. - Roy Goodman
- The secret of happiness is freedom, and the secret of freedom, courage. - Thucydides
- Happiness is good health and bad memory. - Ingrid Bergman
- Give a man health and a course to steer, and he will never stop to trouble about whether he is happy or not. - George Bernard Shaw

While Critical Thinking and Common Sense were alive, one of their favourite friends was Mahatma Gandhi who always maintained that life had shown him that life itself, was like a mirror. When asked why, he answered:

> Life has shown me that
> people are courteous if I am courteous;
> people are sad if I am sad;
> people love me if I love them;
> people are mean if I hate them; people smile if I smile;
> people scowl if I am scowling;
> that the world is happy if I am happy;
> that people get mad if I am mad;
> that people are grateful if I show gratitude.

Don Quixote's Legacy

I also sometimes concur with the thoughts of many that our goal in life should be more like that of Don Quixote de la Mancha (in the classic novel by Miguel Cervantes Saavedra). Don Quixote trotted through life pursuing his own laws, which were based on trying to fix injustice, promote good will, and avoid evil. He pursued the narrowest and most difficult trail in search of glory and happiness. He did not like the easy path.

He saw that it would always end up taking him to the wrong place and haunt him for the future. This seemed to be deeply ingrained in the mind of Don Quixote, so his behavior always followed his deep beliefs.

According to Don Quixote, nothing that is worthwhile is easy to achieve, and nothing that comes easy is worth it in the long term and or will last long. He spent his existence escaping from the easy life of superfluous pleasures, immediate gratifications, and wrong ambitions. He was allergic to hypocrisy and lies. He always tried to be honest, loyal, and true to himself and his principles, goals, and beliefs, regardless of how difficult this was.

Don Quixote always chose the arduous trail, the toughest trail, in which he had to make the greatest effort to overcome all obstacles. He chose that path where he had to battle temptation constantly to test his will and power. He always fought against succumbing to temptation. He was convinced that if you achieve something with hard work, effort, tenacity, and enthusiasm, you will keep and cherish it forever.

It is obvious we are not here on Earth only to look for the most arduous and difficult path, but we do need to stay away from the easiest and fastest "solutions." When we do not, poor quality, lack of depth, and incompetence usually follow and, with these, an unethical professional approach more often than not.

CHAPTER TWO: DEMOCRACY, FREEDOM, PRIVACY, AND SECURITY (HUMAN RIGHTS)

Introduction

The US Department of State says that respect for human rights and democracy are the central components of US foreign policy, although, all "Three Amigos" in North America (Mexico, Canada, and the United States) have fought hard throughout their histories to achieve and maintain democracy and freedom. These "American" values are meant to guarantee our security, stability, freedom and human rights, including our rights to work, choose the religion we prefer, be treated equally and fairly, enjoy our privacy and develop and progress in a free market secure from any foreign threat.

The four concepts of democracy, freedom, privacy, and security are tightly interlaced throughout North America. They have made Canada, the United States, and Mexico great countries to live in, especially compared to many other nations around the world. However, as two academics have reminded us – writing 25 years apart and from very different perspectives (one a conservative establishment historian and the other a radical African-American woman novelist) – these values are under threat in modern North American society.

As early as 1962, Prof Daniel J. Boorstin of the University of Chicago warned in *The Image: A Guide to Pseudo-Events in America* that many events in the United States were being staged simply for publicity purposes or for narrow economic interests and produced little or no real value for society. He famously explained that "the biggest obstacle to discovery is not ignorance; it is the illusion of knowledge." Unfortunately, Canada and Mexico since then have also come increasingly under the sway of pseudo-events.

In 1987, in her novel *Beloved*, Toni Morrison noted that "freeing yourself was one thing, claiming ownership of that freed self was another." In other words, the biggest obstacle to realizing or maintaining democracy, freedom, privacy, and security is the illusion that we have these things and the resulting complacency that prevents us from exercising or protecting them.

Democracy

On January 21, 2004, a lecture took place at Hilla University for Humanistic Studies in Iraq, south of Baghdad, that started by defining the four foundations of democracy as:

1. A political system for choosing and replacing the government through free and fair elections.
2. Active participation of citizens in politics and civic life.
3. Protection of the human rights of all citizens.
4. Rule of law, in which laws and legal procedures apply equally to all citizens.

As these principles make clear, every citizen in a democratic country is protected by an array of human rights and the freedom to choose, but also has obligations that need to be complied with. These obligations include peaceful participation in civil life, tolerance of the views and beliefs of others, and respect for the law and for those who enforce it. Finally, in a democratic country, the people are sovereign, which means they are higher than the political authorities. That at least is the theory.

According to the US Department of State, democratic countries always strive to secure peace for their citizens first and then peace for others beyond their borders. They try to stop aggression of any kind, promote economic and political development, protect open markets, uphold human rights, safeguard the global environment, and fight against national and international terrorism and other crimes. Thus, according to the State Department, the goals of the United States and its democratic allies (such as Canada and the United Kingdom) are to:

- Promote democracy as a means to achieve security, stability, and prosperity for the entire world.
- Assist newly formed democracies in implementing democratic principles.
- Assist democracy advocates around the world to establish vibrant democracies in their own countries.
- Identify and denounce regimes that deny their citizens the right to choose their leaders in elections that are free, fair, and transparent.

The US Bureau of Democracy, Human Rights, and Labor (DRL) is dedicated to promoting democracy all around the world. It gives special attention to the protection and promotion of human rights. The Parliament of Canada, for its part, has declared that:

> In a democratic country, all eligible citizens have the right to participate, either directly or indirectly, in making the decisions that affect them. Canadian citizens normally elect someone to represent them in making decisions at different levels of government. This is called a representative democracy.

According to the Canadian Government (canada-eu.gc.ca), Canada and its allies in the European Union (EU) are committed to "helping other states develop democratic institutions and practices by providing direct support, legal and administrative training, and technical assistance." At the heart of Canada's foreign policy, therefore, is support for democratic governance, freedom, the rule of law, and, above all, human rights.

The Republic of Mexico has been, in theory and on paper, a democracy for close to 100 years. In 1917, the Mexican Constitution proclaimed democratic institutions, but the implementation of democracy has been a steep, troubled and difficult path. For example, the current governing party, "Partido Revolucionario Institucional" (PRI) (Institutional Revolutionary Party), which has held power for 76 of the past 100 years, including 71 uninterrupted years from 1929 to 2000, has always claimed to have won power through free and fair voting, but in reality, people seem to have voted against its "dictatorship" in the past to no avail. By March of 2018, it was still the general public perception as well as the view of many international authorities. More details of Mexico's unstable democracy can be found at these two links:

coha.org/democracy-in-mexico-the-past-present-and-future/

foreignpolicy.com/2016/02/23/obama-pena-nieto-mexico-corruption/

In Mexico, as in many other Latin American countries, corruption is not just widespread, but openly and shamelessly practiced at almost all government levels. In Canada and the United States corruption also exists, but is camouflaged as much as possible and happens mainly at higher levels. More government dollars are invested in public infrastructure and services for the benefit of the people in Canada and the United States than in Mexico and other Latin American countries. Although some find this debatable, after what I have lived and experienced in these three countries, there is not the slightest shred of doubt in my mind that our tax dollars go much further in Canada (and in the United States) than in any Latin American country, including Mexico.

In "Democracy and the Mexican Disease" (*Huffington Post*, January 1, 2015), Rodrigo Aguilera noted that it had been 800 years since the Magna Carta – the original foundation of the Anglo-Saxon tradition of liberal democracy – had been signed, but that, in contrast to this tradition, Latin American states had evolved under more authoritarian traditions that inhibited the personal freedoms of citizens regardless of their right to vote. Regarding Mexico, for example, Aguilera wrote:

> Unfortunately, it did not take long [after the opposition's victory in 2000] to realize that elections alone would not suffice for true democracy to exist. Mexico enjoyed a jubilant transition in 2000, following the victory of Vicente Fox, a Coca-Cola salesman who rose through the ranks and then jumped into politics, campaigning on a platform of kicking the "scorpions, vermin, and snakes" of the PRI out of power. However, the mood quickly soured when it became apparent that the existence of a democratically elected government would not automatically destroy the pillars of political power that the PRI had created (the unions, big businesses, local governments); in fact, it ended up reinforcing them as a result of the vacuum of power left over from a weak presidency. The struggle to consolidate liberal democracy in Mexico has been an uphill one since then: whenever the institutions of good governance have faced up against the opposing force of corruption, the latter has almost always won.

> Mexicans from a young age are brought up in an environment where family connections and special favors play a key role in guaranteeing success in life. One must, however, remain sceptical of the willingness of the Mexican political establishment to do so [democratize] … for the simple reason that expecting it to make the necessary institutional changes to eliminate corruption is *a conflict of interest in itself*.

The same problem can be seen in all Latin American countries. A good example is what happened to President Dilma Rousseff of Brazil, who was impeached by the Senate in August 2016, ending 13 years of leftist rule in that country. Brazil has the largest economy in Latin America, along with the best climate, the longest coastline, and an amazing abundance of natural resources. Unfortunately, due to greed, corruption, and lack of vision, these advantages have not ensured freedom and real democracy.

Freedom

Freedom is an essential cornerstone of democracy. Without freedom, there is no democracy. Freedom exists when a country and its people enjoy self-government, self-determination, independence, and autonomy, and have the liberty to exercise their powers and rights. Freedom obviously requires the absence of slavery and coercion, but it is also the absence of any unwarranted and inappropriate restrictions to the exercise of free speech and other basic human rights.

To many, a key element of freedom is simply a strong and firm presence of the truth. We need to be free in order to search and find the truth. The Buddha once said: "There are three things that cannot be hidden for long: the sun, the moon, and the truth"; but, in a non-democratic and free country, it is easy to hide the truth with a blanket of lies and dishonesty. Even in free and democratic countries such as Mexico, the United States, and Canada, the truth is sometimes hidden so deep it is almost impossible to dig it out. Luckily, in North America, we still have amazing opportunities to defy the government (and powerful private corporations) in search of truth and the protection of our human rights. There are many technical and academic definitions of freedom, but every human being understands what freedom is without needing complicated political theories. As a certain Khalid Ali Haji explained in an online forum (haveyoursay.org/what-is-freedom), freedom for the ordinary person is simply "feeling free to do, to say, to be literally (anything) - whatsoever and however, wherever and whenever. Because I am myself, and only I own me, therefore I can, so come what may; I believe I am free, free as a bird."

However, even though I understand Khalid's point, I am convinced his definition lacks something very important. What he described is indeed freedom, but freedom also requires the actions of a free individual to be within the framework of an established society respecting and adhering to its laws, traditions, and civic virtues. This sounds obvious, but there are a lot of people out there who believe their rights are above and beyond the rights of others. Or they simply believe that others have to tolerate their freedom to act outside the boundaries established by the society they both live in. We all need to remember that, in a free society, respect for others means peace. By the way, who is Khalid Ali Haji? I have no idea, but in his bio, he endorses one part of my own philosophy in life, using different wording than I would, but in a similar spirit. He describes himself as "a fighter":

> A fighter that never backs down, because giving up is not an option and never will be. I will take everything life throws at me and I will keep moving forward. No matter how hard I get hit, no matter how far I get pushed back, no matter how deep I fall down; I will fight till it's over, till the end. I will win this battle.

Here again, however, I believe he misses a very important point. If life brings him down hard for whatever reason, then logic, humbleness, persistence, and the right attitude should prevail and bring him back on his feet to try and improve his performance, and to blend and cooperate in his society in a more efficient and successful manner for the benefit of himself, his family, and his community. We cannot and should not have a "macho" attitude, and, above all, we should comply with our society's way of life and respect our surroundings and our environment in a coordinated manner with the rest of our community. This just confirms that the interpretation of freedom is different for everybody; it all depends on your own life experience. For example, Nelson Mandela gave to the world a very interesting concept of freedom, which might sound surprising to many but is absolutely understandable. He said: "When a man is denied the right to live the life he believes in, he has no choice but to become an outlaw."

In North America we are still free, but we constantly need to defend our freedom. Shackles can easily be attached to our freedom by the growing threats to privacy, security, and free speech, which are seriously threatening our way of life. In fact, they have already done a lot of damage, but it has been done so slowly that many have not noticed, while many of those who have noticed either do not care or have simply given up. We will deal with these issues in more detail later.

Privacy

Privacy is a vital and integral need for every human being on this planet. The Merriam-Webster dictionary defines privacy as "the quality or state of being apart from company or observation. It is the freedom from unauthorized intrusion. It is simply a place of seclusion." According to Privacy International (privacyinternational.org):

> Privacy is a fundamental right, essential to autonomy and the protection of human dignity, serving as the foundation upon which many other human rights are built. Privacy enables us to create barriers and manage boundaries to protect ourselves from unwarranted interference in our lives, which allows us to negotiate who we are and how we want to interact with the world around us. Privacy helps us establish boundaries to limit who has access to our bodies, places, and things, as well as our communications and our information.

The value of being alone and unobserved, analysed, or disturbed by anyone is of utmost importance in the life of every human being. Privacy not only provides a sense of security, peace, and relaxation, but it allows us to think, meditate, and grow mentally and physiologically. All human beings have a right to such privacy, and in North America, the average citizen achieves it with ease. But this is not the case in many other countries around the world, especially those at the lower end of the economic spectrum.

Technological advances are meant to improve our lives in various ways, but at the same time, they often shatter the invisible protective coat around us that used to guarantee our privacy. For example, surveillance in public places is intended to keep us safe, but can also be done (and actually has been done) within the confines of our homes, that is, within what are supposed to be our private sanctuaries. This is done via cameras, heat waves and sound waves, without us having a clue we are being observed 24/7. Our right to privacy is compromised without us having even a clue. With sophisticated technology, the violators of our privacy are completely hidden from us, like a wild cat hides itself before it leaps for its victim's throat.

Privacy is a fundamental human right to be appreciated, cherished, and protected relentlessly against any outside threat. The right to privacy according to Privacy International (PI), is an integral part of the laws, rules, regulations, charters, contracts, covenants, guarantees, and other agreements, pledges and promises of every country. Some examples of international agreements on the importance of privacy as per PI include:

- Articles 16 and 21 of the Arab Charter on Human Rights
- Article 14 of the UN Convention on Migrant Workers
- Article 16 of the UN Convention on the Rights of the Child
- Article 21 of the ASEAN Human Rights Declaration

- Article 8 of the European Convention on Human Rights
- Article 10 of the African Charter on the Rights and Welfare of the Child
- Article 4 of the African Union Principles on Freedom of Expression (the right of access to information)
- Article 11 of the American Convention on Human Rights
- Article 5 of the American Declaration of the Rights and Duties of Man

Canada, the United States, and Mexico have their own laws regarding their citizens' rights to privacy. According to the Office of the Privacy Commissioner of Canada, for example, Canada's Privacy Act:

> governs the personal information handling practices of federal government institutions. The Act applies to all of the personal information the federal government collects, uses and discloses—be it about individuals or federal employees. The Act also gives individuals the right to access and request correction of personal information held by these federal government institutions.

The US Privacy Act of 1974 and the Federal Law on Protection of Personal Data Possessed by Private Persons in Mexico are very similar. But do these three governments really keep citizen's personal information private? Absolutely not! As with Australia's Privacy Act of 1988, all governments that regulate the handling of the personal information of their citizens can disclose it to other institutions when this is considered prudent and in the "best interest" of the nation without even having to inform the affected individuals.

To make matters worse, in the United States then-President George W. Bush signed the infamous Patriot Act on October 26, 2001, as a response to the 9/11 attacks against the Pentagon and New York's World Trade Centre. Although many US citizens protested against the Patriot Act, most did not object. Why? Because they felt afraid, insecure, and insignificant.

However, using this act, the government of the United States can tap into the private life of anybody suspected of being a potential terrorist. There is a short but interesting analysis of the Patriot Act I want to quote as follows:

> The USA PATRIOT Act, as it is officially known, is an acronym for "Uniting and Strengthening the United States of America by Providing Appropriate Tools Required to Intercept and Obstruct Terrorism." Bush hoped the bipartisan legislation would empower law enforcement and intelligence agencies to prevent future terrorist attacks on American soil. While Congress voted in favour of the bill, and some in America felt the bill actually did not go far enough to combat terrorism, the law faced a torrent of criticism. The Patriot Act has faced ongoing legal challenges by the American Civil Liberties Union, and in recent years, some members of Congress who had originally supported the bill have come to mistrust the Bush administration's interpretation of the law. Nevertheless, a Republican-controlled Congress passed the bill and Bush signed a renewal of the controversial Patriot Act in March 2006. Bush exacerbated the controversy over the renewal of the act by issuing a so-called "signing statement"—an executive exemption from enforcing or abiding by certain clauses within the law—immediately afterward. (history.com/this-day-in-history/george-w-bush-signs-the-patriot-act)

Is Privacy an Illusion?

Many believe that true, unlimited privacy no longer exists, that it is an illusion that technology, starting with the first credit cards and ending with the launching of the World Wide Web, has all but destroyed. Technology has the ability to expose publicly, with or without our consent, any of the so-called private information, from our birth date to our most personal thoughts and pictures, that we cherish so dearly under the illusion that we can control it. But as soon as we are connected to the web, we are exposing ourselves to institutions, companies, and any kind of organization we decide to be members of. Worst of all, any of us can be victims of hackers. When hacking happens, our personal information, even our identities, can be taken from us. This is why, in the 21st century, there is no more privacy as we used to know it, except for the few who are completely "off the grid," living in insolation in some faraway corner of the world. It is also why contracts talk more and more about confidentiality rather than privacy. Privacy simply cannot be guaranteed anymore.

In an excellent article entitled "Life With Alacrity" (Apr 20, 2015), Christopher Allen makes a very good effort to explain the concepts of security and privacy and, in the process, brings to our attention an example that clarifies the issue succinctly. He tells of a lady who had been a prostitute earlier in life, but later settled into the comfortable confines of a private and quiet life:

> After settling quietly into marriage, Melvin found herself the subject of an unauthorized movie that ripped apart the fabric of her new life. [She] sued the makers of the film but lost. She was told in the 1931 decision Melvin v. Reid: "When the incidents of a life are so public as to be spread upon a public record they come within the knowledge and into the possession of the public and cease to be private." So, the Supreme Court of Los Angeles had one answer for what was public and what was private. Melvin's case was one where public events had clearly entered the public consciousness. However

today, more and more of what people once thought of as private is also escaping into the public sphere — and we're often surprised by it. That's because we think that private means secret, and it doesn't; it just means something that isn't public.

Allen also mentions in his article how comfortable he used to feel about the Fourth Amendment in the US, which protects every citizen against abusive or unfounded searches and seizures. For Allen, this meant there used to be human rights privacy in the United States, known to many as the number one country for its democracy, freedom, and preservation of human rights. Unfortunately, he says, everything crumbled when George W. Bush and John Ashcroft (Attorney General at the time) decided to modify the Patriot Act to give the government the legal right to keep under surveillance any citizen, if deemed appropriate for reasons of national security, among others. In fact, the First Amendment has also been shattered, because there is no longer any such thing as free speech in the US. Reporters can now be subpoenaed to divulge their sources using the excuse of "national security" or for any other reason the Supreme Court deems appropriate.

Suddenly, after an assumed terrorist attack on September 11, 2001, when George W. Bush was in power, two important things happened that were chiseled into the history books. These were the alteration of the USA Patriot Act and the invasion of Iraq based on inaccurate intelligence. Of course, everybody in the US is aware of the "conspiracy theory" regarding the terrorist attacks and Iraq invasion, and many hope that one day the truth will float to the surface for all to appreciate, if indeed it was an inside job instead of a terrorist attack. But if that happens, it will be the start of the decline of the United States of America as we know it. I personally hope that never transpires. Some truths are better if they remain buried forever!

The Whistleblower: Patriot – Dissident – Traitor – Hero

A whistleblower exposes a specific activity or information that he or she deems abusive, inappropriate, unethical, or illegal, whether perpetrated by an individual or an organization, public or private. He or she is "a person who tells someone in authority about something illegal that is happening, especially in a government department or a company" (Cambridge Dictionary). While whistleblowers are considered snitches or traitors by the organizations they expose, others (usually including the average citizen) consider them patriots and heroes for having the courage to bring to light important information affecting citizens. Among the best-known contemporary whistleblowers are:

Julian Assange, the founder and editor of WilkiLeaks. It is said that, since the creation of his website, WikiLeaks has disseminated over one million leaks on the World Wide Web. Born and brought up in Australia, Assange is currently (as of December 2016) residing in the embassy of Ecuador in London, where he has obtained political asylum against pending charges in Sweden. He is known to the world as a computer programmer, journalist, publisher, and dissident. In 2010, Assange published critical information from the Department of Defense about the Iraq and Afghanistan wars. This is considered the largest leak of confidential information in history. Allegedly, these leaks seriously endangered the US and its allies, and the Taliban promised to track down US informants. Later, Assange was accused of sexual abuse and rape in Sweden, charges he denied and claimed were politically motivated, leading him to seek asylum at the Ecuadoran embassy. Assange is also trying to avoid extradition to the United States, where he would face charges relating to the leaks themselves. In an article in The Guardian, Nick Davies wrote:

> The case against Assange, which has been the subject of intense speculation and dispute in mainstream media

and on the internet, is laid out in police material held in Stockholm to which the Guardian received unauthorised access. Assange denies the Swedish allegations and has not formally been charged with any offence. The two Swedish women behind the charges have been accused by his supporters of making malicious complaints or being "honey traps" in a wider conspiracy to discredit him.

Important Note:
Greg Miller and Ellen Nakashima of The Washington Post reported on Mar 7, 2017, under the headline "Wikileaks says it has obtained troves of CIA hacking tools," that the CIA's computer hacking arsenal has been revealed to the public by Wikileaks. Thousands of files exposed the specific cyber-tools the CIA has used to convert televisions, cell phones, and other devices into spy cameras, without the user having a clue that he or she is being monitored and even video-taped. This leak will certainly cause serious damage. Although the agency initially questioned its accuracy, the story was later corroborated as accurate.

Edward Snowden, from Elizabeth City, North Carolina, started working as a security guard at the University of Maryland and then got jobs with private IT contractors such as Dell and Boos Hamilton. Later, as a subcontractor of the National Security Agency (NSA), he made himself famous by leaking information about the NSA's massive illegal domestic surveillance activities. Snowden acted because he considered it unethical and dangerous for the NSA to be secretly monitoring American companies and citizens without them having the slightest idea. In Snowden's eyes, it was a flagrant violation of people's privacy rights and justified leaking documents about the NSA programs to the press (The Washington Press, The Guardian and The New York Times). After a dramatic manhunt, Snowden was granted asylum in Russia. Although the US government considers him a traitor who violated the Espionage Act, he is admired by millions as a hero and crusader for transparency and ethical practices, which many insist are the true spirit of democracy.

Bradley Manning was sentenced to 35 years in prison for leaking, through WikiLeaks, the largest amount of classified information in the history of the United States. Although he was acquitted of the most serious charge, aiding the United States' enemies, he was convicted on "multiple other counts, including violations of the Espionage Act, for copying and disseminating classified military field reports, State Department cables, and assessments of detainees held at Guantanamo Bay, Cuba" (Julie Tate, Washington Post, Aug 21, 2013). However, thanks to Manning, millions of viewers managed to see with their own eyes how a US Apache helicopter opened fire on a group of innocent civilians in Eastern Baghdad and to learn about other US atrocities in Iraq. Manning has many defenders. As Tate noted:

> Civil liberties groups condemned [Manning's conviction]. "When a soldier who shared information with the press and public is punished far more harshly than others who tortured prisoners and killed civilians, something is seriously wrong with our justice system," said Ben Wizer, director of the American Civil Liberties Union's Speech, Privacy and Technology Project. "This is a sad day for Bradley Manning, but it's also a sad day for all Americans who depend on brave whistleblowers and a free press for a fully informed public debate.

Wizer's statement is not just accurate but also very alarming. Only the naïve or ignorant can disregard the ugly realities taking place behind the scenes of every government in the world, not just the US government. Atrocities and corruption have always been part of politics, and we should not just accept whatever our governments tell us. We need to be free to research, analyze, and come to our own independent conclusions, while trying hard to be true and honest with ourselves as well. It is easy to turn a blind eye and let things slide, while accepting everything you are told. But in search of the truth, we require courage and discipline to face the down-to-earth realities we live in while trying to do something about them. We must not look the other way when there is something we cannot accept. In today's world, there is no excuse not to search for, find, and publish the enlightening truth, which we all know will not just set us free but will make us more self-determined and sovereign in our thoughts and actions. Isn't this the true essence of democracy, freedom, and the opportunity to dream big that many people have fought and died for?

Technology vs. Security and Privacy

There is no doubt that the more high-tech our lives are, the less security and privacy we will enjoy. Let's consider four examples:

1. The more connected we are to the World Wide Web with our laptops, tablets, and cell phones, the more apps we download to stay connected or get more connected. But nothing comes free. Usually we also need to grant permission to the owners of those apps to access and share our private information as they deem appropriate, of course within their "company's privacy and ethic codes." But what does that condition really mean? How many of us actually read an app's "Terms and Conditions" before clicking our "Agreement?" And even when we do read and find something we do not like, 99 per cent of us just let it go; we know that if we do not click accept, we will never be able to use the app we want or need.

2. There are now DNA services being offered to people interested in finding out about their genetic background. They are being widely promoted through TV ads and many other marketing strategies on and off line. The two best-known

services are 23andMe.com and Ancestry.com. While they enable an average person to get their DNA analyzed affordably, there are clearly security and privacy concerns regarding the use of the results. This is intimate genetic data, after all, which can be matched to other people's DNA to find out family ties and even specific locations of origin. Crime laboratories have been using DNA analysis for many years. What would stop a police department from requesting a court order to access anyone's DNA analysis done by these companies to investigate a crime?

Indeed, in an article entitled "Cops are asking Ancestry.com and 23andMe for their customers' DNA," (Fusion, Oct 16, 2015), Kasmir Hill reported:

> When companies like Ancestry.com and 23andMe first invited people to send in their DNA for genealogy tracing and medical diagnostic tests, privacy advocates warned about the creation of giant genetic databases that might one day be used against participants by law enforcement. DNA, after all, can be a key to solving crimes. It "has serious information about you and your family. Your relative's DNA could turn you into a suspect," warns Wired, writing about a case from earlier this year, in which New Orleans filmmaker Michael Usry became a suspect in an unsolved murder case after cops did a familial genetic search using semen collected in 1996. The cops searched an Ancestry.com database and got a familial match to a saliva sample Usry's father had given years earlier. Usry was ultimately determined to be innocent, and the Electronic Frontier Foundation called it a "wild goose chase" that demonstrated "the very real threats to privacy and civil liberties posed by law enforcement access to private genetic databases."

The FBI has its own national genetic database, as Hill notes, and is always keen to expand their database for what they call "national security" reasons but others call "invasion of privacy." If a person's DNA is in the FBI database, that person is a lot more likely to be accused, correctly or not, of being involved in a crime. Why? Because the DNA of others is often transferred accidentally to crime scenes and may wrongly place the person at the crime scene at the time of the murder or assault. The police force or other government agency can easily obtain people's DNA with a court order. Therefore, the more information about yourself you provide on-line or in a sample, the more you are at risk.

3. Some security cameras and other surveillance systems on the market, which are meant to provide you with a better sense of security and confidence that your property is being protected, might be doing the opposite. Why? Because whoever is behind the operating system may use the private information you had to input to get the application started. When a user registers the purchased surveillance cameras on line with the manufacturer, that information is accessible by unreliable employees or hackers, for example. They can access your remote cameras, check on a daily basis when you are in and when you are out, and thus determine a pattern that indicates when it will be safe for an accomplice to break in and steal your belongings.

There are two main methods of surveillance: remote video surveillance and mobile video surveillance. A remote video surveillance allows the user to view live video from anywhere in the world. People simply type their IP address in a browser through a dynamic domain name system (DDNS - previously configured). This gives the user better control and security in managing settings and recording videos. A mobile security app is less secure and requires a mobile data plan. This surveillance is limited to the coverage zones of the cellular company and package. For specific security information in different brands or systems, thorough research needs to be done by the end user to minimize their risk potential.

4. Harris Corp's Stingray surveillance system is a device that had been secretly used by the US government and police forces for at least 15 to 17 years as a weapon against their own citizens. Yes, used against the public in a sophisticated cellular surveillance pursuit. It has been proven in court that law enforcement agencies have used this technology to monitor everything from text messages to images and individuals' precise locations. The technology enables agents to listen to and tape cellular conversations without a warrant as part of their "national security" efforts. Some critics, privacy activists, and freedom advocates insist that enforcement agencies are using this "stingray device" and other powerful surveillance devices and methods that threaten on a daily basis the civil liberties of any citizen. The technology can impersonate any cellular communication tower using "cell site simulators" and can operate in 2G, 3G, 4G, and other signals simultaneously. It intercepts the signal headed to the towers of a regular commercial provider, then re-routes it back to the commercial provider after having snooped and kept any information deemed relevant to "national security."

Imagine you are protesting against oil pipelines in a public demonstration in New York or Toronto. Demonstrators are sending each other "private" information, images, and instructions, and making telephone calls to each other. The enforcement agencies have access to everything being exchanged, including the exact location of the senders and receivers at any given time. Protesters who think they are safe and private and that nobody knows who is under that balaclava should think again, and think very hard. In reality, they are out there in the open. The police know who they are and where they are sleeping that night. All protesters should think twice before attempting anything.

Personal and National Security

For the average person, the concept of security is simply a feeling of being far from danger and any kind of threat, physical or psychological. Merriam-Webster defines security "freedom from danger, anxiety and fear." Every human being works hard and diligently to attain and preserve their personal and family security in the society in which they live. Within the world of personal security, the issue that is of utmost relevance to every citizen, though outside their direct personal control, is the concept of "national security." According to the generally accepted definition of national security, the government makes its best effort to protect citizens against national and international threats. National security therefore involves the protection of the interests of the people and their country as a whole. As uslegal.com states:

> National security is a corporate term covering both national defense and foreign relations of the US It refers to the protection of a nation from attack or other danger by holding adequate armed forces and guarding state secrets. The term national security encompasses within it economic security, monetary security, energy security, environmental security, military security, political security, and security of energy and natural resources. Specifically, national security means a circumstance that exists as a result of a military or defense advantage over any foreign nation or group of nations, or a friendly foreign relations position, or a defense position capable of successfully protesting hostile or destructive action.

The US and Canadian governments have always tried to entice young people to join their armed forces and help protect national security. So has the Mexican government, if less actively. This message on Canada's Ministry of Defence website is typical of the recruitment efforts most governments around the world engage in:

> Discover how we protect the security of Canadians through counter-terrorism, security screenings and the protection of Canada's critical infrastructure. (https://www.canada.ca/en/services/defence/nationalse curity.html?=undefined&wbdisable=true)

The Canadian government attracts recruits in areas of general national security, mainly for the Canadian armed forces and the various services that ensure transportation security, border, and cyber security. National security in every country covers three basic areas: land security, oceans security, and airspace security.

Security and the Police

The motto of most North American police forces is some version of "To Protect and to Serve." The motto originated with the Los Angeles Police Force many decades ago and emphasizes the twin goals of preserving public safety and serving the people, regardless of background or ethnicity. Concerning this subject, there are two quotes I would like to share with you:

> My relationship to power and authority is that I'm all for it. People need somebody to watch over them. Ninety-five percent of the people in the world need to be told what to do and how to behave.
> – Arnold Schwarzenegger

> Educate and inform the whole mass of the people.... They are the only sure reliance for the preservation of our liberty.
> – Thomas Jefferson

Every human being cherishes privacy and freedom. Privacy is essential for peace of mind, while freedom enables us to think, speak, and act as we see fit in order to satisfy our needs and preferences, whatever they may be. However, above privacy and freedom, there is something more valuable – security. If people do not feel safe and secure, they cannot enjoy their freedom or privacy. As per the former Secretary-General of the United Nations Mr Ban Ki-Moon has pointed out, that in many countries our security and peace are now threatened on a daily basis by terrorist extremists. Helen Keller (a famous American educator) even argued that security is mostly superstition, that nature does not provide security *per se*, and that people cannot offer their children full security either. She said: "Avoiding danger is no safer in the long run than outright exposure. Life is either a daring adventure or nothing."

In line with Keller's logic, complete security, especially in cities, is almost impossible to attain and is ephemeral if it ever is attained. Nobody can ensure our security forever, not even the best police force. In fact, in many countries around the world, people fear the police. In North America, we are lucky to be able to feel more or less comfortable with our police forces, not just because they have higher ethical standards, more pride in their work, and a greater sense of responsibility than in many other countries, but because the average police receives a decent salary to support their family (with the exception of Mexico) and they can be taken to court if they do anything improper. Our legal systems in North America works much better than in other countries.

In North America, the average police officer genuinely tries to protect and serve to the limit of their personal abilities. Of course, there are always rotten apples on every tree, but the majority are hardworking and honest, and the rotten minority are usually exposed and dismissed sooner or later. But let's take a closer look at the relationship between security and the police in the three countries in North America.

<u>United States</u>:

Not everyone in the United States shares that secure and comfortable feeling about police officers. This is especially true of blacks and Latinos. In general, every country gives its police too much power, and when an officer feels insecure or threatened, they may in some cases abuse that power. Some end up pulling their weapon's trigger with an amazing ease and apparent lack of remorse. At least that is what has often happened in recent years in the United States, especially in encounters between police officers and black and Latino citizens. Only a few officers behave like this, but a few incidents affect the image and reputation of everyone and seriously erode the trust the average citizen should have in the police. When a police officer is caught in a video shooting a fleeing man in the back and no criminal charges are laid against the officer, it is understandable that people take to the streets in protest. The resentment of African-Americans and Latinos is building up and will certainly explode seriously in the future if things do not change. In fact, some vigilantes have already attacked and killed police officers, and many other vigilantes are being born, because of a system that lacks accountability and fails to punish appropriately the rotten apples that every tree in an orchard develops.

Let me provide five quick examples that have stirred the feelings of African-Americans and Latinos in the United States against their police just in the past couple of years:

- According to German Lopez, writing in VOX Explainer (July 8, 2016), two white police officers in Baton Rouge, Louisiana, responded to a call at a convenience store and apprehended a black man based on the description provided by an anonymous tip. Two bystanders videoed the arrest – and the subsequent shooting of the black man, who apparently was just trying to make a living by selling CDs outside the store. Lopez wrote: "In his last few seconds of life, Alton Sterling seemed completely immobile. Two police officers had pinned him to the floor, flat on his back. But even as Sterling seemed completely unable to move, one of the police officers yelled, 'He's got a gun!' Within seconds, an officer shot Sterling, who was still pinned to the ground by the cops. Sterling died of multiple gunshot wounds, according to an autopsy." The release of the videos enraged people and confirmed what eyewitnesses had reported. No gun was found. According to VOX, of all the people killed by police during arrests in 2012, 31 per cent were black, yet only 13 per cent of the US population is black. Indeed, statistics show that black teens were 21 times more likely to be shot by police than whites, at least between 2010 - 2012, according to Lopez.

- In Ferguson, Missouri, on Aug 9, 2014, Officer Darren Wilson gunned down Michael Brown. Witnesses reported that the unarmed 18-year-old Brown was walking towards the officer, who was in his patrol car, but that there was no apparent reason for shooting him. After a long trial, however, a grand jury determined that there was no probable cause to charge Wilson. Next day, riots broke out in protest and in support of the "Black Lives Matter" movement.

- Kyle Potter reported for Associated Press (July 8, 2016) on the fatal shooting of Philando Castile, who was pulled over and shot by a police officer in a traffic incident. Castile was with a woman, who videoed and streamed his last agonizing moments on Facebook. Before reaching for his license and insurance papers, Castile advised the office he had a gun and also a permit to carry it. According to Potter, the "officer was charged with second-degree manslaughter following an investigation by prosecutors, who concluded that Jeronimo Yañez was wrong to use his weapon in the traffic stop. Prosecutors believe Castile never tried to pull his handgun from his pocket, and Yañez's unrealistic trepidation did not justify the shooting. If convicted, the officer could face up to 10 years in prison. Diamond Reynolds was sitting next to her boyfriend in the car. She said he was shot repeatedly as he reached for his ID after telling Yañez about the weapon and the gun permit." Deadly force under these circumstances should never have been used.

- In July 2015 in Cincinnati Ohio, in another traffic incident, Sam Dubose was shot and killed by Officer Ray Tensing for no apparent reason. After 25 hours of deliberating, the jury concluded, despite convincing evidence of wrongdoing, that they were deadlocked. The judge agreed.

- In Baltimore, Officer Brian Rice was found not guilty in the arrest and death of Freddie Gray. The victim had been taken into custody and placed in the back of a police van without a seatbelt, which caused him to slide and break his neck during transportation to the police station. It is amazing that when an average citizen is legally obliged to buckle up, those that enforce the law fail to do so with their prisoners. Therefore, it seems to many people that the police can do almost anything without consequences.

On the other hand, the average citizen may not appreciate that officers also want to go home at the end of the day and that some of the people they deal with are dangerous criminals who will gun down a police officer without hesitation or remorse. Sometimes officers have only a split second to kill or be killed. They put their lives on the line every day of the week, and we need to understand this before we crucify them with our opinions. People, no matter how funny, angry, or proud, must obey every instruction of an officer and never, but never, make weird moves or jokes that could be misconstrued. For their part, officers must go the extra mile – and be properly trained – to react with cooler heads and more self-control. They should also wear body cameras at all times. With the technology available today, there is no reason an officer should not have a body camera on at all times.

Canada:

In Canada, the Royal Canadian Mountain Police (RCMP) is acknowledged worldwide as a fair and reliable institution. They are organized, systematic, trustworthy, efficient, and proud of what they do – in general. The average citizen feels comfortable with RCMP officers. But, as with anything in life, they are not perfect. They also have some rotten fruit and some serious shortcomings. We have had famous cases where citizens have felt outraged, but because of the silent or tolerant nature of Canadians, few waves have been created. Luckily, these incidents have really had nothing to do with race, as it often does in the United States. A few notable examples where we have all felt embarrassed and worried about our personal security due to the lack of common sense and proper training of some officers include the following:

- Constable James Forcillo shot and killed Sammy Yatim in a streetcar in Toronto. According to Andrew Lupton of CBC News (July 27, 2016): "In January, a jury acquitted Forcillo of second-degree murder, but he was convicted of attempted murder for continuing to shoot at Yatim while the teenager was lying on the floor of an empty streetcar. The acquittal was tied to the first volley of shots, but the conviction on attempted murder was linked to the second volley, fired while Yatim was on the ground." To many people, there was no excuse for an officer to shoot a man from 20 feet away who was only armed with a switchblade and was obviously in distress and needing help and understanding more than a shower of bullets, especially when there were at least 12 to 15 other officers surrounding the streetcar. An average citizen wonders what kind of police training Forcillo could have gone through? Forcillo was sentenced to six years in prison, but between appeals, defence arguments, and lax Canadian laws, only time will tell what Constable Forcillo will end up paying for his crime.

- Four RCMP officers caused the death of Robert Dziekanski in October 2007 at Vancouver International Airport. Dziekanski had only a stapler in his hand and could not understand a word of English, nor could anybody around him speak his language (Polish). The victim was indeed very agitated, but the four young, strong, and healthy officers decided, for no rational reason, to taser him several times, causing his death. After the first taser, the victim fell to the ground and began convulsing. The officers then pinned him down, handcuffed him and, for no logical reason, continued to taser him. To make matters worse, according to Huffpost British Columbia (Canadian Press), "the four Mounties involved in Robert Dziekanski's death 'colluded' to come up with a story designed to justify their actions and then attempted to cover up their collusion by lying to a public inquiry, a Crown lawyer alleged Thursday ahead of the perjury trial of one of the officers." This case has been questioned and criticised by many, regardless of the conviction of the officers years later. Canadians are known for their style of being gentle, quiet, and civilized, so no riots or public manifestations took place. But for how long can people hold their frustration and anger?

- In an article entitled "Somali community demands answers after altercation with police leaves a mentally ill man dead in Canada" (July 25, 2016), Hilary Beaumont reported that the Muslim community insisted the incident was racially motivated, while the officers involved said they were just following their training. However, this training enabled them to shoot a mentally ill man and allowed him to bleed to death, according to all the witness statements. Beaumont wrote: "This isn't the first time that Ontario police have had violent interactions with black and non-white civilians, especially those with mental health issues. But because no agency collects consistent or complete data on use of force and race, it is impossible to determine how often racial minorities are injured or killed by police." I personally do not believe that the RCMP is motivated generally by racism. This is in the eye of the beholder, but in Canada we are definitely not race-oriented, with, of course, a few exceptions like anywhere else. However, if we do not begin selecting immigrants and refugees with similar values to those of Canadians, I feel certain that racial problems will emerge in the future. Unless the government does due diligence on all immigrants' backgrounds, we will end up facing the consequences, as other countries are doing.

- Although many police officers in North America have a "shoot first and ask questions later" mentality, this is definitely far from the norm, although random events still happen and will keep on happening. Officers generally try not to shoot, but if forced, they are trained to shoot to kill, not to injure. Simple as that! But this was certainly not the case of an amazing RCMP officer with courage of steel. Her name is … I cannot tell you, because the media and the RCMP have kept her name secret. This officer drew her gun long before the man decided to attack her. After demanding that he drop his knife and then watching him charging towards her, it appears she decided to shoot at his legs to bring him down. An amateur photographer caught the sequence on camera and the footage shows how she was intentionally aiming low, deciding not to take the man's life. She was purposely pointing all the time at the man's legs, not at his chest. Instead of publicizing her name as a hero and somebody to admire, she has most likely endured the macho attitude of other RCMP officers insisting that she was shaking and afraid, or too weak (being a woman) to lift the heavy pistol. At least that is what Scott Brown surmises in his article in the Vancouver

Sun (May 28, 2016) entitled "Amateur photographer captures moment of shooting."

As a citizen, I am appalled that we do not acknowledge her merits instead of hiding her name and that we continue promoting a shoot-to-kill policy. At the same time, I understand what a friend of mine, an excellent RCMP officer, whom I respect and admire told me once: "We are trained to shoot to the trunk. It is very difficult to hit a man's moving legs, therefore putting yourself at serious risk. In fact, if the attacker is on drugs, you can put six or eight bullets in a man's chest, and he can still come at you with enough force and take your life. Something similar happened to a fellow officer friend of mine." I absolutely understand his position; we all want police officers to go home safe and sound to their families every night.

In relation to the defence of life or the fact of fleeing a violent crime, the use of force is unimportant in itself. What matters is the objectively reasonable belief by the officer that he or she is under lethal threat. That alone gives them the power to use lethal force in return.

Mexico:

The Mexican police, properly known as Federal Preventive Police (*Policía Federal Preventiva*) and familiarly as "*Federales*" are definitely feared more by their own citizens than the police in Canada or the United States. For example, when an RCMP officer in Canada stops somebody, we ask ourselves – what did I do? But in Mexico, if a "Federal" stops you, we ask ourselves – what does he want? This is a big difference. What accounts for it? A study by the Washington Office on Latin America (WOLA) published on May 2014 and written by Maureen Mayer begins by observing:

For more than two decades, successive Mexican administrations have taken steps to create more professional, modern, and well-equipped police forces. While these reforms have included some positive elements, they have failed to establish strong internal and external controls over police actions, enabling a widespread pattern of abuse and corruption to continue.

Mexico's police system is very complicated and it demands serious investigation and analysis. Meyer's article is a good start and can be read in full at:
wola.org/sites/default/files/Mexicos%20Police.pdf

Police Corruption

The image and reputation of the police and other security services such as the coastguard, the army, the navy, the secret service, the National Guard, the FBI, the CIA, and so on have a direct correlation with the sense of security experienced by a country's people. The more efficient and reliable these services seem, the greater the sense of security the people in a country enjoy.

Unfortunately, there is nothing that any institution can do to provide 100 per cent security. Nobody is totally secure on planet Earth. Anything can happen at any moment. However, we can minimize our risks and increase our security if we act under the umbrella of the law and in full cooperation with the police force and other government and private security services. Yes, by doing so, we give away some freedom, but to many people, security is above and beyond freedom, since we cannot really be free unless we are reasonably secure first. But nobody is perfect, of course, and so there are also corrupt elements in the police and other security institutions. This is more evident in Mexico and the United States than in Canada, but even here we have our fair share. The following are just six brief examples:

1. In "Mounties offer apology and $100 million compensation for harassment, sexual abuse against female members. RCMP Commissioner Bob Paulson says sorry for 'shameful' conduct" (CBC News, Oct 06, 2016) Kathleen Harris reported: "The RCMP has delivered a historic apology to female officers and civilian members with massive settlement over harassment, discrimination, and sexual abuse claims that could cost up to $100 million. About 20,000 current and past employees who have worked for the RCMP since 1974 could qualify for compensation, but it is expected that about a thousand will seek payments."

The article describes how, for many years, the RCMP failed to behave properly to their female officers. However, the beauty of our Canadian Royal Mountain Police is that they came to grips with the problem and, as of mid 2016, implemented policies and regulations to ensure that female officers are treated fairly and equitably. Now it is just a matter of implementing these policies and regulations to the letter. The Canadian army went through a similar situation with their "Zero Tolerance of Sexual Abuse" policy. According to Canadian Forces ombudsman Gary Walbourne, the military sexual assault policy needs to be extended beyond the military compounds to protect all those civilian women in the workplace who work alongside men in uniform. Yes, our Canadian system still limps, but contrary to the majority of countries worldwide, we are doing something about it. Acknowledging the problem is the first step, implementing new measures and policies with specific consequences is second, and ultimately the enforcement of these policies needs to be unbreakable and consistent from then on.

2. Recently Constable Trent Milan was removed from active duty in Winnipeg, Manitoba, after being accused of drug

trafficking following a year-long investigation. The case is considered by many as a "dark chapter" for the Winnipeg Police Service. Similar things have happened many times in other countries and still happen on a daily basis as part of "doing business," but in Canada such cases are rare and need thorough eradication.

People will definitely feel insecure when they hear about officers like Milan, but destiny works in a weird and sad manner sometimes, as happened with Constable Milan. He passed away in a car accident (some believe it was suicide) in October, 2016. The Winnipeg Free Press wrote (Nov 3, 2016): "Little more than two weeks after Const. Trent Milan, 42, an 18-year veteran of the force, was charged with 34 offences, including breach of trust, attempting to obstruct justice, possession of prohibited weapons and possession of various drugs for the purpose of trafficking, he was pronounced dead inside his heavily damaged pickup truck after it came to a stop on its side in a ditch on Garven Road at 11:30 a.m. Monday."

3. The next example is quite alarming and concerns an issue many of us do not like to talk about, because it makes us feel betrayed, angry, and impotent. I have never doubted the existence of serious corruption at high levels of our Canadian governments. For example, the ex-mayor of Laval, Gilles Vaillancourt, was found guilty of taking kickbacks in exchange for approving hundreds of municipal contracts. However, one of the worst cases is that of the Canadian senators accused of fraudulent expense claims. They say they took legal advantage of a loophole in the system, but in the view of the average Canadian, they embezzled tax money. In my view, either the Senators are corrupt and unethical or the RCMP grotesquely incompetent. It is one or the other, but the latter seems farfetched, because the RCMP is known worldwide for their high ethical standards and efficient methods of investigation.

Among the most popular senators investigated by the RCMP were Mike Duffy and Pamela Wallin. As CBC News – Politics (July 17,2016) reported: "The RCMP has charged Senator Mike Duffy with bribery, frauds on the government, and 29 other charges related to Senate expenses, the awarding of consultant contracts and the acceptance of a $90,000 payment by the prime minister's former chief of staff." A few years later, Duffy was found not guilty of all charges. In the case of Senator Wallin, CBC News – Politics (May 19, 2016) reported that "an independent audit by Deloitte published in May 2013 recommended she pay back some of her travel expenses, but they found no instance of criminality. The Mounties had also alleged she billed the Senate for trips between her home in Saskatchewan and Toronto that were unrelated to parliamentary business. 'I believe that Senator Wallin's conduct represent[s] a serious and marked departure from the standards expected of a Canadian senator,' Cpl. Rudy Exantus said in an affidavit filed in court."

Sadly, I cannot fathom how, in Mike Duffy's case, not one of the 31 charges stuck, or why no evidence of criminal wrongdoing was found in Pamela Wallin's case. What kind of amateur and unprofessional investigations must the RCMP have done? Or what kind of political "arrangement" was made under the table to enable the Senators to go scot-free? Whatever happened, something smells rotten, but the average citizen will never find out, either because the media do not really know or are incapable of finding the truth or are simply hiding the truth.

Regardless of any loopholes in the system, there is a legal and moral obligation – and an oath Senators swore – that ought to hold them legally accountable. The citizens' trust was placed in their hands, but they betrayed us with a false and unreliable excuse. If an average citizen were accused of something similar, he or she would most likely end up in jail or at least, with a criminal record.

To add insult to injury, the worst is not over. The senators' lawyers may be seeking compensation for the "unwarranted and unnecessary ordeal" their clients were put through! Only time will tell, so let us wait and see what happens. Are we really this corrupt in Canada as well?

4. Another example concerns an issue that is still free from RCMP intervention but might well be added to their future investigations. Let me explain why. The Financial Post has revealed a dicey situation regarding the Trudeau Foundation that has raised eyebrows of many in surprise, concern, and doubt. Apparently, there might be a serious conflict of interest between the Foundation and Prime Minister Justin Trudeau. Conflict of interest is a serious crime that can be punished if proven. In the United States, Congress has passed an extension to the legislation that punishes public corruption in the form of bribery, graft, and conflict of interest. Canadian laws run parallel. According to Claire Brownell and Zane Schwartz in their Financial Post article "Trudeau Charity May Face Probe – donations have surged since Justin became Liberal leader" (Dec 13, 2016), donations surged from $172,211 in 2014 to $731,753 in 2016 – a four-fold increase. The article confirms that the Prime Minister is a former member of the Trudeau Foundation, his brother Alexandre is a current member of the board of directors, and the Ministry of Industry appoints two directors. The Trudeau Foundation also employs two members of the Trudeau family. According to the article, the Prime Minister has been using his position to encourage others to donate to the Foundation, which the authors argue may amount to a conflict of interest.

Brownell and Schwartz wrote:

> The National Post's analysis confirms about 40% of 108 donors, directors and members of the foundation since 2014 – or one in six, if academic institutions are excluded – have affiliations with organizations that currently lobby the government, which could indeed

create the perception of a conflict. Industry Canada – not usually a source of funding for academic research in the social sciences and humanities – granted the foundation a $125 million endowment in 2002. The foundation's net assets grew 1.2% in fiscal year 2015, closing out the year at $150 million.

This article also indicates that, as of December 2016, companies like Suncor, Bank of Montreal, Resolute Forest Products, Google, Lafarge Canada, and Air Canada are registered to lobby the federal government but have also sponsored Trudeau Foundation conferences ever since Mr Trudeau was selected as Liberal Party leader. The article goes into considerable detail indicating the extremely high possibility of the existence of a conflict of interest between the Prime Minister and the Trudeau Foundation. There is an old saying that where there is smoke, there is fire. This situation is certainly surrounded by smoke, but to prove that there is fire (or not), an exhaustive investigation needs to be done. In the meantime, it certainly leaves a bitter taste on every citizen's palate regarding the Prime Minister's ethics. Every Canadian certainly hopes this does not go beyond suppositions. If proven true, it would be a shame for every Canadian.

5. On December 14, 2016, an article by Richard Warnica in The National Post entitled "'Josh, stop. She's out': Documents reveal new details in Toronto Police group sex-assault case" reported that three Toronto police officers had been charged with sexual assault and released on $15,000 bail. Apparently, an inebriated female parking officer was gang raped by the officers. It is not for me to make any conclusions, but what is clear is that a police officer's behavior should be an example to society. A police officer represents an institution and its traditions and should behave above and beyond what animal instincts dictate. Yes, women that get so drunk they cannot even speak, much less consent to sex, put themselves in a dangerous position, but this does not justify anyone taking

advantage of her. In my mind, a real man needs interaction with his partner, not just a flimsy chunk of meat or a rag doll. It makes me uncomfortable to even express it this way, but what is the difference? Again, we are lucky that every tree has only a few rotten apples, while the rest are healthy and shiny.

6. Distrust and even hatred against the RCMP grows when officers or the system itself fail profoundly to serve and protect and, worse, when officers do not face legal repercussions in a timely and efficient manner. Such seems to be the situation in the case of many missing and murdered indigenous women across Canada. It is clear the RCMP has failed to bring justice and closure to the victims' families. Hundreds of articles have been written and published about the failures of the RCMP in this dark chapter of Canadian history. Many insist that a lot of women have simply "vanished" over the years, yet nobody has been brought to justice.

First Nations people have opened numerous cases of sexual assault and excessive force against the police. In "Women feel 'betrayed' police not charged" (Globe and Mail, Nov 19, 2016), Ingrid Peritz sums up the situation: "Aboriginal women talk about sexual violence and intimidation by police. Natives have lost faith in the Canadian justice system." Viviane Michele (President of Quebec Native Women Inc.) confirmed that justice in Canada does not apply to indigenous women in their relations with the police.

Many natives insist that a lot of women have simply "vanished" throughout the years and nobody has been brought to justice. The formula of "police investigates police" simply does not work and is very biased and unreliable. This is why Perry Belgrade (National Chief of the Assembly of First Nations) insists all cases must be researched by independent investigators. So many cases of missing or abused indigenous women have remained unsolved by the RCMP year after year and the situation is a time bomb. Will people start taking the law into their own hands in the near future due to this total lack of justice for victims? As the prosecutor in a famous case against police in Val-d'Or, Quebec, said: "The fact that no criminal charges are being laid in some cases does not necessarily mean the alleged events did not happen." Is that supposed to make people feel better and more secure? The handling of the cases of abused and disappeared native women across Canada has been handled so unprofessionally by the RCMP that average Canadians are losing faith in the force, yet we are supposed to have one of the finest police forces in the world.

Police vs. Vigilantes

Given the levels of corruption and lack of security in many countries, vigilante "justice" ("an eye for an eye") has become common and, alarmingly, is starting to happen more often not just in developing countries but even in North America. Although vigilantism is obviously wrong, when governments do not hold common perpetrators, crooked cops and politicians accountable, they indirectly promote it, and this trend has already started in the United States and Canada. Here are three examples:

1. "Five Dallas police officers were killed by a lone attacker, authorities say." This was the title of an article by Joel Achenbach, Mark Berman, William Wan and Moriah Balingit in the Washington Post on July 8, 2016. Apparently, the lone shooter in this case wanted to get back at white officers for killing innocent black men in various public incidents across the United States. The last straw for the killer, Michael Johnson, was the shooting of Alton Sterling by two white officers, which was captured on mobile phone video and went viral. Johnson's vigilante actions were well planned and ended in the deaths of five officers and the wounding of seven more. What is scary is that, if Sterling could do this alone, what might a group of

vengeful police-haters do if they put their minds to it with the level of planning that Johnson showed?

2. On July 7, 2016, a Missouri man killed three police officers and wounded three others in a calculated ambush. The police had received threats before, which they did not take lightly, a week before this, and still the killings took place. The shooter, Gavin Long, attacked with an AR-15 style, semi-automatic rifle. An avid user of social media, he called himself "Cosmo" for short, had lots of followers, and some of his videos went viral too. Gavin was angry with the police in general, not just white officers. One of the officers he killed, Montrell Jackson, was black, while the other two, Matthew Gerald and Brad Garafola, were white. To make things worse, the shooter was a decorated veteran who had been awarded several medals, including even one for good conduct.

3. In *USA Today* (July 9, 2016), Gregg Zoroya reported a 44 per cent increase in the number of police officers killed in the line of duty in the US in 2016 compared to the previous year. According to the National Law Enforcement Officers Memorial Fund, in 2016 64 officers were killed by the use of a firearm, compared to 38 in 2015. Traffic-related deaths were 53 in 2016 against 47 in 2015. It is clear that aggression against officers is escalating in the United States.

Meanwhile in Canada, a group of vigilantes known as the "Creep Catchers" tracks down sex-predators targeting children and underage women. Their methods are peaceful, but some people do not agree with their actions, arguing, as one UBC law professor has done, that "the end does not justify the means." However, in the minds of many others, probably the majority, when there is a gap in the system not covered by the authorities, citizens have a right to protect themselves as long as they respect the law and operate in a peaceful and careful manner, as the Creep Catchers are doing in Vancouver. Yes, it is true that their "stings" could backfire with violent results, but in the eyes of many, they are justifiable, because even when sex predators are caught by police, our legal system is so lax that a lot of people (and a growing number) prefer a vigilante approach with tough and immediate penalties for those twisted people who lure kids through the internet. I agree, however, that vigilantes should not take the law in their own hands. If they do, they are breaking the law themselves and should face the consequences.

National vs. Global Security

Both types of security hold hands. National security is non-existent without a balanced and properly nourished global security. To achieve international global security, we need consensus and understanding among countries. This can only be achieved through international agreements that can be enforced by organizations such as the United Nations (UN), the European Union (EU), and the Centre for International Governance Innovation (CIGI). As the years go by, and as international relations become more complex, the concept of global security will have to adjust to emerging needs.

In Zurich, Switzerland, there is a Centre for Security Studies that uses "security watches" to evaluate in detail the national and international security implications of events anywhere in the world. For example, their security watch for Dec 12, 2016 evaluated "Germany's new defense policy; the roles of China and Israel in Syria; how evolving media technology is changing the nature of terrorism; last year's top 100 arms-producing and military services companies; and the regional implications of the Rohingya crisis." In their second security watch series, they looked at "the current geopolitics of Central Asia; Russia-related nuclear issues; the micro power of prisons in narco-states; Turkey's new anti-PKK strategy; and whether Central Europe is 'falling out of love' with the West."

Global environmental change is an area that is rapidly gaining importance in many organizations all over the world. A magnificent study entitled "Hexagon Series on Human and Environmental Security and Peace," 1,543 pages long, evaluates the security implications of habitat changes, pollution, economic growth, agriculture, and atmospheric and climate change but is only one of a series of monographs that have been edited from cross-scientific perspectives. The idea is to develop common ground among scientists in both natural and social sciences from countries all around the world and to detect and anticipate challenges to humankind in the twenty-first century and the level of risk in each geographical area.

Human and environmental security and peace are a lot more delicate than many people imagine. Our world is so interconnected in terms of air, water, and land that we need to be super-vigilant regarding what other countries are doing and going through, while trying our best to keep problems at bay in our own country. According to the Hexagon Series, for example, the health aspects alone of human security are dependent on numerous factors such as conflict and humanitarian emergencies, infectious disease crises, and poverty. They all directly affect levels of illness, injury, disability, and death. All influence human survival and flourishing livelihoods and dignity. For the full report, refer to: afes-press-books.de/html/hexagon.htm

National Security in North America

In the United States, the National Security Council (NSC), established by statute in 1947 and chaired by the President, is the agency with overall responsibility for national security. Its members include the Secretaries of State, Energy, Defense, and Treasury, the National Security Advisor, the Director of National Intelligence, the Joint Chiefs of Staff and the Vice-President, and its goal is to advise the President on the coordination of domestic, foreign, and military policies regarding national security.

The NSC's counterpart in Canada is Public Safety Canada (PSC), which is in charge of all efforts to coordinate the activities of the federal agencies responsible for protecting Canadian interests, both at home and abroad. The PSC functions as the nerve centre in coordinating critical infrastructure, transportation security, cyber security, and counter-terrorism activities.

For its part, Mexico has the *Comisión Nacional de Seguridad* (*CNS*) (National Commission for Security), which is in charge of safeguarding peace, order, and public security, preventing crime and protecting people's rights. The CNS oversees various agencies, including city and federal police, along with other development and security departments.

Cyberspace Security

In the Boston Conference on Cyber Security that took place on Mar 08, 2017, FBI Director James Comey stated, "There is no such thing as absolute privacy in America. There is no place in America outside of judicial reach." Comey went further to say that "even our communications with our spouses, with our clergy members, with our attorneys are not absolutely private in America." With these statements, it is fair to conclude that total privacy and security are simply non-existent. Total security has never existed, but before the electronic and computer era, we used to have a fairly good degree of privacy. No more.

In North America, our governments cannot, or should not, invade our privacy and place our security at risk, unless there is a good reason and they obtain a court order. They usually do so only in important criminal cases, in counterintelligence investigations or to address potential terrorist threats. But the question remains: Is it true that they only do this type of surveillance (cyber security) with a court order, or do they reserve the right to use their own judgement in an "emergency"? In today's world, safeguarding intellectual property and personal and financial information is a crucial part of any organization's business strategies. According to techopedia.com, a security attack is:

> Any incident that results in unauthorized access of data, applications, services, networks and/or devices by bypassing their underlying security mechanisms. A security breach occurs when an individual or an application illegitimately enters a private, confidential or unauthorized logical information technology (IT) perimeter.

Those perpetrating the security breaches are called attackers, hackers, or crackers. Their intentions are usually malicious, and organizations use what are known as firewalls to try to stop them. Every network security administrator knows that a security attack is not a matter of if but when. Daily vigilance is required, because a breach can be extremely damaging to the organization's reputation and bottom line.

Among the most damaging cyber-attacks to have ever occurred are:

- The attack on Ukraine's power grids that took place on Dec 23, 2015 when hackers took control of the mission-control systems and shut down energy substations, leaving over 225,000 customers without power. Staff of the Ukraine power grid watched helplessly as the system was shut down, but the attack taught valuable lessons not just to Ukraine but also to the rest of the world.

- ADP (a huge tax and benefit services payroll company) suffered a cyber-attack in which private and sensitive information from some of their clients (more than 640,000 companies) was compromised. One of these clients, Bancorp, a US bank, reported that their W-2 – detailed wage and tax information that can be used to obtain fraudulent tax refunds form the Internal Revenue Service – was stolen. According to RHEA Group, the hackers used "sophisticated multi-stage attack vectors" to breach ADP's complex network and firewalls.

• The Central Bank of Bangladesh suffered a massive cyber-attack on May 17, 2016, in which they lost 81 million dollars. The hackers' target was one billion dollars of the bank assets, and only a printing error detected by a bank employee prevented their plan from succeeding. The hackers targeted what is known as SWIFT (Society for Worldwide Interbank Financial Telecommunication), which operates the worldwide funds transfer network for banks. So that the reader can have an idea of the magnitude of the hacking perpetrated in Bangladesh, the description of SWIFT provided by wired.com is as follows:

> SWIFT dates back to the 1970s, is based in Belgium and is overseen by the National Bank of Belgium and a committee composed of representatives from the US Federal Reserve, the Bank of England, the European Central Bank, the Bank of Japan and other major banks. The SWIFT platform has some 11,000 users and processes about 25 million communications a day, most of them money transfer transactions.

In an alarming article by Kim Zetter (May 17, 2016) on the insecurity and unreliability of SWIFT, which up until then had been considered impenetrable, the depth of the potential problems, along with the lack of privacy for end users, is laid bare. According to Zetter:

The incidents also raise integrity issues about the trustworthiness of SWIFT reporting. The United States government relies on SWIFT transaction records to alert it to suspicious money transfers that could be related to terrorism financing. The so-called Terrorist Finance Tracking Program has, according to the government, allowed the US and our allies to identify and locate operatives and their financiers, chart terrorist networks, and help keep money out of their hands. But if hackers could so easily subvert systems at SWIFT endpoints as they did in Bangladesh Bank's heist, they could conceivably do the same thing to initiate money transfers that feed terrorist groups or countries whose bank account funds are frozen by international sanctions.

Among the most famous cyber-attacks in the United States, the following five stand out:

- In Oct 21, 2014, hackers broke into the iCloud accounts of many of Apple's clients, including Hollywood celebrities, and stole compromising pictures which they uploaded to the worldwide web for anyone to see.

- In Aug 2016, spyware was detected in the iPhone of Ahmed Mansoor, (well-known human rights lawyer in UAE) that enabled an infected iPhone to be used as a mobile camera and microphone to snoop on the user's activities. Owners of iPhones had to download a protective patch to protect them from this spyware.

- In December 2015, Target Corporation was hacked and the personal information of over 11 million consumers compromised. To date, Target is still facing issues arising from that information leak. The hack has reportedly cost the company over $148 million, and some security experts say it could end up costing it one billion. Information on over three million credit cards was sold and used on the black market, before banks managed to cancel all the cards.

- On September 18, 2014, Home Depot's system was similarly hacked and over 60 million people had their credit card details stolen. In this case, the hacking went on for five months before the breach was detected. Home Depot eventually agreed to pay $19.5 million in damages. Just imagine that every time you use your credit card, all your personal information is fair game for a skilful hacker. Many experts say it is just a matter of time before this will happen to you.

- In July 2015, Canadian Wal-Mart customers were hacked through Wal-Mart Canada's Photo Centre online photo processing website operated by PNI Digital Media. PNI Digital is owned by Staples, which was a victim of another cyber-attack in the fall of 2015, when many Staple locations in the northeastern United States were hit by point-of-sale malware. This attack infected over one million credit card holders.

- In Sept of 2017, the Atlanta (Equifax), GA-based credit corporation admitted to a huge credit breach. Names, driver's license numbers, birth dates, home addresses, and social security numbers were stolen. Over 145 million people were affected, mostly in the USA.

Hackers are sometimes professional criminals, but often they are just troubled. They are smart and highly skilled teenagers with a passion for computers. They are usually loners with an uncontrollable sense of curiosity and are known as cyberspace explorers. Readers who google "most famous hackers" will find many amazing cases of youthful hackers who breached complex firewalls and other advanced security protocols just for the challenge of it. In the process, however, they hijacked huge corporations and government agencies, caused millions of dollars in damages, and in some cases triggered national security alerts. Professional hackers, usually work in highly organized international gangs and sell the confidential information they steal. When caught, they are usually sent to jail, but most serve relatively short sentences compared to the damage they caused, mainly because 90 per cent of them are minors, so penalties are lenient.

My "favourite" hacker was Jonathan James, known online as "the comrade." He was only 15 years old when he hacked several major organizations, including NASA, the US Department of Defense, Bell South, and the Miami-Dade school system. When caught, he was tried under juvenile criminal law and sentenced to several years in prison, but was placed under house arrest. He was arrested again and jailed for six months for violating his probation terms. A few years after his ordeal, other companies and organizations were breached, and suspicion fell on James again. The subsequent FBI investigation placed a lot of pressure on the young man, and James unfortunately ended up committing suicide to avoid prosecution for crimes he maintained he had never committed.

Security risks and new technology

Technologies are dynamic and change on a daily basis, especially in the social, mobile, and cloud areas. If users do not protect themselves with proper security measures, data is at high risk. When employees use a tablet or an iPhone as a personal device but share company pictures, images, and data, they are placing the company's future at serious risk. There is a lot of sensitive information that employees share inadvertently with others and that can easily be intercepted by hackers and put to an improper use. However, more and more companies are finally paying attention and implementing adequate information security protocols (controls, certifications, and other processes). Companies offering protective measures against security breaches are in high demand nowadays. People's rights is a very serious concern.

CHAPTER THREE: PEOPLE'S RIGHTS AND NATIONAL VALUES

Tolerance, Respect, and Social Reciprocity

We live in an age when everyone in North America and beyond should fully accept that we are all different and that we need to be tolerant and respectful of others. Tolerance and respect cannot exist, however, without social reciprocity. We cannot prosper in peace without this "rule of reciprocity."

In turn, the rule of reciprocity requires consistency and continuity. Tolerance and respect always have to go both ways. They are not a one-way street. One-way tolerance and respect can only provide short-lived solutions. So, while it is a given that we ought to be tolerant and respectful of others, we should also expect the same in return. Unfortunately, only a few of us demand this reciprocity unwaveringly and persistently in our daily lives. It does not come naturally to many.

Why is this the case?

Well, the key to achieving tolerance and respect is self-discipline, and we know this is extremely difficult for most human beings. If we lack self-restraint, we definitely cannot master the rigorous challenges of being patient and tolerant and showing respect for others. It is a huge challenge to exert the willpower to control our emotions, desires, and actions. Yet self-control is a powerful psychological, self-regulated quality that empowers those who can master it to triumph in sports, business, politics, hobbies, social relationships, etc.

People exhibit their lack of self-control and the tolerance and respect it enables in many different ways that undermine the rule of reciprocity and place societies at risk. The emphasis in this chapter is on the resulting failure to recognize and implement policies and enforcement measures to promote the rule of reciprocity. We will look at three areas:

1. Acknowledging women's, children's, and LGBTQ2 rights.
2. Respecting and protecting North American values.
3. Assisting immigrants to adapt and integrate.

These three points seem obvious and logical. The average citizen assumes they are guaranteed in our North American societies, but the reality is that we are still far from upholding and protecting essential human rights in these areas. They are slipping between our fingers due to political correctness, lax and lenient laws, and lack of two-way tolerance.

These three subjects are extremely important in every corner of our world, not just in North America. Unfortunately, in certain parts of our planet, there are serious problems upholding fairness, justice, and a progressive and peaceful life for all. In particular, respect for women, children, and LGBTQ2 people, although understood and pursued in many developed and developing countries, still seems to be light years away from where it should be.

Social reciprocity (the rule of reciprocity) refers to the manner in which individuals treat and influence one another and are treated and influenced in return, on an equal and fair basis, especially in relation to social interactions between different cultures. As Kendra Cherry defines it in "What Is the Norm of Reciprocity" (verywell.com – Psychology - July 10, 2016):

> The norm of reciprocity, sometimes referred to as the rule of reciprocity, is a social norm where if someone does something for you, you then feel obligated to return the favour.

Although the rule of reciprocity is commonly thought of as a marketing and business norm, it is of utmost importance for avoiding social conflict in our daily social interactions in every country, but especially in multicultural societies.

Rights of Women, Children, and LGBTQ2

Throughout history, women's rights have been ignored, disregarded, and abused all over the world. It is ironic that men owe their lives to their mothers, they grow up with sisters, marry a woman, and have daughters whom they adore, but still do not respect women overall, either physically or mentally the way they should. Even today, in North America (and as sad as it may sound), women are still relegated to second place, regardless of whether men want to accept this or not. Sadly, that is the way it still is in the eighteenth year of this twenty-first century (March of 2018).

It is so bad that, in the state of Michigan, women need to purchase "rape insurance." The legislature there passed a bill prohibiting any insurance company from covering abortions, regardless of the causes (including incest and rape) or consequences. This was reported in Ms. Magazine (msmagazine.com) in their winter/spring 2014 issue by Anita Little, Melissa McGlensey, Lindsey O'brien and Ponta Abadi. According to these authors, women can buy separate insurance as long as they are not pregnant when they purchase the policy.

In Spain, a pending bill will greatly circumscribe women's abortion rights. In the summer of 2014, also in Ms. Magazine, Yolanda Dominguez reported that, in reaction to the upcoming bill, women had started a movement called "Register." In Madrid, Barcelona, Sevilla, Bilbao, and Zaragoza, women actually went to the streets and lined up to register their own bodies. As Dominguez says, they went to the Chamber of Commerce of Personal Property to do so and proclaimed:

> The body is our territory, which needs to be re-conquered by women: It has been molded by and for others, converted into an object, used as merchandise, assaulted, manipulated and subjected to impossible stereotypes.

It is unbelievable that women in today's world do not have full control of their own bodies. Abortion is penalized in many countries around the world. In countries like the US and Canada, anti-abortion activists are real threats to women and to society itself. Most are motivated by religious beliefs, along with a very narrow-minded view of freedom that would deprive women of their right to choose. How many anti-abortionists (or any other men) have had vasectomies to avoid impregnating women who may not want to get pregnant?

Women should have an absolute right to decide what to do with their own bodies. This includes the right to abort. It is not just their bodies but their futures that are at stake and at risk. Anti-abortionists only focus on the "rights" of the fetus, but take no responsibility for the unwanted child. They do not seem to care about actual living and breathing humans, including a woman's right to freedom and self-protection. What is mind-boggling is that even women are marching against abortion, regardless of whether the woman's own father or a serial killer, got her pregnant. It just seems to be a strong religious matter.

Anti-abortion groups call themselves "pro-life" and say their goal is the preservation of life. They include health groups, youth groups, legal groups, economic groups, medical groups, religious groups, and many others. Often, they compete against each other and have different strategies, goals, and objectives in mind. Some have an agenda of their own. An article published by Priests For Life entitled "The Unity of the Pro-life Movement" highlights this issue:

> … while there is good reason for the diversity and number of pro-life groups, there is never a justification for disunity. By disunity, I mean a phenomenon whereby one group sees another as a threat rather than as an ally, as one to compete with rather than cooperate with, despite the fact that the ultimate goal, restoring protection for human life, is the same (priestsforlife.org/columns/column7-20unity.html).

This shows that even anti-abortionists (pro-lifers) cannot get their act together and seem to have different interests above and beyond protecting human life. The same article concludes by citing the Pope: "The Holy Father sums it up: No single person or group has a monopoly on the defense and promotion of life. These are everyone's task and responsibility" (*Gospel of Life*, 91).

As a normal human being, I wonder if what pro-lifers and anti-abortionists state is really what they deeply believe. If so, where is the help for women they persuade to give birth instead of aborting? Where is the help to buy food, pay for the child's education, ensure the child's physical safety, support a better quality of life, provide non-religious mental and health support, buy clothes, and pay for shelter, heating, entertainment, books, etc. Isn't this supposed to be everyone's task and responsibility? Why preach "life" but not practice what they preach? Talk is cheap, but it is expensive to "walk the talk." I sometimes ask myself: isn't it cruel, unfair or even sadistic to prevent an abortion and allow that new life into this world without providing long-term protection, assistance and education, while leaving all responsibility on the mother's lonely shoulders?

It is especially irresponsible, unethical, and cruel to prohibit women from aborting when they lack the mental or economic stability to care for their child. Most will struggle for the rest of their lives without being able to provide properly for their child.

Anti-abortionist groups certainly will not take responsibility for the child; they either cannot or will not. Indeed, it is questionable whether they actually care for the well-being of that new life. Their "pro-life" crusade is more a matter of feeling good about themselves because they "saved a life," even when their efforts put a new life at risk.

Everyone seems to view a woman's decision to have an abortion as an easy thing, like deciding to dye her hair or choosing between a pizza and a salad for lunch. Of course, this is not the case! Abortion is a gut-wrenching decision that women have to live with for the rest of their lives. However, the practice has been going on for thousands of years and will not stop. Surely it is better to have it done in a clinic by a doctor and nurses than by a "back-alley" abortionist.

Neither religion nor misunderstood ethics should ever govern and therefore, control a woman's body. They certainly do not govern men in any shape or form. Here is where gender equality should start. In my opinion, those women marching against abortion are also marching against gender equality and in favour of the subjugation and control of women. This is simply uncivilized and mind-boggling. Go figure!

In my view, women throughout history have suffered, and still do, in four main areas:

- Rape
- Physical and Mental Abuse
- Social Inequality
- Inherent physical characteristics (e.g. pregnancy, menstruation, menopause, etc.)

Rape

There is no doubt that the main causes of rape are men's lack of self-restraint, backward cultural values, mental illness, or simple selfishness and cowardliness. However, these and other "reasons" cannot in any way justify rape. Nothing, absolutely nothing, can justify it, and by the same token, rape needs to be punished as firmly and quickly as possible.

Some people argue that men rape because they feel superior to the opposite sex, which they think exists only to serve them. Such men rape in order to keep or gain control over women. They want to prove they have the power to subjugate the opposite sex. Some men, however, lack the power to control their sexual drive and cannot deal with rejection. For others, rape is a matter of revenge or simply a consequence of being under the influence of drugs or alcohol. Again, however, whatever the "reason," nothing, absolutely nothing, justifies this primitive, cowardly, animalistic, and cruel behavior. It is a barbaric action that should never go unpunished.

A rape often destroys the life of the woman and deeply affects the lives of her family members as well. If she also gets pregnant, other serious problems come into play that can be even more traumatic than the rape itself. When a rapist is caught, and proven guilty, I believe he should have his penis surgically removed. If the reader thinks this is too harsh, how about putting the rapist in prison in a section where there are only rapists and pedophiles, so that he is raped by the other inmates for the rest of his miserable life?

My grandfather used to say "for big problems, big solutions." We all know that rape is a serious problem happening all over the world, yet only a few rapists get caught and, even then, many still get away with their crime due to cultural or religious beliefs, errors in the legal system, and many other reasons. But when they get away with rape, they will repeat the crime time and again. That is just human nature. Thus, vigilantes often have to act because the legal system has failed them.

The issue of rape can be "delicate" due to cultural or religious beliefs. Many perpetrators go unpunished because they live in societies that allow rape to go unpunished. These societies simply look the other way and sometimes blame the woman because she dared to go walking alone in the street, or for other weird, cruel, twisted, cowardly, and unjustified reasons. We live in the twenty-first century for crying out loud!

An article in The Economist (July 19-25, 2014) entitled "A Question of Proof – Sitting on Evidence" notes that, in the United States, only 12 per cent of rapes end even in an arrest. Just imagine, 88 per cent of rapists are going scot-free. To me, this is as unbelievable as it is alarming. Even when a charge is brought, it is usually a battle of "he said, she said." There is rarely objective and reliable evidence.

On the other hand, I think it is just as bad when a woman claims rape falsely. In such cases, the full weight of the legal system should punish her with serious repercussions, provided she is proven a liar without a shred of doubt. Luckily, nowadays we increasingly have the means to collect forensic evidence that, if analyzed properly, will enable the law to identify and punish many more perpetrators.

The Economist article also notes that many convicted rapists are forced to pay parental support when they make their victim pregnant. Unfortunately, they are also granted parental rights, which makes the life of the victim, the child, and the whole family a nightmare for the rest of their lives. According to this article, in Massachusetts (and 16 other US states), there is no specific law restricting parental rights for rapists who impregnate their victim. This is a recipe for disaster. In the rapist's distorted thinking, he probably believes he deserves to have parental rights simply because he was ordered to pay child support. In his weak and unbalanced mind, he feels this gives him the right to participate in the life of "his" child, while inflicting horrible memories and continued torture on the victim and her family. How can a woman who was the victim of rape ever get over the trauma of the assault if she has to respect the rapist's parental rights? This is like adding salt and lemon to the wound!

Many states in the US in effect promote revenge and vigilantism by not taking away the rights of a rapist who has been found guilty. The lack of appropriate legal penalties allows the perpetrator to keep torturing his victim and her family. Is this in the best interest of the child? Absolutely not, yet the system permits it. According to the Economist article:

> The emphasis is always on the best interest of the child. However, the state of Massachusetts allows the court to terminate parental rights if "the parent has been convicted of a felony that the court finds is of such a nature, that the child will be deprived of a stable home for a period of years." Common sense suggests that it should also apply to rape, and most judges are sensible; but not all.

This was exactly the case with Mr Jaime Melendez in Massachusetts, when he was found guilty of rape and forced to pay child support, yet his parental rights had not been revoked at the time the article was published. Now, another delicate and alarming aspect concerns the number of cases in which the police just sit on evidence and do nothing. The same Economist article goes on to explain how, in Detroit alone, more than 11,300 untested sexual assault kits (also known as rape kits) were discovered in 2009. Some dated back to the 1980s. Even more alarming:

> Tests of the first 1,600 kits have already matched the DNA of hundreds of known criminals, including nearly 90 serial rapists, who have gone on to offend in 23 other states.... Tens of thousands of untested kits have been discovered in police warehouses in [other parts of]

the US alone, including as many as 20,000 in Texas, 4,000 in Illinois, and more than 12,000 in Memphis [Tennessee], where three survivors are now suing the city for mishandling evidence. In addition, crime labs are estimated to have a backlog of 100,000 rape kits. Such delays betray victims. Most rapists are never caught.

We all have to do something to improve as much as possible the statistics in rape cases. You hear and read about rape everywhere and all the time. It is a serious matter that needs serious attention. And as if this were not enough, rape does not happen only to women. Young boys are also victims of sadistic, twisted, sick adults. Usually, the perpetrators in these cases are individuals in positions of trust, such as coaches, priests, and even police officers. A recent article in The Canadian, entitled "Former Mountie Charged with Sexual Assault," reported:

> Saskatchewan RCMP say a former Mountie is charged in the sexual assault of three boys under the age of 18 while he was an officer in Yorkton. Police say Alan John Davidson lived in Yorkton from 1986 to 1993 and had contact with children as a member of the RCMP and as a hockey coach.

Davidson was arrested at age 59 and sentenced for crimes going back many years. When rape is committed by people we trust, it is not just painful and sad but extremely delicate and worrisome.

Gang rape is perhaps the ultimate crime against women. During wars, the women of the defeated country have suffered this throughout human history. All conquering armies have done it. In general, in war, the men are killed, the children spared, and the women imprisoned and usually gang-raped often repeatedly. However, gang rape is not confined to wartime. In many countries, such as in India, gang rapes are a common, serious problem for local communities and authorities. In such cases, it is a cultural problem that needs a drastic and immediate solution. The Huffington Post (January 22 of 2016) published an article entitled "Four Convicted in India Bus Rape Case." Written by Katy Daigle and Shivani Rawat, the article reported:

> An Indian court convicted four men Tuesday in the deadly gang rape of a young woman on a moving New Delhi bus, a brutal crime that galvanized public anger over the widespread – yet widely tolerated – sexual violence faced by Indian women. As word of the verdict filtered out, protesters outside the courthouse chanted, "Hang them! Hang them!" The men were convicted on all 11 counts against them, including rape and murder, and now face the possibility of hanging.

Indeed, there seems to be an "epidemic" rape in India. A woman is raped in that country every 20 minutes. It is a cultural problem that has existed for thousands of years there, as well as in many other countries in Asia, the Arab world, and Africa. Some countries in Latin America, although not as bad, are not too different.

In Saudi Arabia, women of all ages require a male companion to accompany them if they leave the house. It is just until Sept 26, 2017 that a new decree was issued to allow Saudi women to drive. But it is to be implemented only until June 24 of 2018. Women represented 13 per cent of the labor force by the end of 2015. By the end of 2018 is forecasted to reach 17 to 18 per cent. Though, in general, they are expected to be kept "safe" at home doing only "womanly" duties such as cooking, cleaning, knitting, dusting, laundry, and getting pregnant and caring for children. Is that the only future a woman can look forward to?

All people, men and women, should have the freedom to choose how they wish to live their lives, yet people everywhere still make jokes based on women's' supposed weaknesses – "you run/throw/cry like a girl!" That style of demeaning comparison must stop. Throughout history, men have shown their disrespect for the opposite gender. Even in the 21st century, men continue to trample on the dignity and rights of women. Of course, this is denied and rarely tackled head on, but it is a fact that is easy to prove, as we will be doing later in this chapter. If men have no tolerance or patience for women's rights and equality, how can they expect to have respect for themselves or the environment?

In the twenty-first century, there are many countries and religions that still relegate women to third-class citizenship and disrespect them in many social and professional activities. Their opportunities to succeed are not even close to those of men. This is also happening, although to a lesser extent, in North America. It is obvious that the will to stop the abuse of women and to be respectful, fair, and gentlemanly towards them, is still not present in many men.

Physical and Mental Abuse of Women

Women have been victims of both physical and mental abuse throughout history. In more "civilized" countries, women more often endure verbal rather than physical abuse, but this is not the case in much of the developing world. For example, in the journal Archives of Women's Mental Health, an article entitled "Violence against women in South Asian countries" by Unaiza Niaz (Feb 5, 2003) from the Psychiatric and Stress Research Centre in Karachi, Pakistan, exposes the alarming and unsettling way women are treated in that corner of the world. Among many important observations, I want to quote three:

1. In South Asian countries the amalgamation of Buddhist, Confucian, Hindu, Islamic, and Christian traditions have shaped the personalities of women and determined their social status. Rigid cultures and patriarchal attitudes which devalue the role of women result in the widespread occurrence of violence against women. The family structure, in which the man is the undisputed ruler of the household and activities within the families are seen as private, allows violence to occur at home. As well as traditional forms of violence such as wife-battering and sexual assault, women in these countries are also exposed to dowry crimes such as bride burning, kidnapping for the purpose of prostitution, and "honor killings." Laws permit discrimination against women and discourage reporting of violent acts. Efforts to remedy this situation must include changes in local laws and assistance from the United Nations and the international community.

2. In Hindu culture patriarchal values support female inferiority (Segala 1999). On the Indian subcontinent, the "theory of perpetual tutelage for women" was formulated by Manu, the Hindu lawgiver. He preached that education for girls should be stopped and that they should be prohibited from public life and restrict themselves to their homes. His dictum that a wife ought to respect her husband as God and serve him faithfully, even if he were vicious and void of any merit, was accepted as applicable to all women. Buddhism, very much like Hinduism, considered women subservient to men. Buddhism further taught that women lure a man away from the path of NIRVANA or SALVATION. The Buddha had to leave his kingdom, wife and child to attain purity. Women were considered to be temptresses who hinder a man's rise above the worldly status. Islam is relatively new in Asia. It penetrated the Sindh province of Pakistan through the historic Khyber

Pass, on the border of Pakistan and Afghanistan in the 12th century A.D. and through other countries of Asia via sea route. The status of women in Islam was much higher than the one granted by Buddhism and Hinduism. Islam gave women the legal right to own property, marry, and divorce. Her status in the community was very much like [that of] a man and determined by her deeds. In early Islam, women excelled in scholarships, medicine and warfare. However, with the passage of time and due to its basic teaching of tolerance and respect for other religions, Islam absorbed much from the local cultures of India, and changed its view of women's status according to the culture of the host country.

3. Islam absorbed the Hindu culture's patriarchal values, which support female inferiority, and these values were transmitted to the younger generations, resulting in family violence tolerated as a male right to control those who are dependent. Hence Islam in most countries of the world today is the male interpretation of uneducated or semi-educated Maulanas (Ulema-priests). This interpretation came to include all the negative implications of other religions such as the inequality and subjugation of women, denying women's rights of inheritance, divorce and marriage etc. Today the culture prevalent in the South Asian Muslim countries is completely contrary to Islamic religious teachings. In Afghanistan, for example, under Taliban rule, women were totally deprived of the right to education, work, health care, legal recourse and recreation.

Why do men feel the need to abuse those who depend on them? Where is the sense of love and protection instead of domination?

Niaz wrote a very detailed article that is more alarming because things have not changed much, if at all, since she wrote it. She mentions other countries, such as Japan, where the traditional family structure is very much patriarchal, being the father the leader of the family. Japanese culture may not be as violent as other cultures, but still treats women without the respect they deserve. As a result, fewer and fewer women are getting married there, and more are remaining single and independent, while still fighting for equal job opportunities and equitable salaries. On Japan, Niaz observes:

> In Japanese social systems and practices, there are many policies and systems that are based on gender stereotypes. Even those which seem to be gender-neutral on the surface function differently for men and women, reflecting their different status in society.

According to Niaz, the second most common cause of divorce in Japan is physical abuse of women. Often, they endure it for years until finally "enough is enough," and they acquire the valor to separate themselves from the abuser. In her article, Niaz writes clearly and in a very eloquent style, but her words are painful to read and digest.

Just imagine for a second what it must be like for a woman to live in such countries. And what is worse, there are other hideous acts taking place on a daily basis against women in those countries, yet practically nothing is being done to help them. There are no effective social programmes for women's protection. As Niaz mentions, kidnappings, "honor killings," and dowry violence are rampant. Added to the everyday sexual harassment and rapes, these make the lives of women extremely difficult, to say the least. In many countries, women also have to be cautious with the police, who tend to be unreliable, or even dangerous and cruel. In fact, Niaz writes, "incidents of abuse of women detained by police and the involvement of policemen in the rape of women during imprisonment are commonly reported." In many parts of Asia, Africa, and Latin America, women's human rights and fundamental freedoms are challenged every day. In North America and Europe, unpleasant things also happen, though at a lower rate, but, if apprehended, men at least will not go unpunished.

Women protect and care for the well-being of all little boys and girls. They nurture and love them throughout their infancy. All little boys are brought up mainly by their mothers, grandmothers, aunts, or sisters. Yet in many cultures, these innocent boys grow up influenced and ultimately misguided by their society into adopting a vicious attitude against the "weaker sex," and like rabid dogs, they bite the hands of those who protected and fed them during their infancy and childhood, now including even their own wives and daughters. How can anybody justify these barbaric acts against women? It seems that grandparents, fathers, and elder brothers are teaching boys from an early stage in life that the way to "be a man" is to abuse women. Perhaps they do not even teach this intentionally, but boys learn by observing the examples their elders provide. It is obviously doubtful that women are teaching boys that they want to be abused!

These sexist attitudes are much more widespread in cultures with markedly different values from those of North America. This is the reason why a former candidate of the Conservative Party in Canada, Ms. Kelly Leitch, was demanding the screening of refugees to ensure that they will respect our Canadian values if they are admitted into the country. The majority of the Canadians are in favour of such screening.

The United Nations must do something about enforcing everything related to the Convention on the Elimination of All Forms of Discrimination Against Women (CEDAW, 1992;

Burney and McArthur, 1999). Pakistan is one of the countries that stands out for its government's lack of action to enforce CEDAW. In Canada, by contrast, a valuable program to prevent rape trains women to avoid difficult and dangerous situations and other "rape scenarios." As reported by Erin Anderssen in The Globe and Mail (June 11, 2015) in her article entitled "Resistance Works." The programme has helped reduce rape incidents by 50 per cent, but according to Anderssen, we still need a profound "cultural change" to eliminate rape entirely. Clearly, this will take time, and meanwhile women need to protect themselves by, among other things, avoiding risky situations. Among the things women are taught in this programme are:

- To avoid offending others.

- To control the amount of alcohol they consume.

- To behave appropriately in other cultures by respecting their customs and traditions.

- To avoid travelling or going out alone where the local culture frowns on unaccompanied women.

- To always be aware of their situation and surroundings.

- To practice forceful verbal strategies such as yelling, swearing, screaming, etc. if attacked.

- To apply forceful physical strategies such as punching, scratching, kicking, biting, hair pulling, etc. if assaulted.

- To practice the "buddy system." To be responsible for each other until everyone is back home safe and sound.

- To avoid misunderstandings that may give others "ideas."

- To practice self-control and show others that nothing can

make them place themselves in a dangerous situation.

- To practice zero tolerance for sexist jokes. Such "micro-aggressions" can escalate.

- To leave a party or any event if they observe or foresee risky behavior and, if that behavior is directed towards them, to either look for immediate support or simply walk away.

- To avoid going to the bathroom alone in crowded, isolated, or unfamiliar places.

- Never to leave drinks unattended.

- Never, under any circumstances, to consume unknown substances (e.g. pills., free drinks, snacks, etc.), especially from strangers.

- Never to go alone into an empty parking lot or garage at night and to keep a safe distance from buildings, shrubbery, wooded areas, etc. when walking outdoors.

- To always carry a repellent spray for protection.

- To avoid using ear pods or headphones in public areas and to stay attentive and connected to their surroundings instead of to their iPods or cellphones.

- To use common sense, discretion, and logic in every situation.

- To dress appropriately for the occasion and to avoid dressing provocatively or wearing clothes that send the wrong messages. This last piece of advice is tricky, of course, because it may seem to blame a woman's clothing for a man's inability to respect others and control himself. I absolutely support a woman's right to dress as she pleases, but please: use common sense and "feminine intuition" to dress safely wherever you go.

According to Anderssen, sexual assault can be categorized into five basic types:

1. Complete rape
2. Attempted rape
3. Coercion
4. Attempted coercion
5. Non-consensual sexual contact.

A study of the programme found that:

> In all five categories, the rapes for the groups receiving the training were consistently lower. The rape events were reduced by half. Researchers believe this is because women learned to avoid risky situations and were more likely to stop coercive behavior before it escalated.

There is evidence that introducing such programmes at earlier stages in life (when young girls are discovering their sexuality) will give participants a decisive advantage in avoiding sexual assaults.

Victims of Social Inequality

Women are often victims of social inequality. They do not receive the same opportunities and rewards as men. This is more evident in underdeveloped and developing countries, but is also a serious problem in developed countries. In many industries, the "boys' club" is simply impenetrable to the opposite sex. Does this make sense? Not at all, but it is there, and will most likely stay forever unless something changes.

Two articles in The Economist (May 30-June 5, 2015) throw some very interesting light on this issue. The first article, "The Weaker Sex" points out that more than 90 per cent of prime ministers, presidents, and CEOs are men and that men also dominate areas such as music, finance, sports, film, and technology. Women have been gaining ground, but mainly in the education and health sectors.

However, the second article, "Men Adrift" observes that in schools and universities, men are losing ground compared to their female counterparts and are therefore having more problems adapting to the rapidly changing demands of the workplace. In particular, men with older skills who do not update their knowledge are falling behind. If they lose their jobs, especially in manufacturing, the odds are they will never work again. When this happens, men can lose more than their jobs. They often lose their partners and their families as well. The risks are highest among men who only have a high school diploma; those with university degrees tend to adapt better to the changing job market. The article nevertheless regards the increasing equality of the sexes as one of the greatest social achievements of modern times, arguing that nowadays anybody can accomplish their goals and ambitions regardless of gender.

Although "Men Adrift" also confirms that 95 per cent of Fortune 500 CEOs, along with 93 per cent of the self-made billionaires on the Forbes Rich List, are men, it points out that, since World War II, the "real money" has increasingly been made in work requiring intellectual skills, and this is where, slowly but surely, men are falling behind. For example, women now outnumber men on most college campuses, especially in Asia and sub-Saharan Africa.

The article also confirms that, in Organization for Economic Cooperation and Development (OECD) countries, males now achieve only 42 per cent of university degrees, in contrast to women who achieve the remaining 58 per cent. The OECD includes 34 democratic governments with free-market economies that interact on a daily basis and that work with another 70 non-member countries to promote sustainable growth and prosperity.

One of the main problems with men is their attitude, which tends to be less pleasant and understanding than women's, who tend to be more customer-oriented, especially in the 30 occupations expected to grow most rapidly in the future, according to Hanna Rosin in her book "The End of Men". According to Rosin, women now dominate in 20 of these 30 occupations, most notably in nursing, accounting, eldercare, childcare, food processing and preparation, and hotel services.

As Peggy Orenstein, author of *Schoolgirls* and *Waiting for Daisy* comments:

> Men have been the dominant sex since, well, the dawn of mankind. And yet, as journalist Hanna Rosin discovered, that long-held truth is no longer true. Women are no longer merely gaining on men; they have pulled decisively ahead by almost every measure.

The Economist article "Men Adrift" gives some very interesting figures on degrees earned by men vs. women:

- In the United Sates alone, the percentage of women with only high school education or less fell from 32.9 per cent in 1979 (one per cent higher than men) to 11.4 per cent in 2013 (one per cent lower than men).

- The percentage of men who reach the peak of their working age still holding a job fell from 95 per cent in 1965 to 84 per cent in 2010. This an alarming drop. By March 2018, this trend was still strong.

- In Great Britain, the percentage of men aged between 16 and 64 who are in work fell from 92 per cent in 1971 to 76 per cent in 2013, but for women it rose from 53 per cent to 67 per cent. By March of 2018, this trend was still continuing.

Similar trends are happening in Canada and Mexico. The gap in social equality that used to exist between men and women in North America is closing, and closing fast, to the benefit of the social and economic fairness of future generations.

Victims of Their Own Biology

Does the fact of women being in a less advantageous physical condition compared to men (i.e. less physical strength, prone to difficult menstruation and menopause, subject to pregnancy) mean we should abuse and take advantage of them? If we say yes to that preposterous question, we are authorizing men to act like Neanderthals. By not acknowledging women's different biology, some men are being real bullies in our society and setting a bad example for our children. The Capital News of November 06, 2012 published a letter entitled "School yard bullies graduate to workplace" by N.W. Smith, in which she writes: "We teach our children that bullying is not to be tolerated and to report it to a parent or teacher." As adults, we all have the right to a safe environment to work in, free from harassment, bullying, and sexual discrimination, which are even recognized as criminal offenses in some cases. In her letter, Smith argues that, regardless of how workers and co-workers ought to behave, people, and especially men, still behave improperly towards female and even other male co-workers. It happens everywhere, though in some industries more than others, such as the health care industry as per Smith's letter to the editor.

Aparita Bhandaria, a journalist living in Toronto, observed in the Globe and Mail (May 8, 2015) that "a culture of shame is more dangerous than sex education." Many parents complain that sex education in schools starts too early and that, in any case, it should be taught at home by mom and dad. Unfortunately, by making sex education taboo, we create a silence that could be worse than any miseducation. I agree that introducing very early sex education in schools might not be the best decision. Not all children are created equal. They do not develop at the same speed, and selecting the proper age to begin sex education is very important. To shame and blame women because they *are* women and, for example, experience menstruation, is aggressive, shameful and unnecessary. Bhandaria writes:

> I was around seven years old when I was told I was impure. It was at a family get-together in India that involved a religious ceremony. My mother had her period at the time, and had been segregated to a cold, dark room. I had no idea what was wrong with her, only that I never wanted to have what she had. I was impure by association. I was told I needed to take a purifying bath if I wanted to sit with my cousins. Eager to please, I splashed cold water on my shivering body. But I could not wash away the sense of shame.

Bhandaria also reveals that she never had an opportunity to have "the talk" with her parents, yet everybody around her (friends and family members) told her to be very careful in what she wore and how she acted, because she could be raped. Thanks to the more open society where she now lives, she understands that it is better to have sex education than to live in shame and silence. When people avoid talking about sex, they create fear and shame about something that comes naturally and instinctively to humans, as to all other animals.

Fixing Feminism

The most basic definition of feminism relates to equality between men and women and to any movement seeking to achieve the goal of equality. The premise of feminism is that women have not been treated equally and that this unfairly disadvantages them. Feminism holds that women are accorded a diminished and false sense of equality. Feminism is therefore about social, economic, and political fairness and equal rights. It works to end sexism, gender-based abuse, and misogyny and to place women's rights and interests on the same level as those of men. It fights to end sexism, patriarchy, and all forms of abuse based on gender. Women worldwide deserve equal rights for education and personal development.

A more in-depth definition of feminism is offered by Eastern Kentucky University's Women and Gender Studies programme (http://wgs.eku.edu/what-feminism-0):

> Feminism is an interdisciplinary approach to issues of equality and equity based on gender, gender expression, gender identity, sex, and sexuality as understood through social theories and political activism. Historically, feminism has evolved from the critical examination of inequality between the sexes to a more nuanced focus on the social and performative constructions of gender and sexuality. Feminist theory now aims to interrogate inequalities and inequities along the intersectional lines of ability, class, gender, race, sex, and sexuality, and feminists seek to effect change in areas where these intersectional ties create power inequity. Intellectual and academic discussion of these inequities allows our students to go into the world aware of injustices and to work toward changing unhealthy dynamics in any scenario. Feminist political activists campaign in areas such as reproductive rights,

domestic violence, fairness, social justice, and workplace issues such as family medical leave, equal pay, and sexual harassment and discrimination. Any time stereotyping, objectification, infringements of human rights, or intersectional oppression occurs, it's a feminist issue.

In "How to fix feminism" (New York Times, June 11-12, 2016), Judith Shulevitz discusses how tough it remains for women, especially mothers, to compete with their male counterparts on an even basis, but also offers the example of Hillary Clinton, whose story gives hope to every woman in North America and every corner of the world, that tomorrow can be better. Shulevitz writes: "To me, Mrs. Clinton's sheer professional survival is as inspiring as any as her other accomplishments." This feeling has reverberated across the world.

Hillary is a vivid example that where there is a will, there is a way, and that anything is possible. Shulevitz is convinced we live in a rich age of feminism, which also celebrates a full range of diverse identities that range from a different colour of the skin to a different sexual orientation. She argues that "women…who scale back in the face of impossible expectations feel themselves morphing into caricatures: attachment freaks, helicopter moms, concerted cultivators, neo-traditionalists."

Shulevitz also pursues an idea that the average man has probably not even thought about. She notes that Hillary's generation has always aimed to free women from domestic work but points out that work outside the home can be a different type of prison. In her article, she uses the word "caregiver," which she defines within the boundaries of those who "demand dignity and economic justice for parents (male or female) dissatisfied with a few weeks of unpaid parental leave, and who try to mitigate the sacrifices made by adult children responsible for aging parents." She believes that more "family-friendly policies" should be implemented and that any woman celebrity could be the champion of a campaign for these. In all spheres, fairer working opportunities are essential for giving women a stronger position in society but are not a complete answer to women's problems. Women need a lot more than just equal employment opportunities and fair pay.

Women as Sex Objects

Some women seem to feel that portraying themselves as sex objects will give them power. This is utterly incomprehensible. In fact, it is demeaning and embarrassing, especially for the educated younger generation that can see how men have taken advantage of that mistaken conception that the exploitation of female sexuality will open fair and equal doors to women. Yes, men may respond to women who use their sexuality to get ahead, but after gratifying themselves, they will regard those women as inferior, to say the least, and never look at them again. Unfortunately, however, we live in a hyper-sexualized culture in which some girls end up believing that being sexual object brings power and success. This can end up being detrimental in their future. But they fail to see it.

As Anne Kingston in "Outraged moms, trashy daughters" (Maclean's, August 16, 2010) observes, "for these girls, Snoop Dogg's misogynist 'Bitches Ain't S—t' is not an affront but a ring tone, and *slut* and *bitch* are not put-downs but affectionate greetings between female friends." The problem is that social media, television programmes, pop songs, and computer games hound and almost harass young girls into adopting a sexualized and self-diminishing culture that has a negative impact on many. These young girls feel an unrealistic sense of empowerment. This feeling crumbles after they have been around "feeling good," falsely perceiving themselves as mature women and having fun only temporarily. In social gatherings, they drink over their limit and go wild, doing things that are caught on cellphone cameras for the world to see. They do not see the risk they are inflicting on their reputation, but rest assured, those photos will come back to haunt them, in some cases for the rest of their lives. Any young man full of testosterone will respond to a lady's sexual advances, but will certainly never take them seriously or as the basis for a lasting relationship. If that is a woman's distorted sense of sexual feminism, she is in for a rude awakening and a very different future reality. Men who have had lots of women are envied and admired by other men, but it is the opposite with women. They are seen as promiscuous and slutty. I know this is an unfair double standard, but for now it is the world we live in, whether we like it or not.

According to Kingston, the wrong information regarding popular culture is coming at warp speed through social media. This is "junk food" that distorts behavior and reasoning and inhibits logical thinking and common sense. Kingston contends that "millennials" (born in the late 80s and early 90s) have been bombarded with a false sense of "empowerment" that pushes them into sexual misbehavior and illogical and blatant overconsumption. She ends her article with this heartfelt message: "I am so deeply pained to see girls being groomed to believe their purpose in life is to be sexual beings that please men."

Discrimination against Women by Women

In 2012, the Harvard Gazette published a study by Mahazarin R. Banaji that exposed prejudice by women against other women based on race, gender, weight, skin colour, sexuality, disability, and religion. In a report in Time magazine (Oct 4, 2012) on the study's finding that even women prefer to hire men, Ericka Christakis comments:

You would think that people with a history of being discriminated against in the workplace might give those whom they resemble a break. But a growing body of research confirms exactly the opposite: women are just as likely as men to show sexism toward women in hiring practices, salaries, and professional mentorship. One study … [by Banaji] even found that people of both genders would forgo thousands of dollars in salary to have a male boss. The pervasiveness of cognitive bias is depressing. It's more palatable to think of sexism or racism or ageism as a symptom of a few rotten apples than as a fundamental human trait. But if we're all doing it, even to ourselves, how on earth can we move beyond the stereotypes?

What is worse, some women even promote female genital mutilation (FGM), in which the female's clitoris is cut in an effort to diminish the girl's sexual desire so that she is more likely to be a virgin when married. Although many Muslim-majority countries follow the practice, it is done for cultural, not religious, reasons.

Empowerment of Women

Robert Engelman has been directing some very important research at the World Watch Institute, while acting as the president. The Institute's challenging mission is "to accelerate the transition to a sustainable world that meets human needs":

> The Institute's top mission objectives are universal access to renewable energy and nutritious food, expansion of environmentally sound jobs and development, transformation of cultures from consumerism to sustainability, and an early end to population growth through healthy and planned childbearing (worldwatch.org/mission).

Engelman's research is focused on family planning and its relationship to a sustainable environment. In an article in Scientific American (February 2016) entitled "Six Billion in Africa," he begins by exposing something we all should know and be doing something about, although it seems the great majority is failing to do so. Engelman writes:

> Earth is a finite place. The more people who inhabit it, the more must compete for its resources. Globally, women are giving birth to 2.5 children, half as many as in the early 1950s. In 40 percent of the world's nations, the fertility rate is at or below the "replacement" level of 2.1 children per woman.

However, he notes that Africa is an exception. Its population is expanding at a faster rate, well beyond what was previously forecast by the United Nations. The UN had projected a global population of 9.1 billion people by 2100. It has now revised this to 11.2 billion. The burden on Earth's natural resources is obvious and likely to be catastrophic, regardless of how much our technologies progress in relation to agriculture, food processing, housing, job creation, water consumption, and energy. According to Engelman, in Africa alone the population could easily jump from 1.2 billion in 2015 to between 3 billion and 6.1 billion. He poses two key questions:

1. How can the fertility rate in the African continent be slowed to no higher than the replacement level of 2.1 to 2.3 children per woman?

2. How can other countries in Latin America, Asia, and South East Asia achieve these fertility rates as well?

Engleman's research suggests two main potential solutions:

1. Empower women socially, economically, politically, and, above all, educationally. If governments and industry implement programmes to protect and educate women,

amazing things can happen due to a more educated and confident female population base.

2. Provide men with social, economic, political, and educational guidance and support. The expansion and diversification of their economic opportunities (combined with a reduction in corruption at all levels) will help create new jobs for both men and women.

A strong government programme to promote the use of contraceptives can do miracles. This has been proven in Tunisia, for example, where the fertility rate fell from seven to two children per woman, and in Mauritius, which brought its fertility rate from six to 1.5 children per woman (*below* the replacement rate). However, Engelman notes that "for such efforts to succeed, government leaders must encourage public and policy conversations about slower population growth." At the same time, the growth of local economies is required. Economic power, particularly the empowerment of women, expands freedom of choice.

Despite economic expansion and the strengthening of democracy, most African countries still suffer high levels of corruption, exploitation, and oppression, along with high fertility rates and a slow pace of economic development. Other negative factors affecting the African continent include droughts, inefficient farming, poverty, food insecurity, and limited opportunities for education. Fortunately, some countries are pushing hard to overcome these problems. Such is the case of Mauritius, where according to Engelman, the steepest drop in fertility happened in the 60s and 70s when the government overcame pressure from religious groups (mainly Muslim and Catholic) and vigorously promoted family planning. Luckily, women and men in Mauritius are more educated than their counterparts in neighboring countries, and they responded positively to fertility control measures promoted by their government.

In the case of Tunisia, it is worth quoting Engelman's article:

> In 1957 Tunisia's first President, Habib Bourguiba, set in motion a sea of change in the legal status and reproductive health of women; hard to imagine in a mostly Muslim country. Bourguiba guaranteed women full citizenship rights, such as voting and removing their veil. He pledged universal primary school attendance for girls as well as for boys, banned polygamy, raised minimum marriage ages and granted women the right to divorce. He legalized contraception and then subsidized abortions for women with large families. By the mid-1960s, mobile-family planning clinics were offering oral contraceptives throughout the country.

Tunisia's example proves that any country can dramatically improve its future through good governance and economic policies geared towards the protection and well-being of citizens. Engelman's article also discusses changing male attitudes and recommends an integrated strategy to empower women to control their own fertility and their future.

Progressive Women

Over the past 40 years, almost all societies on the American continent have considered men as leaders and the pillars in professional arenas, while women have been considered more nurturing and supportive rather than as potential leaders. Fortunately for women, this is changing and, in some professions, such as veterinary care, accounting, financial services, insurance services, catering and events management, the apparel industry, and medicine, has been turned around already.

During 2018, the workplace dynamics in North America, especially in Canada, is undergoing a drastic and progressive change. Women are actually reversing the gender gap in many universities and professional careers. There are more and more females in colleges and universities on the American continent and around the world. "Gender blindness" in universities and in the work force is definitely gaining momentum. If men do not keep pace, they will be left behind. In fact, as previously noted, they have already been left behind in many disciplines, and the gap is bound to increase.

The Changing Face of Saudi Women

This is the title of an article by Cynthia Gorney in *National Geographic* (February 2016). She starts by observing:

> In a deeply conservative culture, women are carefully redefining the boundaries of a respectable public life. Modesty around strangers is obligatory, but some women now feel comfortable using social media like Instagram to celebrate their identities.

According to Gorney, although Saudi Arabia remains the "most profoundly gender-segregated nation on Earth," it is now undergoing extraordinary changes in the daily lives of the women of that country.

In the rest of the world, Saudi women are seen as victims or as so brainwashed that they feel indecent talking unsupervised to a man who is not a member of the family. The abuse of women throughout Saudi history is so ingrained in that society that few women even realize they are under complete subjugation by men, to the extent that they end up feeling guilty and remorseful if they are seen in the unsupervised company of a man not related to them. No wonder that when Europeans or Americans hug or simply shake hands with women outside of their family radius, it is unacceptable in the Saudi culture. Luckily, change is arriving, though at a slow pace, but it has started. There are now more women at university in Saudi Arabia than men. Eventually, this will empower women. By March of 2018, Saudi Arabia still forces women to live under the supervision of a legally authorized male guardian (father, brother or husband), and requires them to have their guardian's permission to get a passport or to travel abroad. Many Saudi women have little understanding of liberty and independence because of thousands of years of control and submission. Gorney says that Saudi women are obliged to hide the "female form" from any non-family men. As astonishing and disturbing as this can be for foreigners, it is normal for Saudis, even though some women (and men) are beginning to question it. Gorney writes:

> Nearly every woman who talked to me about covering invoked traditions, social pressure, religious devotion, and the primacy that Saudi culture places upon respectability, the assurance that a woman's honor – her fidelity and probity, if she is married; her modesty and virginity, if she is not – remains unimpeachable.

Men wear whatever they want to wear, from jeans, to suits, to "thobes" (white Arabian long robes), while women have to wear the "abaya" (long-sleeved or sleeveless, floor-length, traditionally black dresses) when in public, while covering their face as well, especially if they meet men outside their family (with or without supervision).

Gorney asked several people why the abaya needs to be black, which absorbs heat in one of the hottest countries in the world? The explanations were many. The most common was that black "is unappealing to man's gaze." Another cited the tradition that in Prophet Muhammad's time, women wore clothing resembling black crows. There is no law or any specific Islamic scripture that requires the abaya to be black. It is just a tradition. Even with the more relaxed social attitudes and higher education levels that exist in 2018, Saudi working women confront steep challenges due to factors such as lack of day care, gender segregation rules, and fewer opportunities for women to work in industries such as manufacturing and construction. For example, Gorney notes that 54 per cent of women 15 years old are homemakers, while 60 per cent of men the same age is employed.

Not All Women Earn Their Respect

Every woman, like every man, needs to earn respect from others within their society. Our conditioning, beliefs, and actions will either gain the respect or disrespect of others. A good example is that of Muslim women who immigrate to secular countries but insist on wearing the niqab (which covers everything except the eyes) or the burka (which covers everything including the eyes) regardless of the traditions, way of life, and feelings of the locals. To many, this amounts to disrespect and leaves the door open for cultural retaliation.

Many argue that anyone should be free to wear what he or she wants in their own society, but tourists or immigrants in foreign countries should respect and adapt to the traditions and ways of life of the society they are visiting. Many foreign women adopt the niqab or hijab in Muslim countries out of respect and to avoid being harassed by local men. Wouldn't it be wiser for Muslim women (and men) to adapt in turn to the country they are visiting as tourists or to their new country as recent immigrants or refugees instead of disrespectfully imposing their own traditions publicly? Or should secular societies respect these traditions and even embrace them as something new, interesting, and exotic?

Clothing styles are a matter of personal taste, but not when they represent a potential threat to peace and security. The Canadian Charter of Rights and Freedoms (CCRF) confirms that everybody has the following fundamental freedoms:

- Freedom of conscience and religion

- Freedom of thought, belief, opinion, and expression, including freedom of the press and other media of communication
- Freedom of peaceful assembly
- Freedom of association.

When the government of Prime Minister Steven Harper banned facemasks at citizenship ceremonies, it was found by the Federal Court of Appeal to violate the CCRF. But this ruling arguably violates the rights of all women to be free and equal. In fact, one Canadian Muslim woman, Raheel Raza, publicly stated that "Canada should ban the niqab and the burka in public" (Huffington Post, Sept 24, 2015) The great majority of North Americans agree. Why? Because, according to Raza:

> The argument ... [that] concealing one's face [is] ... a religious obligation [for Muslims] is contentious and is not backed by evidence. In Western societies, the niqab is also a symbol of distrust for fellow citizens and a statement of self-segregation. The wearer of a face veil is conveying: "I am violated if you look at me." It is a barrier in civic discourse. It also subverts public trust.

Is it not a violation of women's rights to enable them to be oppressed and controlled in their new country by traditions from thousands of years ago? Does this not end up being offensive to the rights and freedoms of local women? It is also clear that problems of security, oppression, and integration are going to follow, as I argue later in this book.

Domestic Violence

Domestic violence against women is a well-known disease in almost every culture and unfortunately is still very much present in Canada and the United States. In some areas, it remains a very delicate problem that needs proper and immediate attention. Nevertheless, according to the Canadian Women's Foundation (CWF), domestic violence in Canada has fallen over the years, partly because of government programmes promoting equality and respect. The greater financial freedom that more and more women enjoy has also strengthened their position in society and, as a result, their treatment by spouses and partners.

The CWF attributes the decrease in domestic violence mainly to the following factors:

> improved public awareness, more treatment programs for violent men, improved training for police officers and Crown attorneys, having the police lay charges rather than the victim, more coordination of community services, and the creation of domestic violence legislation in some areas of Canada.

But the CWF also acknowledges that rates of domestic violence remain much higher than what is reported. They say that 70 per cent of domestic violence is not reported. Men are also victims of domestic violence, but about 20 per cent less often than women (per the CWF). Domestic violence includes physical abuse, moral abuse, sexual abuse, verbal abuse, emotional abuse, spiritual abuse, and financial abuse, but many cultures accept such abuse as a matter of tradition, and some immigrants bring these traditions into their new countries. Often it takes two or three generations for these traditions to be abandoned.

According to The Province newspaper (June 24, 2016), the City of Surrey in the Metro Vancouver area, which has large immigrant populations, has only a "short critical window of opportunity to intervene … to increase the chances of keeping women and children safe and keep the offender accountable" for domestic violence. This matter is so important that the title of the article explains itself: "Only domestic violence on the docket."

Personal Note:

We need to utterly eradicate discrimination against women. For the great majority in North America, all gender bias needs to be abolished, because it impairs or endangers the recognition and acceptance of women on an equal level with men and with the same rights and standards. This should be directly correlated to human rights and the freedom for equal opportunities. But it is equally important to acknowledge that men should have the same rights as women in all areas and that both men and women should be punished for wrongdoing equally, regardless of where it takes place. We all know that gender-based aggression, abuse, and violence directed at the "weaker" gender is wrong and can never be justified. I put the word "weaker" in quotes, because I would love to see a man and a woman giving birth at the same time. I would bet everything I own that the man would scream more loudly and strongly and probably faint. Strength should be measured from the eyebrows up (brain mass), not how big the biceps are.

Unfortunately, women tend to be profoundly restricted in the enjoyment of their freedom and their rights on an equal basis with men. As a society, we need to teach the true value of equality from a very early stage of life, starting at elementary school and continuing through all education levels, while monitoring and enforcing behaviors as needed. Discrimination against women, and indeed discrimination against anyone, based on colour, religious beliefs, sexual orientation, or gender needs to be totally eliminated from our society.

In an article entitled "It's time to fulfill the promise to end violence against women" (unwomen.org, Oct 30/14), Phumzile Mlambo-Ngcuka, (Exec Dir at the United Nations) notes:

More often than not, violence against women is committed by an intimate partner. Of all women killed in 2012, almost half died at the hands of a partner or family member. It is not an exaggeration but a fact that the overall greatest threat to women's lives is men, and often the men they love. In some conflict situations, it may be more dangerous to be a girl or a woman than to be a soldier. Violence against women has become a real epidemic that must definitely be stopped. (beijing20.unwomen.org/en/ news-and-events/stories/2014/10/oped-evaw-phumzile-mlambo-ngcuka-un-women).

For its part, the World Health Organization has declared that violence against women worldwide has gone rampant and is reaching epidemic proportions.

We all need to support women's organizations, which often are the ones that deal with the actual victims of violence against women. They are on the frontline, but Mlambo-Ngcuka makes a point of inviting more men and boys to take a firm stand against violence towards women and girls. She also urges political and religious leaders to lead the way by teaching and guiding men to be gentlemen in their relationships with women. And as Mlambo-Ngcuka adds, everyone should "support efforts to end impunity and ensure justice for those attacked."

There is a formidable lady with guts of steel, strength of spirit, clear vision and determination, but with a sweetness and a delicate touch. Her name is Mary Black. She wrote a poem entitled "Quiet," where she says she will *not* be quiet whenever she sees or experiences spousal abuse, violence against women, rape, women disappearing, the killing of women by their partners, etc. She exhorts every human being not to be quiet about these things in any shape or form. She believes that being quiet is a disease and that people who see, hear, or experience anything evil should face it and talk about it, vehemently avoiding silence. Nobody should ever be afraid of speaking the truth. Breaking a silence makes us more human, and we all ought to break the silence if that means helping or even saving a woman. To watch a video of Mary Black's poem, visit Youtube and search her name and the title of the poem, "Quiet". It is a very impressive and valuable message, because, as Ms Black says, remaining quiet does not heal, and many women, "beautiful beyond expectations," have been victims of a system created to protect them. She also insists that the time has arrived to stop being quiet about how the current system pushes women (and men) to addiction and suicide, and to refuse to carry the guilt of shame anymore.

I also recommend visiting these websites:

- Break the silence – violence against women (*afn.ca/uploads/files/violenceforum/jr_larose_-_bc_lions,_be_more_than_a_bystander.pdf*)
- amnesty.ca/our-work/issues/womens-human-rights/violence-against-women

It does not matter where we come from or the society we are living in. It is important to make an effort to accept people for who they are. This is the only way we can all get along and participate in a progressive society for our own benefit and that of our family and friends. Unfortunately, tolerance is a concept that not everybody understands, especially when it means accepting women on the same playing field as men or accepting immigrants and refugees while providing them with social and economic support and hoping they will fully integrate and blend harmoniously in their adopted country.

Sexual Harassment and Assault in North America

Sexual assaults and harassments happen even in the places we least expect, not just in unsafe areas such as big city outskirts. It is inconceivable that men still behave barbarically in every country in the world in the twenty-first century. We have not developed and evolved as we think we have, and as we should have. This is mainly due to lack of education and lax punishment for perpetrators that does not match the severity of damage to the victim. Whether people believe it or not – or like it or not – harsher penalties assist drastically to bring down the "uncontrollable need" of rapists.

There are three quick examples I would like to bring to the attention of the reader to show how serious sexual assaults and harassments have become:

1. The Toronto Sun - Associated Press published an article on Nov 4, 2016 entitled "Harvard Suspends Men's Soccer Team Over Sexual Comments." University President Drew Faust said that after an investigation into allegations of sexual misconduct by the 2012 team, the findings were so "appalling" the soccer season should be cancelled. Quote:

> The decision to cancel a season is serious and consequential, and reflects Harvard's view that both the team's behavior and the failure to be forthcoming when initially questioned are completely unacceptable, have no place in Harvard, and run counter to the mutual respect that is a core value of our community.

Faust said that the misconduct continued through the following season even though the team was under investigation. Athletic Director Robert Scalise commented:

> Harvard Athletics will partner with the Office of Sexual Assault Prevention and Response and other Harvard College resources to take additional steps to further educate the members of our men's soccer team, and all our student athletes, about the seriousness of these

behaviors and the general standard of respect and conduct that it is expected.

What I do not understand is that Harvard University is where the most educated and brightest students are expected to be found. For crying out loud, Harvard students are supposed to be among the cream of the crop, right? If these assaults can happen there, imagine what must be happening in less elite universities, or in high schools, throughout North America. The thought alone is scary and primitive. I refuse to believe that all athletes are just muscle and no brain. All my friends and I have loved and practiced sports and always respected women. We were taught to control our urges and channel them the right way. It is simply the ethical, civilized, and manly thing to do and reflects how we were educated and raised. But people are the result of the general moral values of their society, which is reflected, unfortunately, by what people are fed by the media, computer games, television, movies, religion, their elders, their parents, their teachers, etc. Our society is failing to bring up our young with strong, balanced, healthy minds.

2. The BBC published an article by Rajini Vaidyanathan on June 7, 2016 entitled "Will Stanford sexual assault case silence future victims?" The article reported that in January 2015 a female student suffered a brutal and aggressive sexual assault, which she detailed during her declaration against the perpetrator when interviewed by the authorities. The case has been very controversial due to the lenient sentence handed out. The law allows for up to 14 years' imprisonment in a situation like this, but as the Palo Alto Weekly reported:

> In January 2015, Stanford University freshman-swimmer Brock Turner was arrested after two graduate students found him on top of an unconscious woman outside a campus fraternity party. A jury later found Turner guilty of three sexual-assault felonies after a

three-week trial in Palo Alto. Santa Clara County Judge Aaron Persky sentenced on Thursday former Stanford University student-athlete Brock Turner to six months in county jail and three years of probation for the sexual assault of an unconscious and intoxicated woman, acknowledging the "devastation" the woman has suffered yet also the "severe" impact imprisonment would have on Turner.

The moral and psychological damage a rape can inflict on a victim is different for every person, but it certainly leaves deep scars and impacts behavior and self-esteem for the rest of the person's life. A six-month jail sentence for a rape like this was an insult to every woman on campus and beyond. If the Stanford University freshman-swimmer Brock Turner suffered a severe impact in prison, as Judge Persky feared he would if he were sentenced to a longer term, so be it. He chose his path by doing something uncivilized, barbaric, criminal, and stupid to a defenceless woman. Yes, she put herself at risk by drinking and behaving stupidly, but she certainly did not deserve what happened to her, much less in a "prestigious" place like Stanford University.

Fortunately, one good thing has come out of this ordeal. Attorney Jeff Rosen proposed new legislation requiring a mandatory sentence of three to eight years for sexually assaulting an unconscious person, and in August 2016 the proposed bill passed unanimously. I still wonder, though, whether three years is harsh enough to stop a perpetrator. Is it comparable to the "punishment" suffered by the victims for the rest of their lives?

3. The New York Times published an article by James C. McKinley Jr. on Mar 24, 2016 entitled "Former Mt. Sinai Doctor Charged with Sexually Abusing 4 Women." Several women who had attended the emergency room at the Mount Sinai Hospital in New York when Dr. David H. Newman was on duty

complained that the doctor drugged them, touched their private parts, and, in one case, masturbated on the patient, according to McKinley. It is astonishing that women who went to receive emergency help suffered such assaults. However, after a long trial, Dr. Newman was sentenced to two years in prison and registered as a sex offender. Perhaps too little, too late!

Gang Rape

While uncommon in North America, gang rape is very common in many African and South Asian countries. Unfortunately, gang rapes also happen in some Latin American countries. On May 28, 2016, The Vancouver Sun reported under the headline "Gang rape of teen shakes Brazil" that the authorities there "have identified and are searching for more than 30 men suspected of gang raping a 16-year-old girl. This case rocked Latin America's largest nation and highlighted its epidemic problem of violence against women." By March of 2018, proper arrests were still pending.

To make matters worse, some Brazilian men joked about the incident and posted pictures of the unconscious and naked 16-year-old on Twitter. It appears that instead of maturing and advancing in society, we are falling back into an abyss as dark as our past. With the technology and fast means of communication we now enjoy in the twenty-first century, this should not be happening. Something fundamental is wrong in our societies. Frustration and a desire for vengeance against the weak and innocent (women and children) motivates many of us. Tougher laws and harsher punishments are required, along with proper education and in-depth social programmes. If we do not do something about this problem within the boundaries of the law, more and more vigilante enforcers will emerge, and there is nothing we will be able to do. People have a right to expect justice, and if they do not find it within the system, they will take the law into their own hands.

Quebec Tackling Sexual Violence

On Oct 28, 2016, the Canadian Press reported on a long-awaited strategy to prevent and fight sexual violence in Quebec. Among many measures, a new police unit will specialize in sexual crimes using top technology tools to keep in touch with victims during the investigation. Victims tend not to trust the system, and Quebec authorities are trying hard to make every case more personal so that victims can trust the system and come forward. Awareness campaigns, along with personnel training, are priorities for working with and protecting victims while trying to prevent incidents. According to the article, however, many groups still complain that the new strategy is too little too late, that sexual violence is still not being taken seriously and that budgets are falling short of the real needs posed by the problem. Meanwhile thousands of Quebecers are going to the streets to march against what they call "a culture of sexual violence."

Nevertheless, we have to keep in mind that sometimes women do accuse men of sexual misconduct when nothing really happened, often as revenge for something that took place between the two parties. When an accusation is found to be false, the accuser should be punished severely. She should perhaps get the same punishment she was demanding for her alleged assailant. The law should always apply to all involved.

Stop Sexual Assault!

During the 88th Academy Awards ceremony last February in Los Angeles, US Vice-President Joe Biden introduced Lady Gaga and invited all viewers to take the "It's on Us" pledge to put a stop to sexual assault. What does it mean to take this pledge? It means to make your best effort and commitment to assist in keeping women and men safe from any type of sexual assault. It also means to commit to the following (http://www.itsonus.org):

- To recognize that non-consensual sex is sexual assault.
- To identify situations in which sexual assault may occur.
- To intervene in situations where consent has not or cannot be given.
- To create a strong environment in which sexual assault is absolutely unacceptable and survivors are fully supported in every aspect.

The Rape, Abuse, and Incest National Network (RAINN) adds that, as well as taking the pledge, we all need to go the extra mile and take these extra steps to end sexual assault:

- Take action in your campus, workplace, and anywhere within your community
- Share the National Sexual Assault Hotline with a friend or a loved one. For North America, call 1-800-656-4673 or visit online.rainn.org
- "Tell your ideas using the hashtag #ItsOnUS. What should schools be doing to address sexual assault on campus? Share your thoughts on social media — and be sure to tag RAINN (@RAINN01)"
- Encourage intervention by both women and men on campus and beyond before somebody commits another crime. Promote respect for women and insist on self-control and discipline for men. If you feel that a situation is risky for a woman (or a man) and may get out of control, find a non-combative or non-confrontational way to dissuade the potential perpetrator(s).

At the Academy Awards ceremony, Lady Gaga sang a beautiful and meaningful song as part of a worldwide effort to stop the sexual assault of women and men. The song is called "Till It Happens To You." The lyrics can be found in YouTube.

Me-Too and Times-Up Movements (#MeToo) / (#TimesUp)

There was a lady whose name was Tarana Burke. She survived sexual violence and decided to start the "Me Too" movement (#MeToo). This movement has brought down some of the most powerful men in their industry, especially in politics and entertainment. The most resonated example was that of Harvey Weinstein (a Hollywood mogul) in Oct of 2017, when him and other powerful players in the entertainment industry, were accused of sexual harassment by many women. Several lawsuits were launched and the anti-sexual harassment movement #MeToo went viral, deeply resonating in many cultures around the world. Almost in parallel, another hashtag went viral called #TimesUp, which represents a legal defence fund and an anti-sexual harassment initiative. Many prominent women are behind these two movements, but it has echoed in almost every culture and at all levels.

Oprah Winfrey made a powerful statement during her speech at the Golden Globes in January 2018, insisting that for all girls and women, "a new day is on the horizon." Oprah thanked all those women "who felt strong enough and empowered enough to speak up and share their personal stories of harassment and abuse." She especially promoted the voices of those women, like her mother, "with children to feed and bills to pay and dreams to pursue." She dedicated her speech to those women that are never heard, such as workers in factories, domestic workers, farm workers, restaurants and academia. To all those women working in the police force, in the army, in sports, and in different industries such as engineering and technology. Before she finished her speech, she brought to the attention of everybody present (and beyond) the case of Recy Taylor who was ambushed and raped by six white men in 1944. The perpetrators were never arrested. Oprah said, "Taylor's spirit still stands strong, will never be forgotten and lives on every woman who chooses to say 'me too' and every man who chooses to listen."

Tolerant vs. Liberal

A liberal society is one in which there are no challenges to the moral beliefs and values of others. It is a specific political philosophy of pluralism, equality, freedom, and liberty. The more different behaviors a society accepts, the more liberal that society positions itself compared to others. Every liberal society accords an intrinsic value to tolerance. In any liberal society, many people are tolerant rather than just accepting. They learn to live with different behaviors, regardless of whether they agree with them or not. They acknowledge, accept, or adapt to difference and respect others' ways as long as they are not forcefully imposed. A good example is how more and more societies accept lesbians, gays, bisexual, and transgender (LGBTQ2) people. We have definitely become more understanding and open to LGBTQ2 people's affection for each other and their right to get married and adopt and raise children. In the twenty-first century, everybody should have equal rights under the law.

In Canada, we now recognize the following four categories:

- Gender assigned at birth
- Gender expression: each person's individual and internal sense of gender
- Gender identity: how an individual decides to openly show their gender
- Sexual orientation: sexual preference.

The above does not apply in many other countries, but in Canada, same-sex marriage is legally accepted, and the Trudeau administration recently passed Bill C-16 in the House of Commons, providing full legal protection to transgender people throughout the country. For other countries, these are strong messages of progress, fairness, equality, unity, and strength. In January 2017, National Geographic published a special issue entitled "Gender Revolution." It should be read by everybody and will help people, not just in Canada but in every other country around the world, to understand, grow, and mature individually and as a nation in the proper understanding of gender and sexuality for the benefit of their own people.

Metrosexual

In a liberal society, it is more common to find "metrosexual" men, that is, men who are heterosexuals yet have a refined sense of beauty, taste, and artistic values. These kinds of men want to portray themselves as well-groomed, modern, and fashionable, with a high sense of aesthetics. They like to feel and be seen as trendy and dandy. Some people see them as a bit feminine and not necessarily virile, but they are solid heterosexuals. They seem to be more inclined to show their class rather than their "manly" qualities, and they feel comfortable and secure in themselves. To many, metrosexual men are known as the male peacock or the bird of paradise.

There is no equivalent term for women. Women interested in fashion, taste, and beauty are simply lady-like women who are feminine and attractive to the opposite gender. In today's world, while there are more and more metrosexual men in our society, there are unfortunately fewer and fewer lady-like women. In fact, there seems to be an epidemic in North America of women who do not care how they look or how others perceive them. Let me give you an example. There is a website famous for its discussion forums called LPSG (lpsg.com). In that website, I found a comment posted about the antithesis of being a metrosexual, but in relation to women. It describes so well what the average man thinks of such women that I quote it in full:

> Maybe a really sporty woman, hair in a ponytail... interested in her cats but doesn't give a rat's ass about her appearance. Maybe no makeup and lots of baggy

attire. :smile: I feel sad when I see women with no makeup at all, uncombed and messy or dirty looking style hair with clothes that does [sic] not look good and far from feminine. They tend to wear clothes that are either too loose and baggy or too tight for their clearly unfit and usually large bodies. They seem to have completely given up in their desire to look and feel neat and tidy. They seem to have lost their pride and "joie du vivre avec classe."

It does not matter if you are a man or a woman. Not caring how you dress, behave, and portray yourself in your community sets a bad example for the young. Of course, we live in North America and are free to do as we wish without being censored or openly segregated, although these things happen quietly and discreetly.

Child Abuse

Anything that results in direct harm to a child or places a child at risk through an intended lack of care is considered child abuse. Physical abuse is temporary, but emotional and psychological abuse can last a lifetime. If a person neglects an animal or a child; both are abuse. Neither a child nor an animal has the ability to care for themselves. A grownup has the ability and the duty to care and provide for them.

There is a fine line between educating a child and forcing something on a child to the extent of constituting child abuse. For example, Rob Cooper in Mail Online (Apr 22, 2013) reports that, according to atheist professor Richard Dawkins (author of *The God Delusion*), "forcing a religion on your children is as bad as child abuse." This might be difficult to accept by religious parents, regardless of their denomination. But Dawkins argues that there is more psychological damage in forcing a religion on a child than even perhaps in sex abuse. He agrees that every child should be taught about the existence of religion and about the different types of religions, but without *indoctrinating* them in any religion. Now, David N. Elkins, a former fundamentalist Christian minister, wrote in Psychology Today (Nov 19, 2015) on the topic of "Fundamentalist Christianity and Child Abuse: A Taboo Topic." He starts by sharing three sad stories that, in my view, absolutely amount to child abuse:

- An American child is dying at home. The parents are members of a Christian sect that does not believe in modern medicine. They pray fervently, but the child grows worse and dies. "It was God's will," says the father. The mother agrees.

- A five-year-old boy says a dirty word. His Christian father spanks him with a wooden paddle. The paddle leaves welts and bruises. "Spare the rod and spoil the child," says the father, quoting the Bible.

- Kristy is eight. Her father leads the congregational singing at church. "When I get big, I want to lead the singing just like Daddy," Kristy says. Her mother tells her, "You can serve God in many ways but only men can lead the singing." Kristy says, "Why?" Her mother says, "God doesn't want women to usurp the authority of men." Kristy says, "Oh, I didn't know that."

I leave it to the reader to judge the examples above. From the point of view of extreme religious sects, it is all good, but from the legal, psychological, and moral points of view in any "normal" society, should it be construed as child abuse or not? Those who abuse children are usually individuals who are trusted and loved by the children. It is abominable when parents or a church abuse innocent lives while marking them psychologically forever; many victims turn out in the future to be sexual predators or even serial killers. On Apr 11, 2014, the BBC, under the headline "The Vatican's child abuse response," reported that the United Nations had "accused the

Vatican of systematically adopting policies allowing priests to sexually abuse thousands of children." The article describes how it was not until the late 1980s that the first cases of child molestation by priests started to come to light in the United States and Canada and not until the twenty-first century that other countries started uncovering similar abuse perpetrated by the church on thousands and thousands of children around the world. Since then hard-core proof of child abuse has been found in every country. It has become so bad that, although Pope John Paul II always protected the priests and turned a blind eye to the suffering of children, Pope Francis has had to acknowledge the abuse, stating: "dealing with abuse is vital for the Church's credibility, and ... sanctions must be imposed against perpetrators." For more information on this gruesome story, please refer to: bbc.com/news/world-europe-25757218.

LGBTQ2 Issues

Non-discrimination against LGBTQ2 people, which stands for lesbians, **g**ays, **b**isexuals, **t**ransgender, **Q**ueer, and **t**wo-spirit people. LGBTQ2 is still not accepted in many parts of the world, but in Canada it has been steadily gaining ground, and LGBTQ2 people have now achieved the same rights as any other person. Fortunately, in North America as a whole, the LGBTQ2 movement has gained a lot of support towards mainstream social acceptance. Their struggle for equality has been tenacious and, luckily for them, is now paying off. There are still some so-called normal people, and perhaps always will be, who will never accept or understand LGBTQ2, but we are confident that the great majority in generations will accept them as their friends, neighbours, and co-workers. They are just normal human beings, often with high human standards, with their own taste, flair, and ways of being, and we should all open our doors and respect that fully.

Everything in life is a two-way street. LGBTQ2 people need to understand and accept the fact that they are different from the "norm". They do not need to push themselves in or try and make a point of who they are, but just act normally and respectfully in front of others. In this way, they will gain the respect of their peers, keep their dignity, and show respect for others as well. Let's face it: between a white supremacist, a Muslim hater, a macho-style trophy hunter, an anti-Semite, or an LGBTQ2 person, I would choose the last for a long-lasting friend any day of the week. The others reflect hatred, revenge, and selfishness, which are detrimental to everybody around them. LGTBQ2 people are just like any other normal person who are also usually friendly, loving, and caring. Simply put, they are just like an average human being.

In the past in North America, accused gays or lesbians were usually charged with indecency or indecent exposure. They were portrayed as dangerous sexual offenders, as mentally ill, unbalanced sexual predators, or psychopaths. Society was extremely aggressive and unfair towards them. Worst of all, the treatments they received behind doors from psychiatrists, doctors, and scientists in efforts to "cure" them, such as applying electric shocks that seriously affected their genitals and brains, were inhumane and barbaric. Other treatments included addictive and torturous drugs, lobotomies, and castrations. A company called Farrell Instruments patented and manufactured several aggressive treatment products such as flash lighting and wave-shock monitoring techniques that never proved successful and that nowadays are being used in other countries to torture prisoners. An article by Jamie Scott in The Huffington Post (Feb 2, 2016) describes typical treatments:

> In the more brutal therapy sessions, the shock was delivered directly to the male patient's genitals every time the patient experienced any form of positive response to the slides being shown to him. The following excerpt from a Farrell Instrument catalogue advertising electroshock therapy products details how

the therapies worked: "Aversive conditioning has proven an effective aid in the treatment of child molesters, transvestites, exhibitionists, alcoholics, shoplifters, and other people with similar problems. Stimulus slides are shown to the patient intermixed with neutral slides. Shock is delivered with stimulus scenes but not with neutral scenes. In reinforcing heterosexual preference in latent male homosexuals, male slides give a shock while the stimulus relief slides of females do not give a shock. The patient is given a 'slide change' hand button, which enables him to escape or avoid a shock by rejecting a shock cue scene."

Fortunately for the LGBTQ2 community, times have changed. Pierre Trudeau decriminalized gay sex for the first time in Canada's history back in 1969 with Bill C-150. In 1996, the Supreme Court confirmed an amendment to Section 15 of the Charter of Rights and Freedom guaranteeing the "right to equal protection and equal benefit of the law without discrimination and sexual orientation." Many years later, "Prime Minister Justin Trudeau raised a Pride flag on Parliament Hill today for the first time in the country's history, in recognition of the people who have 'fought a long time' to secure equal rights for LGBTQ2 Canadians" (John Paul Tasker, *CBC News – Politics*, Jun 1, 2016). There is still a long road ahead in North America, but like some European countries, we are setting an example for other countries to follow and hopefully change their laws. In fact, something wonderful just happened in Ireland, where the first gay Prime Minister Leo Varradkar was elected on Jun 2, 2017. Irish boys and girls can now dream whatever they want to be without any hesitation or fear, and bring those dreams to fruition.

CHAPTER FOUR: RESPECT FOR NORTH AMERICAN VALUES

Introduction

Immigration is a great thing for any country. It is how North America (and many other countries worldwide) has grown, progressed, and improved their standards of living throughout history. But the concept of immigration (especially regarding refugees) has drastically changed in recent years. We need to adapt to the changes or we might end up regretting the so-called "tolerance" for which Canada (and the United States to a lesser degree) is acknowledged and admired throughout the world. Our tolerance and "political correctness" are now being pushed to the limit, in fact to the brink of a potential dangerous and dark precipice. We need to adapt to the real needs of our people without hypocrisy while protecting our country's values, for which our soldiers fought to protect, and are now at risk.

The message on immigration sent by US voters in electing Donald Trump is clear. The old school of American politicians failed (or did not care) to see the need for changes in the immigration laws and policies. If they did, they failed to place the proper importance, focus, and effort on this issue and lost the presidential race as a result. Personally, I think it was their shortsighted vision along with excess confidence in the system, which the average voter does not believe in anymore. Political incorrectness has been a problem for many years, but it cannot be ignored any longer. Yes, it is politically incorrect to say: "Stop illegal Mexican immigration. We need to build a wall and have it paid for by Mexico." But even though he knew he was going to get into hot water, Trump's vision was above and beyond that of the media and, of course, the Democratic Party. He wanted votes, and he knew very well that almost every Mexican legally established in the United States (and allowed to vote) did not want more competition for jobs from illegal immigrants from Mexico (or elsewhere). This is why many more legally landed Mexicans with voting rights voted in favour of Trump than expected. And yes, to the surprise of many, as Trump strategically envisioned and planned it from the beginning. Now, stop to think and really understand what the majority of the country has been feeling about immigration for many years. Among many accusations, Trump was tarnished for being racist, anti-immigrant, anti-Muslim, anti-Mexican, etc., but he gave the average voter what they were hungry for. He offered hope for better job opportunities and a greater feeling of security within American soil, from external illegals and extremist sources.

There is a saying in Mexico that goes like this:

Si vez a tu vecino rasurar, pon tus barbas a remojar, porque tu eres el siguiente. ("If you see your neighbour getting a shave, put your beard in hot water, because you are next.")

I truly hope this message is loudly resounding in countries such as Canada, France, Australia, and others where lots of immigrants and refugees are going, and where locals (at least in Canada) are afraid of saying "enough!" Why? Because they think it is politically incorrect, intolerant, and racist, when in reality it is their right to self-preservation, security, and growth that is at stake. In Canada, PM Trudeau, to my mind, made a big mistake by accepting, in the speed in which he did, so many Syrian refugees as part of his first mandate when he took power. Why? Because if PM Trudeau fails to pay attention to the "silent roar" of the average Canadian regarding an open-door immigration policy, we are all going to regret it. Indeed, I think we already are starting to regret it. This subject will be dealt with in more detail later in this book. Every country is safer with a selective immigration process in which people with similar values are chosen, but above all, with a proper and full background check.

Kathie Michaels wrote an article in the Capital News (Nov 11, 2016) on "The sacrifice for freedom of thought and expression", which according to her, has been achieved and earned thanks for every Canadian (man or woman) that gave their lives for their land, their people, and their beliefs for freedom of thought and expression. According to Michaels, an Afghanistan veteran told her that Canadian soldiers there had defended our values. Michaels then wrote this powerful thought:

> As Canadians, we are fortunate our values are enshrined in the Charter of Rights and Freedom. We live in a world where those who do not accept what we take for granted are willing to use violence against innocent people to oppose those values.

Immigrants and National Identity

Every country needs its own identity, not selected or imposed by the government but by the people through their traditions, preferences, food, music, and pride in their flag, national anthem, sports, and other deep national symbols. In Canada, PM Trudeau claims that we need to "adopt progressive values", but that concept is never clearly explained.

A website (mpvusa.org) that focuses in the progressive values of the Muslim community around the world uses the motto: "Be Yourself. Be Muslim." Their message to the world is: "We envision a future where Islam is understood as a source of dignity, justice, compassion and love for all humanity and the world." I personally wish we could all see Islam in such a positive light. Muslims are just normal human beings like anyone else. After all, it is only the puritanical and radical Muslims that people fear, and the mainstream Muslim community condemns these types of Muslims as well. As a country, we need to stand unified against any racial, religious, social, or educational extremists. There is no real difference between members of the Ku Klux Klan, anti-Semites, or any other hate group. But one thing should be crystal-clear: refusing to accept radical Muslims does not make a person

Islamophobic. Islam and radical Islam are two different things. Shame on those exploiting the word Islamophobic for their own twisted purposes.

PM Trudeau constantly says our country is strong not despite our differences but because of them and that our differences make this country strong and progressive. I quasi agree with him, but he goes further, however, and maintains that we are a multicultural country. But our public school system is meant to integrate immigrants into the Canadian values we cherish and protect, such as freedom, equality, democracy, and free speech, which do not exist in many of the countries that immigrants, and especially refugees, come from. As Canadians, we must always remind ourselves of our Canadian values so that newcomers can adapt and conform as much as possible. The Canadian system should be a tuned-up system for integration and ultimate assimilation, not segregation.

Unfortunately, some immigrants who come to Canada do not want to fully integrate. They practice their own ways and even impose them on others, who are afraid of being called racists if they complain. In many cases, these new immigrants even try to change our ethical way of doing business, and we are expected to tolerate and accept this, even though it goes against our values and, in many instances, our laws. A good example is all those mainly Chinese restaurants in Richmond and Vancouver that only accept payment in cash. They usually display a small sign, not necessarily in an obvious place, and when it is time to pay, they surprise with "cash only." They even force you to go and get cash at the closest ATM and have precise instructions for how to get there. They do not accept any kind of card. They probably under-declare their annual income to reduce their tax commitment, but they certainly still demand high quality government services. Otherwise, why practice something so unbusinesslike. If they were paid with debit cards, they would not even need to pay interest to the merchant banker. Even worse, why doesn't the government do something about this and stop this open practice that looks to many Canadians like tax-evasion?

Immigrants vs. Refugees

There are two main types of immigrants in Canada (and in any other country in the world): immigrants by choice and immigrants by force. Immigrants by choice select a country to which they want to immigrate and apply through the proper procedures. They are accepted or rejected based on specific immigration policies created for the short and long term benefit of Canada. Immigrants by force are usually refugees in search for asylum (protection and safeguarding) who are pushed to leave their country. According to dictionary.com, a refugee is "a person who flees for refuge or safety, especially to a foreign country, as in times of political upheaval, war, etc." Refugees usually move to escape danger, persecution, and nowadays even climate change.

Immigrants who come to Canada by choice are likely to integrate easier and faster than those forced out of their countries and accepted by other countries as refugees (for example, the "supposedly" 25,000 Syrian immigrants in Canada). Why "supposedly"? Because that was what Prime Minister Justin Trudeau and Immigration Minister John McCallum promised every Canadian they would bring. But by Dec 18, 2016 close to 36,000 Syrian refugees actually did land and more than 30,000 new Syrian refugees kept on landing during 2017. By April of 2018, more Syrians were still arriving. A big difference from the 25,000 originally promised. More than 66,000 will actually be arriving from Syria alone. This figure does not include all the refugees crossing the borders from the US to Canada after Donald Trump's election. These refugees are now in the thousands and are crossing mainly to BC, Saskatchewan, Manitoba and Ontario. According to Michelle Zilio in the Globe and Mail (Mar 9, 2016):

> Immigration Minister John McCallum says Canada plans to accept between 280,000 and 305,000 – with a target of 300,000 – new permanent residents this year, an increase from the updated target of 279,200 for 2015. "It [annual report to Parliament on immigration] outlines a significant shift in immigration policy toward reuniting more families, building our economy, and upholding Canada's humanitarian tradition to resettle refugees and to offer protection to those in need."

This certainly sounds nice, altruistic, and admirable to many Canadians and to the outside world. To many other Canadians, however, it sounds like a bit of a lie, a bit of a trap, and a bit of a betrayal. Other countries say they "admire" Canadians for accepting more refugees, but they also scratch their head in wonder and confusion. These countries also know the financial problems and potential security issues this will undoubtedly bring to every unsuspecting Canadian. Why aren't other nations accepting more themselves instead of closing their doors as they are actually doing in a rush? In fact, some have completely closed their doors to refugees from Syria and elsewhere. To my eyes, and to those of many other attentive and analytical Canadians, we are enduring a political charade that is difficult to prove wrong at present, but with the passage of time will be seen as a mistake. By then it will be too late in areas of financial debt per capita, economic burden and in social security issues.

Before I continue, I want to make clear that the world has nothing personal against Syrians or refugees from any other corner of the world. We all feel deeply for them and wish we could help them even more. The majority have gone through extremely difficult times and there is no doubt they require a helping hand from abroad. It is our human responsibility. But it is important to make extremely clear that if some countries are closing their doors, it has nothing to do with being racists and much less Islamophobic. It has to do with other reasons such as lack of service and accommodation capabilities, economic and financial restrictions and potential security concerns.

Let's face it; those same young child refugees from various Muslim countries, cute as a button, are just like the kids that Europe granted refugee status 15, 20, or more years ago. Just like Syrian children and other African and Middle Eastern countries now, they were originally accepted from similar nations in distress, and a large percentage failed to integrate. I strongly believe the same thing will happen in Canada in the future. For specifics about the economic and financial impact I foresee, please refer to the concluding section of this book under the subtitle "Critical Path."

In Canada, the weak and improvised government integration plans for Syrian refugees seem to lack real and tangible long-term opportunities from the educational, social, and professional points of view. Many Canadians are concerned that an invisible time bomb might be in the process of being assembled. I sincerely hope I am wrong, but I sometimes share the same feeling. This was another reason the CIA, FBI, and Homeland Security in the US criticized the Canadian government last year. Regardless of the real possibility of harbouring camouflaged extremists pretending to be refugees, the reality is that all refugees are being forced out of their country. They are not leaving it behind by choice. That alone makes a huge difference from the situation of an average immigrant who leaves by choice and decreases our risk to the country. My real fear is in relation to the economic impact. All these refugees deserve to have legal advice after their arrival, proper medical services, a roof over their heads, clean clothes, decent food, proper entertainment, sport related activities, English classes to all, school for their children and job opportunities for the adults. Both Dad and Mom need to support their large families; some with 10 to 12 children plus other family members such as the grandparents. But how is Mom supposed to work with so many children to care for?

Grandparents are in many cases too old to take care of the children. They need taking care themselves. What kind of income does the father need to earn to support them all? These questions are difficult to answer when the great majority of refugees arrive with low levels of education, as all European countries have already corroborated.

The Real Threat:

The immediate problem is not necessarily related directly to the refugee's background, religious inclinations, values, or social behaviors. Although important, these may actually be less critical than the following two points:

1. The financial burden to our country. Why? Because aside from our financial responsibilities to every refugee as soon as they land, Statistics Canada has confirmed that the household credit market debt in Canada for 2016 increased to $167.3 of adjusted household disposable income. This means that for every dollar of disposable income in a household, there was $1.67 of credit market debt, and it is still on the rise. In the fourth quarter of 2016 Canadians borrowed an additional $28.4 billion on a seasonally adjusted basis. This is up from $18.7 billion added in the previous quarter. Quote: "Total household credit market debt, which includes consumer credit, and mortgage and non-mortgage loans, totaled nearly $2.029 trillion in the final quarter of last year." For more information, please refer to the article published by Craig Wong on March 15, 2017 by CTV News: "Canadian household debt creeps up to another record in fourth quarter."

The Fraser Research Bulletin published a study in Jan 2016 of "The Cost of Government Debit in Canada, 2016". The authors, C. Lamman, M. Palacios, H. Macintyre and F. Ren, accurately forecast a $1.3 trillion-dollar debt by the Federal Government. They added:

Debt accumulation has costs. One major consequence is that governments must make interest payments on their debt similar to households that pay interest on borrowing related to mortgages, vehicles, or credit card spending. Spending on interest payments consumes government revenues and leaves less money available for other important priorities such as spending on health care and education or tax relief.

How then are we supposed to cover all the financial needs of refugees until they become productive? The Bank of Canada is forecasting 2.1 per cent inflation by the end of 2107 (up from 1.7 per cent in 2016), though we all know that in reality the inflation rate is already way higher than that. As of March 2018, the Canadian dollar is still considerably devalued. Naturally, this has not improved our balance of trade, and the oil industry needs to pump considerably more barrels of oil to compensate for previous losses and a lower international price per barrel. That is part of the reason that PM Trudeau gave the green light to Enbridge's Line 3 and Kinder Morgan's Trans Mountain pipeline against serious environmental concerns and our commitments to reduce CO_2. Fortunately, he at least rejected the Northern Gateway pipeline.

2. How are Canadians going to respond to the altruistic efforts of the government and many foundations, institutions, and church organizations regarding the refugee crisis now and ion the future? Many Canadians feel they are being left behind without government or private social programs and financial assistance. A good example is all those native people committing suicide up North due to lack of proper support, or all those people (young and mature) that cannot find a job with decent pay, or all those elderly Canadians whose pensions are insufficient to live on with dignity.

The immediate concerns of the great majority of Canadians involve questions such as: What is the government doing in relation to our lagging productivity and innovation across Canada and our excessive reliance in the exploitation of our natural resources? What kind of new incentive programs are being offered for private corporations to support industry diversification and job creation? What is the government really doing to renovate our cities' old and crumbling infrastructure without printing more money and getting into deeper debt? What is the government doing about public corruption at many levels? How can the government tackle alcohol and drug addiction across Canada? How can the Trudeau administration solve the crisis in our courts, as outlined in an alarming article by Ian Mulgrew in The Vancouver Sun on Mar 18, 2017? Criminals are walking free in the streets due to court backlogs and shortages of judges. And these are just a few of the more immediate concerns of the average Canadian, who does not share the Trudeau government's infatuation with being seen as great humanitarians. It is the average working class Canadian who really supports this country through their taxes. A fairer and more responsive tax system is more important than supporting refugees beyond our financial means. Fortunately, on Mar 29, 2018, the Liberal Party tabled an important piece of legislation to improve the Canadian justice system. According to Justice Minister Wilson-Raybould, "Every single person in Canada has the right to a fair and timely trial." We just hope that with time, this holds true.

According to Jared Lindzon, "Canada is cracking down on offshore tax evasion and aggressive tax avoidance" (Vancouver Sun on Mar 4, 2017). We all hope that the Canadian Revenue Agency (CRA) can improve their taxing tools and train their auditors assigned to offshore non-compliance and high-net-worth individuals. Lindzon reports:

> The CRA already has a proven track record – with over $218 million in third party penalties against promoters and tax preparers who advise their clients to participate in aggressive or illegal tax arrangement plans or

schemes – and will continue to increase the application of penalties to all cases of serious non-compliance.

Kudos to the CRA. As Barbara Shecter wrote in the Financial Post (Mar 23, 2017), "all Canadians must pay their fair share." According to Shecter, the federal government has pledged over one billion to "crack down on tax evasion during the next five years." The government has promised to hire more auditors as well as specialists on what they call the underground economy. They will try to focus mainly on the hospitality and construction industries, says Shecter. Their main target are large corporations and high net-worth individuals

We certainly hope the above will assist in the battle against poverty across Canada and help hard-to-employ people to find jobs, if the new tax money is spent wisely. We need to give our own needy citizens a purpose to wake up to and a life of pride and dignity. They need opportunities as much as the refugees do. Unfortunately, it seems that many Canadians do not want to see or accept this. People in need due to addiction or poverty are invisible to the average Canadian, yet they should be our first priority. An article by Lori Culbert and Bethany Lindsay in the Vancouver Sun (Mar 4, 2017) talks about the thousands of homeless people who want to work and could bolster the economy more quickly than waiting a generation or two for refugees to become productive. The title of the article says it all: "Thousands of former homeless want to work, and could bolster B.C.'s booming economy". In the same issue of the Vancouver Sun, an article by Arlen Redekop notes that Prime Minister Trudeau has publicly acknowledged that the "opioids crisis is devastating communities and families across Canada," with "families ripped apart, communities forever altered, loved ones lost too soon." Trudeau has also acknowledged that "social policies that tackle mental health, housing, and economic opportunities are key components in the fight." But if he is so conscious of this, why does the refugee crisis seem more important to him than the plight of his own people? Is it because everybody silently sees homeless Canadians people as a write-off, hopeless, useless, incompetent, a liability and of less value than foreign refugees? I sincerely hope not!

Issues around the social integration of newcomers are arising all across Canada, and many Canadians are not happy. Resentment is building against those demanding that we accommodate our values to theirs, when in fairness it is newcomers who should make an effort to adapt to their new country. On its website, the Canadian Human Rights Commission (CHRC) starts its discussion of non-discrimination by saying:

> Sometimes people need to be treated differently to prevent or reduce discrimination. As an employer or service provider, you have an obligation to take steps to eliminate different and negative treatment of individuals, or groups of individuals based on prohibited grounds of discrimination. This is called your duty to accommodate, and it applies both to your employees and the public you serve.

However, the CHRC also notes that:

> Under the *Canadian Human Rights Act*, an employer or service provider can claim undue hardship when adjustments to a policy, practice, by-law or building would cost too much, or create risks to health or safety. There is no precise legal definition of undue hardship or a standard formula for determining undue hardship. Each situation should be viewed as unique and assessed individually.

The last sentence clearly leaves the door wide open for assessments to be unbalanced and unfair depending on the situation. In practice, the principle of "undue hardship" is being pushed aside more and more in order to "accommodate" minorities, because employers do not want to put their foot down and be accused of discrimination and racism. This is becoming a serious and dangerous situation in Canada, with potential safety repercussions. Let me explain why.

According to an article published by The Associated Press on Jan 30, 2017, Tracy Lindeman wrote, "Canada is generally very welcoming towards immigrants and all religions, but the French-speaking province of Quebec has had long-simmering debate about race and religious accommodation. The previous separatist government of the province called for a ban in ostentatious religious symbols such as the hijab in public institutions." When employees from a minority group ask for accommodation to pray during certain hours in the day, the company has to abide by it. If the praying takes place during working hours, they need to provide them with a proper location to pray. Whether or not the minority employees make up for the time lost, the accommodation is likely to be resented by their coworkers. Tension is going to build, especially when others also start asking for accommodations based on their religious practices. A special-treatment "phobia" will arise and cause social problems in the future. Everybody is going to ask for special holidays at school or at work based on his or her background, like the Jewish holidays granted to Jews. Why not allow Christians to say grace and hold hands at lunchtime? Shouldn't we all respect the use of religious symbols, holidays, and expressions just as we should respect the use of the hijab as an Islamic symbol of modesty and privacy? I think we should, as long as the acceptance and respect go both ways. But if minorities only want to impose their own practices, then all should be banned in public to keep everyone on equal footing.

The average Canadian is afraid that minorities are "silently" starting to rule our country. Many feel Canada will soon cease to be a democratic country where the majority should rule. Our multiculturalism is allowing minorities to demand accommodations for more and more of their practices and to impose their cultural identity on the rest of the country, blocking Canadians from discovering and claiming their own identity. My identity is Mexican-Canadian (or Canadian-Mexican), but that of my children is just Canadian. How can you define their real Canadian identity? Should it just be a multicultural identity? That is very difficult to grasp for many and a bit confusing for people abroad.

But isn't the whole world heading towards a "one-world" situation in which multiculturalism will be the basis of everyone's, with Canada being the pioneer? If that is the case, it would be an honor, wouldn't it? But what about integration and assimilation, which is the most important and challenging issue regarding new immigrants and refugees?

I have asked many people in Canada to describe their Canadian identity. They all gave very different answers, and few were completely sure about their identity. To many, there simply is no publicly acknowledged Canadian identity to feel proud of. However, I feel they are wrong. There is a Canadian identity embedded strongly in some Canadian minds. The best definition was given to me by my Canadian-born son who, strange as this may sound, feels more Canadian than maple syrup itself. His definition of being Canadian is as follows:

> A strong component of our culture is that of acceptance, tolerance, and understanding. We strive to uphold and protect human rights, while challenging the norms of history. The former is inherent in our bilingual beginnings, and [in our] quickly evolving nation that is working to reconcile and recognize the indigenous populations. The latter comes from our unique position as a relatively young country. Now, paradoxically as it may be, it is in this relatively brief history, that a rich

culture, compassionate values, a strong moral compass, and a pride for the nation's unique heritage that the Canadian identity emerges.

Canada is the place where basketball was created, where curling was invented, where some of the world's best hockey players are born. The origin of the poutine, maple syrup, the Nanaimo bar, a London Fog, and the best cheddar cheese in the world, to only name a few. A place where one can go skiing or snowboarding in the morning, and swimming in the Pacific Ocean in the afternoon of the same day; try their luck at riding a bull or betting on horse races; engage in ecological, innovative, and sustainable farming practices; experience fresh water lakes so large (the largest in the world in fact) they have waves you can surf; portage through the deciduous and pine forests and fresh waters of 'cottage country'; taste the wonders inside a cabanes à sucre; sit back on a grassy hill as you watch an ice glacier float by a fishing boat harbour on the most eastern coast; or star-gaze at the northern lights across our true north, strong, and free.

It goes without saying, our nature and land is one of a kind, and extravagantly diverse, just like the mosaic of peoples and culture of our country, which includes unreservedly the peoples and cultures of our indigenous hosts as well. Indeed, we are all global citizens. However, it is this beautiful and youthful land that promises a brighter future for many today, while aiming and working hard to provide a brighter future for even more tomorrow. It is a place where we can support our differences in harmony and unity for the mutually beneficial growth of our country and its people. It is a place that is an example and global leader for the rest of the world.

All this being said, I'll be the first to admit, we are not perfect, and there is work to be done; but as Canadians, because we are Canadian, we are just as keen and motivated to keep co-creating our nation into the best version of itself that it can be.

This drive for perpetual improvement of the lives of all – Canadians and our global neighbours alike – is possible only because of our contagiously kind, holistic, and integral moral compass passed on by our Canadian heritage and our values, that have been enshrined in the Canadian Constitution. Simply put, the reason I am proud to say where I am from, a place of wildly diverse landscapes, a place of unity, a place where our strength is drawn from our differences and played out on the common ground that is our identity: we are all, and I am, Canadian.

A Question to all North Americans

There is an important matter that average North Americans do not even question themselves about: if they were in the same Syrian situation, what would they do? For example, after all these years of Syrian civil war, and with no solution in sight by April of 2018, would they still keep having children? Is it fair and human to bring children into a country torn to pieces by war? Should I have more children who will go to bed with an empty stomach? Am I not being selfish by wanting to have sex regardless of how many children I already have, thereby putting them at mortal risk in the future? Is it ethical to use my children as shields and display their suffering to the world on social media so that I can be accepted as a refugee? Now, I certainly do not have complete answers to such questions, but as North Americans, I doubt we would answer "yes." Our values are different. Isn't this why our fertility rate per woman was 1.59, as posted by Statistics Canada for 2016. This is a low figure, and the reason we need immigrants and refugees.

Many countries have cultures with values and social behaviors very different from ours. Consequently, they tend to procreate at a noticeably higher rate than people in Europe and America. Now let us pause for a moment to consider a matter that worries many Canadians: the lack of proper provision and planning by the Canadian government when they offered to accept the initial 25,000 Syrian refugees. To my mind, the real reason seems to be PM Trudeau's international popularity and his goal to be seen as the humanitarian leader in the world. Equally important, however, is our government's desperate need for more immigrants and refugees to cover the country's internal debt and aging population. Just take a look at an article by Laura Glowarcki on CBC News (Oct 12, 2016) entitled "Canada caught off guard by number of Syrian refugee children, says federal minister." At the time, the cabinet minister concerned, John McCallum, admitted that the government had failed to foresee the real number of people per family. The article explains the difficulties the federal government is already having in dealing with the heavy load of Syrian refugees. Imagine what may be coming in the future.

As of December 2016, more funding has been promised to Manitoba to support Syrian refugees and help the province deal with problems such as job training, housing, and language barriers. It is well known that many Syrians are relying on food banks to support their families. Manitoba took 1,200 refugees in 2016 alone, but with services stretched to the maximum, they were not sure how they would tackle the Syrians' needs and other asylum seekers for 2017 and 2018. This is why they were asking for more federal funding as well as more support from the local community. Under federal rules, said McCallum, the Ministry of Immigration can only provide one year of support to immigrant refugees. How are they expected to survive with dignity after this? According to McCallum, the whole idea was for Canada "to step up to the plate." But stepping up to the plate without knowing what they were going to deal with? Hard to believe but, if that is true, imagine what future awaits the poor Syrian refugees. If the government failed to anticipate crucial aspects like the number of children in their large families (a very basic aspect of immigration policy), how and when did it perform due diligence regarding the background of every refugee, when the majority do not even have proper documentation? This is why the United States is still worried about who really is being harboured in Canada as a refugee, although, in the short and medium terms, the more urgent issues for Canadians are the refugees' potential health issues and the diseases they may be bringing into our country.

Now, do not judge me as racist or anti-Muslim. I am absolutely neither. I am just stating the realities. I do not want to sound harsh or heartless, so let me go further and bring to your attention some facts highlighted in an article by Soeren Kern entitled "Germany: Migration Crisis Becomes Public Health Crisis" (gatestoneinstitute.org, Nov 18, 2015). The article is very alarming, and we in North America need to learn from Germany's experience. Here are some of the key problems the article reveals:

- German hospitals are increasing security to protect doctors and nurses from violent attacks by migrants unhappy with the medical treatment they are receiving.
- Critics are warning that German taxpayers will end up paying billions of euros to provide healthcare for a never-ending wave of asylum seekers. This is in addition to the billions of euros already being spent to provide newcomers with food, clothing, and shelter.
- In addition to the massive economic and social costs, as well as the burden of increased crime, including a rape epidemic, Germans are now facing the risk of being exposed to exotic diseases and tuberculosis.
- Roughly five per cent of asylum seekers are carrying drug-resistant germs, according to Dr. Jan-Thorsten Gräsner, director of the Institute for Rescue and Emergency

Medicine. In real numbers, this works out to around 75,000 newcomers with highly infectious diseases.

- Twenty vaccines are now in short supply, and 16 others are no longer available at all. Because of production bottlenecks, some vaccines will not become available until 2017.
- Muslim women refuse to be treated by male doctors, and many Muslim men refuse to be treated by females, according to Max Kaplan, director of the Bavarian Medical Board.
- German media outlets are downplaying the extent of the healthcare problem to avoid provoking anti-immigrant sentiment.

The immigrants our immigration minister should focus on are those applying through the proper channels, who are eager to come to Canada, and willing to adapt and integrate in their new country. They should have been pre-screened and selected due to their backgrounds, professional skills, language knowledge, age, health, and other pertinent factors. Most importantly, these immigrants are legitimately interested in Canada and the opportunities it provides. Immigration to Canada is their own choice (they have not been forced by external circumstances), and they are eager to prove themselves in their adopted country. All this makes them an asset to our economy and our well-being.

By contrast, many refugees feel that we are obliged to extend a helping hand and assist them and their family members for many years to come. Many refugees have a "give me" attitude instead of asking "what can I offer?" John F. Kennedy once said: "Ask not what your country can do for you. Ask what you can do for your country." Do these refugees understand that philosophy? Or do they think that we owe them just because some developed countries, such as Great Britain, France, Belgium, Netherlands, etc., invaded theirs in the past, exploited their resources, and in some cases even instigated conflict and social unrest. Does this mean we are now obliged to provide for them forever?

Refugees love their mother country. They miss their own food, their music, their land, their social rules and laws, their ways of life, their ways of doing business, their manners and modes of expressing themselves in public, their language, their history, their traditions, their warm climate, etc. They did not want to immigrate to another country and learn a new language, adapt to new laws, new traditions, new customs and values, and make new friendships. They did not want to deal with Canada's harsh, freezing winters.

Some will integrate well, of course, but others will become frustrated and resentful and will miss what they left behind. Why? Because they never wanted to integrate into a new society in the first place, or perhaps because they do not feel fully accepted or provided with the same opportunities in their "adopted" country. Their new country, after all, is not just being kind. It needs newcomers to do the jobs that locals do not want to do and at wages many locals will not work for. It needs a larger tax base to cover the future financial requirements of an aging population. Let's face it; we are not entirely the kind and generous country we portray ourselves to be. We need the immigrants and even the refugees. But even more than this, we need proper, meticulous refugee scrutiny.

A good example is that of Abdullah Almugharbel, a Syrian refugee who, after a year in Canada, does not speak English and was not able to enrol his children in school. As in many other cases, the fault was not his but that of the government, which failed to assist the family properly during their settling-in process. As the old Chinese proverb says, "give a man a fish and he will eat for a day; teach a man to fish and he will eat for a lifetime." It is sad, but many of the people who are not given the chance to learn, adapt, and integrate will develop bitterness and animosity that could be dangerous for their future and that of Canadians as well. This is happening in Europe and many other countries with refugees who have grown into home-made extremists. We just hope and trust it never happens here!

Human vs. National Values

Not even people born and brought up in the same community or city have the exact same values. However, their overall and core values are usually within the same parameters that have been developed in their country over its history. Thus, their *core* values are very similar, although the values embraced by personal choice during their upbringing might be slightly different. For example, one of the main reasons marriages fail is because of differences in the values chosen by the partners during their respective upbringings, which are sometimes dramatically different.

Clifford Sharp in *The Origin and Evolution of Human Values* describes human values as:

> the "habits of thought" each of us acquires as we mature so that we can assess and deal with "ethical" problems (where "ethical" relates to the fundamental question of how we should live). Should we aim at happiness or knowledge, at virtue or the creation of beautiful objects? If we choose happiness, will it be our own or will it make proper allowance for the happiness of others? And what of the more particular questions that face us? Is it right to be dishonest in a good cause? Can we justify living in opulence while elsewhere in the world people are starving? What are our obligations to the other creatures with whom we share this planet, and to the generations of humans who will come after us? What do we regard as a "good" quality of life? For us? For others?"

All human values evolve according to particular cultures. Concepts of truth, responsibility, ethics, morals, manners, discipline, religion, trading practices, justice, traditions, and laws differ in every culture. Some are similar, but others are drastically different. Kellie Leitch a former Conservative Party member pledged to make Canada safer and stronger through unified Canadian values if she were to become Prime Minister. Her goal was to bring a stronger identity to Canadians that should feel proud of being diverse and multicultural, but according to some critics, that same diversity could end up being its Achilles heel. I hope these critics are mistaken and that our differences with our common Canadian values, end up being our strength, but sincerely, I have my doubts.

Kelly Leitch did not have a strong regard for political "taboos." She said loud and clear that she wanted to protect Canada's national values through a "Canadian values test" for all potential immigrants (refugees or not) similar to the proposed "extreme vetting" of immigrants to the United States. Personally, I believe she made a strong argument and that the great majority of Canadians still want standardized values to protect their country and its identity. This will bring pride and strength, just as the protection of the French language has brought strength and unity to Quebec's true identity.

Usually, the more religious a person is, the more they want to help immigrants, especially refugees. This is very noble, no doubt. However, I decided to research what the average Canadian thinks about allowing refugees into Canada. I consulted a Christian magazine called Faith Today and found an article in the Nov/Dec 2016 issue acknowledging that:

> Canadians are split in how we feel about refugees, but usually more positive than 21 other countries in an Ipsos 2016 study [Ipsos is a global market research and consulting firm with worldwide headquarters in Paris]. The results of that poll are: 34% of Canadians feel that

the borders for refugees should entirely be closed, 41% of Canadians feel that refugees will not fully integrate into their new society, 58.5% believe that there is big potential for terrorists pretending to be refugees who will enter Canada to cause violence and destruction and 55.5% feel that most foreigners who want to go to Canada as refugees really are not refugees. They just want to go to Canada for economic reasons, or…to take advantage of the welfare services.

Note: The people who answered "not sure" in the above survey were split in this analysis for fairness and accuracy.

These statistics clearly show that the average Canadian has serious doubts about refugees, asylum seekers, and the lax government policies of PM Trudeau. This should open a serious window of opportunity for candidates like Kelly Leitch in her efforts at the time, to gain the support of people who do not dare to say out loud what they nevertheless believe is the truth. In a country like Canada, such people are bombarded and coerced by the media and government policies into pretending to be tolerant, accepting, and politically correct, but in their hearts, they feel very differently (insecure, fearful, und deeply uncertain). Canada could be facing something similar to what happened in the United States election contest between Trump and Hilary Clinton, when the "establishment" failed to understand that "where there is smoke, there is fire".

An even more accurate statistic emerged through a national polling partnership between CBC News and the Angus Reid Institute. On Oct 3, 2016, Jason Proctor from CBC reported in an article entitled "CBC-Angus Reid Institute poll: Canadians want minorities to do more to fit in" that over 68 per cent of Canadians want immigrant minorities to make more of an effort to fit into mainstream Canadian society, regardless of their home customs and languages. The poll also found that most Canadians also believe that immigration policies should put Canada's economic needs first, not the needs of immigrants. According to Shachi Kurl, executive director of the Angus Reid Institute:

> It does seem like a very surprising finding, especially when you consider this is a country that has been living with 45 years of official multiculturalism as government policy. It is maybe not what conventional wisdom might expect. But what these findings show is there are real limits on what Canadians — regardless of their own heritage or walk of life — are prepared to put up with in terms of accommodation and the sense of the mosaic versus the melting pot.

Unfortunately, the Canadian government and media are sending mixed messages about immigration that in the future may end up dividing Canadian society and causing serious problems by promoting "multiculturalism as strength" and hurting the true national pride of every Canadian citizen. I humbly suggest we all need to understand that the past is just that. It is gone, so we need to treasure our background and teach it to our children, preserve our mother tongue and our traditions at home and in doing business honestly as much as possible. This requires immigrants to make an effort to integrate.

Their new country is the future for them and their children. Immigrants should therefore respect and defend their new land, its national flag and anthem, its values, and above anything else, follow strictly all Canadian laws. If some want to live their lives as they used to do in their mother country, feeling sad or bitter for what they left behind without honestly trying to integrate, they should in my opinion think about going back to where they came from. We need devoted and loyal people with faith in their new country, so we can all prosper and grow strong. This applies to any immigrant in any country around the world, not just in Canada.

Values and Survival

On Dec 28, 2016, in an article by Kathy Michaels in the *Kelowna Capital News*, a picture of a proud Syrian man with his daughter and wife was shown. It was a beautiful, humane, and positive picture. The article explained that this family was trying to get settled in the Okanagan Valley (in British Columbia, Canada) and described their admirable efforts to do so. However, the girl in the picture was only the youngest of 11 children.

My point concerns the large number of family members that people from Africa, the Middle East, and other developing areas of the world tend to have. For the great majority of people in North America and Europe, two children are already a lot, but this is contrary to the philosophy of many other countries, even countries in turmoil like Syria. For example, the tragedy of the three-year-old Syrian boy, Aylan Kurdi, whose body was washed to shore on a Turkish beach, rocked the world when the picture of his drowned body was published in September 2015. The picture was absolutely sad to see and made us all want to help refugees even more. But with absolute respect, I need to ask a few more questions for which again I do not have concrete answers.

If Syria was already at war when Aylan Kurdi was born (like hundreds of thousands of other children), what kind of personal values do you have (or lack) to bring a new life into such a horrible reality surrounded by war, scarcity, and death, and where, even worse, there is no immediate end in sight? Does this match our North American values? Is it a matter of religious beliefs or of the need for men to prove themselves fertile? I am nobody to judge, but isn't it true that the more educated and free a woman is, the less children she tends to have? Are women in those countries forced to have sex regardless of the consequences, knowing very well that they are bringing another child into the world only to suffer? Are women there living under oppression? Are men so obtuse and ignorant that they really do not care to bring more children to danger and suffering? Is it just their selfish attitude to have more children to take care of them during their elderly years?

In my mind, and at the risk of sounding politically incorrect, whatever the reasons, they do not justify what I see as an extreme selfish and irresponsible act of bringing innocent children into this world under such detrimental conditions. Other examples are all those children being born in Sudan, Nigeria, Yemen, Somalia, and several other countries. An overwhelming percentage of the population in these countries is being born into suffering, famine, and a short and agonizing life. Are these our North American values? I do not think so!

Human Tolerance

To avoid misunderstanding, I want to pause in order to make it clear how the concepts of tolerance and patience are interpreted and applied in this book.

A tolerant person needs to be patient, but a patient person does not necessarily need to be tolerant. Google defines tolerance as "the ability or willingness to tolerate something, in particular the existence of opinions or behavior that one does not necessarily agree with." However, tolerance can also mean giving in rather than taking a stand on what one truly believes. It can indicate a lack of self-confidence or a weak personality as well as a strong, fair personality.

There are certainly different definitions and interpretations of tolerance among people depending on their specific backgrounds. For some, tolerance means the willingness (or weakness) to put up with opinions and behaviors one does not necessarily agree with or like. It is also seen as the ability to accept or to survive something unpleasant or even harmful. But some people legitimately wonder how much tolerance we need to have before we are seen as lacking in character or simply as stupid or weak. Some people believe they are seen as "tolerant, humane, and nice", when in reality they are seen as weak and naïve. This is the reason many refugees and immigrants abuse the Canadian system in various ways, as well as that of many European countries.

Study.com gives an interesting definition of tolerance that is worth quoting:

> Tolerance can be defined as a fair and objective attitude towards those whose lifestyle differs from yours. The level of tolerance in your life can be attributed to levels of happiness and contentment.

There is no doubt that tolerance is an important value, but how acceptable is it for people, in the name of tolerance, to adapt to the sometimes-inflexible lifestyles of others? The answer is easy. Not everybody is all that tolerant. Most are certainly not as tolerant as our government portrays everybody as being. In fact, the government is trying hard to impose a false sense of "pride" regarding tolerance.

Why? The following important technical definitions of tolerance may help provide the answer:

Scientific Definition: Tolerance is the allowable deviation from the known standard. Therefore, it is a range we should not go beyond for security reasons. For example, if the pressure in a gas pipe of an oil rig is exceeded, it puts at risk the security and well-being of all the operators and the oil platform itself. It is unacceptable and dangerous to go beyond the calculated tolerance of any system.

Medical Definition: Tolerance is the immunological state distinguished by indifference and passiveness to specific antigens. An antigen is a toxin or other foreign element that provokes our immune system to kick into gear to protect our body by creating antibodies. But not everybody is immune to a specific toxin, so people cannot all be dealt with as if they were immune to that specific toxin. The great majority may not tolerate the toxin or may even die.

According to Prime Minister Trudeau, we Canadians are a "tolerant society and we are proud of it," but many people across Canada do not agree with this imposed tolerance. It is a nice word that sounds altruistic and friendly, but if truly and fully applied in a country like Canada, it can go against the interest and well-being of the average citizen in the medium and long term, financially, economically, and even from the security point of view. In fact, Trudeau's vision of complete blind tolerance is not really accepted in any country of the world, including the United States and Mexico.

Other countries would never apply this philosophy of so-called political correctness that is being forced on Canadians. In fact, European countries that tried to be tolerant for many years and that worked tenaciously to help new immigrants and refugees adapt to their new countries, while assisting them to be an integral part of their new nation and its traditions have clearly failed. The proof is all the problems that have recently been happening in various European countries due to immigrants, especially those with a Muslim background. Their traditions, customs, and general way of life are simply too different from those of the European Union. Sooner or later, social unrest was bound to happen.

North America is unique. It is different from other countries, including the European Union. But what makes us think that we will not import similar social problems along with our refugees? It is either ignorant or naïve to believe these problems will not happen to us if we open our doors to refugees without proper planning, strategies, and security checks, regardless if they already have family members in Canada. It is not practical. It is arguably crazy from an economic and social point of view, though strategically sound from a political point of view, if a "tolerant" political image is your only goal. Therefore, we cannot deny that there is a potential risk of importing external terrorism along with the refugees. Wouldn't it be naïve or ignorant to do so? Time will tell, but in the meantime, we should all work together to try to prevent that from happening.

But what about internal terrorism by Canadians who feel that the government is admitting too many refugees with values hostile to Canadian traditions? In fact, regardless if it is right or wrong, many North Americans already perceive some Muslims as intolerant and imposing. When I first started writing this third book of the Runaway Trilogy, I had already anticipated that retaliations by Canadians would happen. Six immediate examples now come to mind (and without being negative, I am afraid it is just going to get worse):

1. Benjamin Shingler from CBC News reported on June 20, 2016, that a pig's head left outside a Quebec City mosque was the latest in a "string of incidents pointing to a rising tide of Islamophobia in the provincial capital and across Quebec," according to a prominent anti-discrimination activist.

2. The Toronto Sun posted "Quebec mosque attack: What we know" on January 29, 2017. This was after six people were killed and many more injured by an internal terrorist attack against the Centre Culturel Islamiqué de Québec (Islamic Cultural Centre of Quebec). This is definitely an extremely sad event for Canadian efforts trying to achieve only tolerance, multiculturalism, diversity, and integration, but completely ignoring the power of assimilation to make Canada stronger.

3. The Huffington Post reported on Feb 02, 2017, "Montreal Mosque Vandalized on Day of Quebec Victims' Funeral". According to the article, "the window at the Khadijah centre was smashed and an egg thrown at it. Fatima Ahmed, the

daughter of the mosque's director, says the building was also spray-painted with graffiti a few months ago."

4. The National Post published an article by Stewart Bell on Mar 01, 2017, "Arson attempt suspected at Toronto Islamic centre." The police found a circular burn on the roof and a gas canister. Stewart Bell wrote: "This incident comes amid a divisive debate over the Liberal government's anti Islamophobia motion and follows the Jan 29 attack at a Quebec City mosque that left six worshippers dead."

5. Andy Riga reported in the National Post (Mar 1, 2017): "Concordia building evacuated as Montreal police investigate bomb threats against Muslims." The cause was a letter threatening to target Muslim students in two Concordia University buildings after one of the buildings hosted an Islamic Awareness Week. Riga says that the letter was apparently sent by a group that calls itself Council of Conservative Citizens of Canada, complaining about Muslim students at Concordia. The letter said "Now that Trump is in office south of the border, things have changed." The scary part is that these groups live in silence among us, and they only need the slightest provocation to surface. Similar situation has happened in Europe along with the radicalized born Europeans committing terrorist attacks as well, not just from radical terrorists coming from abroad.

6. Nick Boisvert from CBC News posted an article on Nov 8, 2017, entitled "Muslim community slams Peel District School Board over 'stigmatizing' Friday prayer restrictions. The Peel District School has suspended the policy after complaints from students, religious leaders." Boisvert reported that Imam Ibrahim Hindy had insisted that, if the school board restricted student from praying, it would evoke memories of dictatorial regimes where freedom of speech is restricted. Does that mean anybody should be allowed to practice their religion at school or, for that matter, at work? News Anchor Marcia

MacMillan from CTV News interviewed Janet McDougald who is the chairperson of Peel District School Board. McDougald said that "all students are allowed to use vacant rooms for their prayers." To many Canadians, that statement will be alarming. Almost everybody, including myself, is in favour of "religious freedom," but most also believe religion should be a private practice and not brought to school or any other public place for that matter. To enforce on others the religious practices of Muslims in the name of multiculturalism, diversity, and tolerance is simply wrong, especially when Muslims are seen as intolerant and imposing. Isn't that a lack of reciprocity? The great majority of Canadians believe that minority groups should adapt and not impose their practices on others in public places. The issues about "accommodation" are a disagreement to others who unfortunately, are starting to develop a new sense of negative feelings, hate, and even some sort of retaliation. Schools cannot be a breeding ground for religious confrontation, reason why religion should be kept out of school grounds.   In her morning news, Marcia MacMillan said: "The confrontation in the Peel region of Ontario turned out ugly, very ugly on what was being said. It was like a bad episode of Jerry Springer".

There is no doubt that what Trustee McDougald was trying to achieve is positive, even noble, but the reality is that it is also dangerous. History has shown that religion has been the cause of horrible wars and crimes, abuse of women and children, political conflict, financial exploitation, and much more. As examples, we have the Crusades, the uprising of Buddhists against Christians in Myanmar, the Croatian and Bosnian wars where Orthodox Christians, Catholics, and Muslims clashed, the continued war between Israel and Palestine, and countless other conflicts. In my humble opinion, religion needs to be exempt from school and any other public places. Forcing religious traditions and practices on others is like trying to teach a cat to bark or a dog to meow. It will simply fail.

Tolerance of Immigrants vs. Political Correctness:

At the beginning of this section, I want to reiterate that I am totally in favour of the following three objectives of Canadian immigration policy:

1. Sustain a steady development and fostering of immigration to assist in populating our vast country and stimulating our economic expansion.

2. Continued tolerance and protection of legitimate refugees and asylum seekers, but with a proper screening process beyond that required for a regular immigrant applicant. Everybody deserves the opportunity of a fair, safe, equitable, and progressive lifestyle, unless they forfeit their rights due to criminal acts. In that case, they should be sent back where they came from. But our government needs to do due diligence and rigorous follow-ups. The media also needs to be fair and honest in reporting what is really going on, fully disclose both the good and the bad, and not simply follow government guidelines and interests as to what is the best story and angle to publish. They should avoid at all costs being biased and selective and have no fear of sounding politically incorrect.

3. Peaceful Canadian interventions in other countries to assist their populations to deal with violence or economic hardship. Any such interventions should comply with international law and be coordinated through the United Nations in cooperation with the country in need. In Canada, we are very lucky to have either been born here or to have had the opportunity to immigrate to this great nation. It is our moral duty and responsibility to cherish and protect our country and fight for the freedom and values we cherish. Tolerance is certainly one of our most valuable, defining Canadian traits, but let's be realistic about its limitations and social boundaries. Unconditional tolerance will never work in Canada (or

anywhere in North America). It will certainly be opposed by many Canadians and will spark future discontent and conflict. In fact, as of April of 2018, a backlash has continued and even doubled in some places across Canada in the form of graffiti, slurs, and other more serious types of attacks.

It is important to be as tolerant as possible of new immigrants and refugees, but we need to draw the line when our lifestyle, freedoms, confidence, safety, or financial security are at risk. Does everybody need to succumb to tolerance regardless of their background and beliefs? If we do not, would tolerance be forced upon all by the authorities regardless of people's values and freedom? Many are concerned there will be a negative reaction, as it has happened in many parts of Europe and other countries. Unfortunately, in Europe the backlash is just getting worse as the days go by. When our lifestyle, security, and peace are at risk, or when the abuse of women is justified by ancient traditions or contorted religious beliefs, we are definitely beyond tolerance and patience.

It is clear that "political correctness" can suddenly turn into an imposition and into what the poet Mary Black rebelled against. We cannot keep quiet because we are afraid of repercussions or being shamed. As Canadians (and as North Americans), we have a responsibility to protect our social and economic lifestyle. Black implied that we keep quiet because we have been affected by fear or guilt and forget that our system was created for our well-being and protection. She warns everyone not to keep quiet when we see the abuse of women in any shape or form. I want to extend her warning to many other areas of life. We should never remain quiet when we see any threat, unfair treatment, or potential danger in any aspect of our society, whether it comes from abroad or within. Breaking the silence makes us responsible and honorable human beings. Shouldn't we all feel a moral and ethical obligation to speak out if that means helping the community and the country we live in?

It is the opinion of many Canadians, though most are afraid of saying it openly, that the government should not impose tolerance on its citizens unevenly and unfairly. Although I am in favour of a controlled refugee protection programme, since 2015, the government of PM Trudeau literally dropped the weight of the "initial 25,000" refugees on the shoulders of every Canadian without proper planning, an adequate budget, sufficient housing, and, above all, adequate security precautions. All this happened in a very short period of time, and the Minister of Immigration at the time, Mr John McCallum, publicly admitted the government was ill-prepared to manage and settle so many refugees. Added to this, by the end of the second quarter of 2017, Canadians were having the problem of thousands of refugees crossing the border from the US to Canada. It became so bad that thestar.com reported on Feb 26, 2017 that Manitoba Premier Brian Pallister had called Ottawa for help because of the problems the province was having coping with the flood of refugees crossing the border, which was bound to increase as better weather arrived in the spring, which it did. The title of the article was "Despite calls from Manitoba premier, immigration minister not convinced of asylum trend." How can this be possible? Numbers do not lie? Unfortunately, some politicians disregard facts.

As a result of its haste, the government was forced to look for private donors (religious groups, private companies, or good Samaritans) to provide the required funds and housing for the immigrants. The same government could also fail to provide security to Canadians in case a few radicals get in while pretending to be refugees. Contrary to what the average person in Canada might believe, this can certainly happen.

It is clear to many educated and hardworking people that immigration policies sometimes favour foreigners above citizens for political reasons. This takes advantage of the good will of the country's population, especially that of the average person who lacks a deep understanding of how immigration will impact the society, the economy, and even their personal budget in the medium and long term. It is like favoring somebody else's child over your own. How many parents would go for that?

We also have many people in our country who live in poverty and whose situation is similar to or even worse than that of some refugees, but our system does not protect them enough. We should take care of our own people first and then focus on foreigners or at least do both at the same time and in proportion to their needs. If the government wants to increase our population density, why not coordinate a balanced programme of immigration instead of simply opening the doors to more and more immigrants indiscriminately? For that matter, why not develop new government policies to motivate Canadians to have more children and make it economically feasible for the average family to have another child?

Good examples of Canadians in need include the homeless, the poor, remote native communities, and all the unemployed people affected by the oil crash of 2015 and earlier. In July 2014, the price of a barrel of oil was slightly above $100. By January 2015, it had dropped to $50 per barrel, with clear indications that it was heading to even lower levels of perhaps $40 or even $35. Every economist knew this would impact the economy severely, not just the oil industry, as was soon reflected in the Canadian-US dollar exchange rate.

When the price of oil goes up, our goods and services go up due to the higher price of gasoline and higher transportation costs. But when the price of oil goes down, the Canadian dollar tends to suffer serious devaluation, causing imported products, materials, and services to go up. The Canadian economy is natural resource-based, and we therefore need to import a lot of finished products and services from Asia, Europe, the United States, and other places. The rising cost of imports pushes inflation higher. Regardless of whether the cost of a barrel of oil goes up or down, the average Canadian family was financially worst off by April of 2018, except for the privileged minority.

The writing was on the wall from the beginning of 2015. Any prudent and intelligent government officer at medium and higher levels should have seen it coming. The average Canadian was given a bit of "circus and distraction" with the new Prime Minister's election campaign during 2015, along with his potential and future new cabinet. In my mind the writing on the wall clearly said: "There is an oil crash approaching that will seriously impact our economy, so buckle-up, plan accordingly, and be prepared." The only difficult part was to predict how low the price of oil could go. Nevertheless, at higher levels of government, private enterprises, and research institutions, professional people knew the crisis was going to hit Canada and hit it hard.

Among many articles on the oil industry published around the beginning of 2015, I want to bring to the reader's attention an article entitled "Saudi Arabia 'engineered' oil crisis: Dallas Fed chief. (CNN, Feb. 11, 2015). Written by Heather Long, it reported:

> Saudi officials have repeatedly blamed supply and demand for the price meltdown. They say they were caught off guard by the price decline, and acknowledge this is putting a lot of pressure on US shale. [Prince Alwaleed bin Talal, a member of the Saudi royal family and a well-known global investor said that] "although Saudi Arabia and OPEC countries did not engineer the reduction in the price of oil, there's a positive side effect, whereby at a certain price, we will see how many shale oil production companies run out of business."

Unfortunately, instead of preparing our economy, which could have lessened the impact on the average Canadian family,

Trudeau's Liberal party created another distraction by suddenly promising to allow 25,000 refugees to come to Canada over a very short period of time without proper background checks and without thinking through the real costs, especially in terms of housing problems and the help that refugees would need in order to settle permanently. To make matters worse, the government then proceeded to authorize hundreds of millions of dollars of additional funding for the Syrian refugee programme while requesting donations from private industry, religious groups, and the general public. How professional is that?

Questions:

We are a country made by immigrants, and we have a moral obligation to help others in need (like the Syrians), but we should do so in a rational, measured, intelligent, and well-organized manner. So, several questions arise:

- Why hasn't the government implemented a similar strategy for all those families that have lost their jobs and or businesses due to the economic crisis driven by the oil industry downturn and its impact on the Canadian dollar?
- Why do private companies or tax-exempt religious groups not assist further their own fellow Canadians by creating funds to assist families whose breadwinners lost their jobs?
- Have the oil industry companies and private magnates who owe everything to their committed and devoted staff done anything to help their ex-employees during those hard times? These are companies and individuals with billions and billions of dollars. Instead, the oil industry in Alberta was asking for bailout money from the federal government.
- Doesn't everybody have the responsibility to save money when times are good, instead of increasing their spending levels by buying new toys to emulate their neighbours? In corporations, shouldn't business owners and enterprises should have the same philosophy?

Answers:

The answers are relatively simple:

- In Canada people lost their jobs, but unlike refugees, they did not lose "everything," nor are their lives at risk.
- As Canadians, we tend to have unemployment insurance (at least for a while) and are not starving.
- We Canadians do not have a government that is fighting rebels and bombing their own people.
- Canadians do not need to risk their lives and cross oceans to look for better opportunities while escaping from hunger, bombs, rebel attacks, and lack of protection from their own government, police, and military.
- The average Canadian has fewer mouths to feed at home compared to Syrian families that can easily have 8 to 10 children (or more).

These reasons are genuine, but they do not justify the lack of special programmes by the federal and provincial governments to prepare for what was clearly coming. Programmes, such as anti-inflationary policies, tax benefits for the newly unemployed, stronger assistance programs to their families, and the creation of new jobs in other industries to diversify and expand our economy, which should have been previously planned. The government should have implemented policies to minimize the exploitation of our natural resources and expand the economy through the diversification of high-tech industries, expansion of national production levels, growth of export markets, promotion of renewal and sustainable energy, and development of our infrastructure, with the overall goal of minimizing the importation of finished goods. On a slightly different note, to encourage the development of renewable energy will also be welcome, such as hydropower, geothermal, wind, solar, and biomass (ethanol, biogas, biodiesel, landfill waste gas, etc.).

The Canadian "Fast-Track" Refugee Process and US Security Concerns

On February 3, 2016, the United States' homeland security committee held a hearing regarding the Canadian "fast-track" refugee policy and did not treat Trudeau's policies as those of a celebrity. They saw them as irresponsible, reckless, and politically self-serving and felt they put both Canada and the United States at potential risk of future terrorist attacks.

As Alexander Panetta reported in "Canada's refugee plan on hot seat: US Congress holds hearing on policy" (Canadian Press, Jan. 26, 2016):

> A union representing border guards will argue that there aren't enough border agents to guarantee that the country is protected from terrorists infiltrating from the north.... "It is a source of concern," said Shawn Moran of the National Border Patrol Council. The nearest agent could be 100 miles (160 kilometres) away. By that point, you could easily cross into the US from Canada – and be on your way.

Some lawmakers in the United States have already been ominously questioning how vital the border is to Canada's economy. Trudeau's Liberals should have asked themselves this question before making an offer to accept so many refugees without consulting our neighbours to the south and without being properly prepared ourselves. Why? Because the United States has always been our ally, and they also buy 76 per cent of all Canadian exports. As Panetta notes, after 9/11 the United States tightened the border and adversely affected many Canadian businesses selling goods and services into the United States. Let's face it. Yes, we are supposed to be an independent country, but if the United States sneezes, Canada or Mexico can get pneumonia. Why provoke our neighbour to the south and put them at risk of infiltrated terrorist attacks through our extended and unguarded border?

Before the hearing, Canada's ambassador to the US, Gary Doer was invited to attend, but he declined and instead sent a letter explaining the specific security measures that Canada was implementing to appease the United States. According to Panetta, the main security measures included:

> The collection of biometric information from refugees; a zero-acceptance policy when doubts surface about any individual refugee candidate; use of US security databases; the prioritization of low-risk refugees like women and families; and the fact that the refugees would be non-citizens for years, and couldn't travel to the US without visas.

But the question arises: Are terrorists going to try and get a visa for the United States or simply cross the border on those stretches of 160 km between border patrol stations that are not possible to guard by the border patrol? The answer is obvious and unsettling to the United States.

Immigration Problems: European Union and Beyond

Before I go any further, I need to restate once again that I firmly believe in immigration and in providing a helping hand to all *legitimate* refugees or asylum seekers. Accepting them will not only help them get established in a safe country, but it will also strengthen our economy and enrich the beautiful cultural mosaic that makes us a unique country to live in. However, I also believe we need to plan and respect specific quotas per country, to avoid alienating our own people with waves of refugees and immigrants, as has happened in the City of Richmond, BC. In Richmond, the Asian population has overwhelmed commercial and residential areas. Many have imposed their traditional ways of doing business, which are often different from those practiced and accepted in Canada. Rich Asian immigrants (not refugees) have been pushing the prices of real estate above and beyond the possibilities of the average Canadian working person, forcing their exodus.

People come to Canada (and North America in general) in search of peace, freedom, justice, and safety. You will find all these benefits in North America (with slight variations in degree among Canada, the United States, and Mexico). All three countries follow a similar philosophy and political framework. As Canadians, we all feel proud to stretch our hands out to help others in need. But there is a saying in Spanish that is famous for being scarily accurate. It says: *Farol de la calle, oscuridad de la casa* (lights in the street, darkness at home). It is a difficult translation, but it refers to a person who does good on the street but not at home. In English, we call such people "street angels." That is exactly how many Canadians are starting to look at certain politicians like Angela Merkel in Germany and PM Trudeau in Canada. Both are very different from politicians like Donald Trump (US) and Marine Le Pen (France). The latter fought for justice, equality, and reciprocity, by putting French values and the interests of the French people first, but she was defeated by Emmanuel Macron, French president since May 14, 2017.

If justice and safety are compromised in our country, we will not be able to offer these wonderful benefits to refugees or any immigrants. Worse, these benefits will also end for our own citizens. Just look at what is happening in Western Europe with all the immigration and refugee problems. Look at what is happening in Australia, Southeast Asia, Eastern Europe, and even some Middle Eastern countries. They all started by accepting immigrants and assisting refugees, but after a decade or two, they have serious social problems with refugees or the refugees' children, some of whom have been born in their adopted countries. The following sections give some examples for readers to evaluate for themselves and to research further if they wish.

Turkey:

As Jason Hanna and Hamdi Alkhshali report in "Ankara blast: At least 28 dead in Turkish capital explosion" (CNN, February 17, 2016), 28 people were killed and many more were seriously injured when a vehicle full of explosives was detonated as a military convoy was passing by. To date, nobody has claimed responsibility. Turkish Deputy Prime Minister Bekir Bozdag said that many of the victims were civilians and that it was clearly an act of terrorism. This is hardly the first-time terrorist attacks have taken place in Middle Eastern countries such as Turkey. Civilians are always at risk when venturing into the streets of Ankara. The article quotes Turkish President Recep Tayyip Erdogan stating that:

> Our determination to respond in kind against such attacks against our unity and future from outside and inside is even more strengthened through such attacks. Turkey will not hesitate to use its right to self-defense anytime, anywhere, and in all situations.

But on Dec 11, 2106, bomb attacks outside a stadium in Istanbul killed 38 soldiers and wounded 166 people. On Dec 17, 2016, two Istanbul synagogues were bombed, killing more than 23. The terrorists struck at almost the same time three miles apart. One of the blasts destroyed the façade of Neve Shalom, the biggest synagogue in Istanbul. In another terrorist attack on Dec 19, 2016, the Russian ambassador to Turkey, Andrei Karlov, was shot dead by a Turkish police officer who shouted at bystanders to pledge allegiance to Islam and not to forget the city of Aleppo in Syria.

Turkey has worked very hard to assist large numbers of refugees to integrate successfully in their country, but not all Turkish people are happy or comfortable with these efforts, and this is why terrorist attacks (by outsiders and insiders) are happening. By Dec of 2017, they closed their border to refugees.

Sweden:

In "Sweden's Ugly Immigration Problem" (Globe and Mail, Sept 11, 2016), Margaret Wente reported:

> In Europe, refugees from Syria and Iraq have been cramming the ferry-trains heading from Germany to Denmark. But once in Denmark, many refused to get off. Where they really want to go is Sweden, where refugee policies are more generous. When the Danes said no, they hopped off the trains, and began heading towards the Swedish border by taxi, bus, and foot.

This has deep implications. There is a saying, "use caution when giving a helping hand; they might rip your arm off." The Danes offered to assist refugees who then turned their backs on the Danes and quasi invaded Sweden. If they do that without even having arrived as landed immigrants, imagine what their demands be few years down the road when they have gained the same "human rights" as any Swedish or Danish citizen.

According to Wente, Sweden is the most generous European country in everything related to immigration. The words "immigrant" and "refugee" are considered synonyms, unlike in any other country (including Canada). A registered immigrant gets the equivalent of about 700 USD per month plus access to various social programmes to assist them. Sweden is the most immigration-friendly country in the world, yet their immigration programme is not working as expected. The main reasons are lack of proper integration, lack of job opportunities, lack of job skills, ghettoization, and the fact that immigrants and even their children are failing to acquire the knowledge and skills required to compete in the job market. Wente interviewed Dr. Tino Sanandaji, a Kurdish immigrant with a PhD in Economics from the University of Chicago who now lives in Sweden. He works in immigration and says that Sweden has always strived to achieve social equality, but in the last decades they have suffered the biggest increase of social inequality of any country in the OECD. Sweden has tried to integrate the children of immigrants and refugees as best as they can to help them grow up as "native" Swedes. They have been very generous with all their immigration programmes. They have provided good medical services, schooling, housing, and job opportunities, yet they have failed due to lack of trust, inequality, and economic pressures.

According to Wente, the Swedish government spends an average of 4 billion USD a year to help settle new refugees, yet social unrest is escalating. Immigration problems are rarely featured in the "mainstream media" to avoid inciting racism, which unfortunately is increasing anyway and at a very fast rate. Rapes, assaults, break-ins, and murders are perpetrated daily by some immigrants, with very little, if any, prospect of change in the future.

Many immigrants expect to be given welfare by the government for years. At the same time, they do very little to create opportunities for themselves. Instead, they complain and demand to be given more and more. Dr. Sanandaji says:

> If you're offering generous welfare benefits to every citizen, and anyone can come and use these benefits, then a very large number of people will try to do that. And it's just mathematically impossible for a small country like Sweden to fund those benefits.

Over 58 per cent of those on welfare in Sweden are immigrants, and according to Wente, the great majority of murders, rapes, and robberies are committed by either first or second generation immigrants. So where is the integration and the equality? Where is the immigrants' appreciation for the opportunities granted to them by a friendly country built by people who treasure freedom and equality? The situation has become so bad that the government recently decided to deport 80,000 asylum seekers, only for them to disappear and stay on illegally. This is weakening Sweden's social stability.

Note: A similar situation is happening in Denmark and other countries. The Danish government decided to encourage immigrants to be more productive by cutting their benefits by half. The results are yet to be seen. As in Sweden, many immigrants have settled in "welfare ghettos," which only increases social stress.

Germany:

Germany has accepted over one million refugees from Africa, the Middle East, and from Asia. This is mainly due to the country's low fertility rate. They need to open their doors to immigrants and refugees. Unfortunately, the newcomers also bring health concerns such as diphtheria, HIV/AIDS, Congo hemorrhagic fever, polio, mumps, tuberculosis, hepatitis whooping cough, typhus, scabies, tetanus, etc. Their needs are pushing the health care system in Germany beyond its limits. Doctors, nurses, and volunteers were all screaming for help and rest. The immigrants' trauma issues and the health care they require (for issues that were not all detected prior to their arrival) is overwhelming the unprepared German health care system and placing a hefty economic burden on the country and its citizens.

According to Soeren Kern (German Interior Minister):

> Critics are warning that German taxpayers will end up paying billions of euros to provide healthcare for a never-ending wave of asylum seekers. This is in

addition to the billions of euros already being spent to provide newcomers with food, clothing, and shelter. Many say the German government failed fully to consider the unforeseen consequences of opening the door to so many migrants.

Now, regardless of the years, let's briefly compare Germany to Canada using Nation Master (nationmaster.com). They are known to compare statistical information among countries. The average figures we have for Canada and Germany for 2012 through 2014 are the following:

2013 / 2014	Canada	Germany
- Government Budget	690 Billion	1.54 Trillion
- Gross National Income	682 Billion	1.9 Trillion
- Unemployment	7.3%	5.4%
- Exports	462 Billion	1.46 Trillion
- GDP	1.82 Trillion	3.4 Trillion

The German population was just over 80 million in 2013 compared to 35 million for Canada. The economy of Germany is much stronger and more diversified than the Canadian economy. Germany has helped to keep the European Union afloat due to its financial and economic strength, yet in 1945 they had been completely destroyed. From the rubble of the second world war, they now stand proud and strong, assisting and aiding other countries that lack their discipline, pride, hard work, and productive mentality. Germany is a country with few natural resources, but a very creative and inventive population and a highly industrialized, capital-intensive economy compared to Canada's. Germans are leaders in technological advances worldwide, and they have been so throughout modern history.

Even though Germany has helped over one million refugees to the best of its ability, it has been the target of many Muslim extremists. As an example, a recent attack took place on Dec

19, 2016, when a Tunisian refugee drove a truck into a busy Christmas market, killing 12 people and leaving 48 badly injured. The attack took place in the heart of Berlin near the Kaiser Wilhelm Memorial Church. ISIS claimed responsibility and said it was proud of one of its "soldiers." To add insult to the tragedy, the suspect (Anis Amri) had been under police surveillance and was scheduled for deportation. Isn't it sometimes unfortunate that everybody has a right to due process? Sometimes we have to wonder about the price to pay for being politically correct and following "proper procedure" in cases where previously collected evidence clearly indicates someone might attack. Why wait and respect his or her rights as a refugee waiting for an asylum decision when the police already had solid evidence? Shouldn't deportation follow immediately?

Note: If Germany, with one of the most developed and diversified economies in the world, cannot control and provide full care to all immigrants, what makes us believe we will not encounter similar or even worse problems in North America and specifically in Canada?

Belgium:

There is a good article by David Graham published on February 17, 2015 entitled "What's the Matter with Belgium?" The small nation has become a major source of violent jihadists, both from Syria and Iraq and also inside Europe. According to Graham, one of the smallest countries in Europe has been providing a steady flow of fighters to ISIS in the Middle East, and it is also where many terrorist plans to attack various parts of Europe have been hatched. The radicalism problem in that country is underground and expanding. It is beyond the control of the Belgian police, which tends to underestimate its real impact and strength within their country and beyond their frontiers.

With only 11 million people, it is estimated that seven to eight per cent of their Belgium population was Muslim in 2015. But that is not the problem, because not all Muslims are created equal. There are very respectable, productive Muslim families who are strengthening Belgium's economy, but it is unsettling that some poisonous vipers are sprouting and slithering their way out from the dark underground. Some are second or third generation Belgium radical Muslims. The government acknowledges that hundreds of these Belgian extremists are going to fight with ISIS, as well as for other groups in the Syrian civil war. Graham wrote:

> Belgian jihadism seems to mimic French Islamist militancy, only more concentrated – as befits a smaller country. Both have large numbers of immigrants who are poor and isolated from the dominant culture. Both countries have also seen far-right, anti-immigrant parties rise by loudly declaring a Muslim menace.

Note: How can you stop radicalization after the seeds have germinated? How do you incorporate the isolated and radical people into a culture that is not offering enough for them to be busy and devoted? Isn't it more important to bring people and help them integrate in their new culture without professional barriers for the immigrant to practice their profession? If Canada (or any other country for that matter) does not offer the new immigrants solid jobs that are fairly paid and fully recognize their professional backgrounds, we will start pushing them, slowly but surely, into their own little ghettos.

But if we are not able to offer those needed full-time jobs to our own people (6.2 per cent of whom were unemployed by Oct of 2017), how can we offer fair opportunities to the new immigrants? How will we stop them from feeling segregated and from lashing back in the future against the society that "opened its arms" and offered them new "opportunities"?

Getting an underpaid job is not a fair opportunity. We can either provide them with full-blown assistance or we will have to become vigilantes of the immigrants' future activities. I hope for the first and repudiate the latter. But only time will tell!

France:

This country has suffered some of the worst terrorist attacks in history. Some have been direct retaliations against "freedom of expression," which is a valuable right that every country should practice. But freedom of expression should not include freedom to insult and humiliate other races, religions and beliefs. At least that is what many critics believe, and I concur. You should be able to write well-researched articles on whatever subject you want, but nobody should be free to ridicule, insult, or humiliate anybody using the excuse of "freedom of expression." Many acknowledge so-called satire as needing to be provocative, critical, and sarcastic, including even mocking other's deficiencies and weaknesses. However, it sometimes goes too far, and that can be very dangerous. Why? The answer is simple: because it can expose the author(s) to retaliation by people or groups that do not acknowledge the justice system in that specific country. They only believe in their own twisted and distorted "justice" based on killing and blowing people away, instead of engaging in equitable, honorable, impartial debate and reasoning. This is why Charlie Hebdo's offices were attacked on January 7, 2015, by Cherif and Said Kouachi (two brothers).

According to BBC News in an article entitled "Charlie Hebdo attack: Three Days of Terror" (Jan 14-15):

> The men opened fire and killed the editor's police bodyguard, Franck Brinsolaro, before asking for the editor Stephanie Charbonnier, known as Charb, and other four cartoonists by name and killing them, along with three other editorial staff and guests attending the

meeting. Witnesses said they had heard the gunmen shouting "We have avenged the Prophet Muhammad" and "God is Great" in Arabic while calling out the names of the journalists.

There is another interesting article published by Journalist's Resource – Research on Today's New Topics (authors: Leighton Walter and John Wihbey) on Nov 16, 2015. I urge the reader to read it at: (journalistsresource.org/studies/international/conflicts/france-muslims-terrorism-integration-research-roundup).

It is worth understanding what France is going through. This is why I suggest you read this article for yourself. I will only quote its first two paragraphs:

> A Nov 13, 2015 string of terrorist attacks across Paris that killed 129 people has again raised concerns across French society about jihadist violence and ISIS-inspired domestic terrorism. The tragedy comes in the wake of several other attacks in France in 2015, including an attack on an American-owned chemical factory near Lyon in June 2015 and two in January 2015, when 12 people were murdered at the satirical news outlet *Charlie Hebdo* and then, days later, four hostages were killed at a kosher supermarket.

Like other European nations, France has a long and complicated relationship with the Muslim world and its own immigrant population, many of whom have been in the country for generations. French Muslims are highly diverse. Some are secular, while others are observant. One of the policemen killed in the *Charlie Hebdo* attacks, Ahmed Merabet, was himself a Muslim. Some are at the centre of French society — for example, soccer player Zinedine Zidane, born in Marseille to Algerian parents, led France to a World Cup Victory in 1998 – but many remain excluded. Research from INSEE, France's national statistical agency, indicates that, in 2013, the unemployment rate for all immigrants was 17.3 per cent, nearly 80 per cent higher than the non-immigrant rate of 9.7 per cent. Descendants of immigrants from Africa have a significantly more difficult time finding work. The report found that education and skill levels only explained 61 per cent of the difference in employment rates between descendants of African immigrants and descendants of non-immigrants.

Why has France been chosen for attack by Muslim terrorist groups? Among the main reasons are:

- Many Muslim immigrants fail profoundly to integrate into French culture due to totally different backgrounds and values.
- Muslim job candidates are two to three times less likely to be offered a job than their Christian counterparts.
- The French understanding of freedom of expression has expanded to include insults against and humiliation of the Muslim religion and its followers.
- The average Muslim household in France has a considerably lower income than the average Christian household.
- Discrimination against Muslims is more obvious in France than in other countries that are more "tolerant."
- Public services, assistance, and overall support go further in Christian communities than in the Muslim communities. By the same token, the appreciation and positive response for integration runs deeper in Christian families than in Muslim families, whose beliefs are so strong and deep that they weaken the spirit of integration, despite adopting the French way of life and way of doing business.
- Some Muslims try to bring their religion into schools or public places, while Christians, Buddhists, Hindus, Jews, Sikhs, Chinese, Taoist, and other religious groups tend to leave their religious practices at home.

Norway:

More and more asylum seekers are crossing the Norwegian border seeking asylum as refugees. Some of them have been living in other countries (such as Russia), and they are simply looking for a better lifestyle, not because they are hungry or their lives are at risk.

Norwegian Prime Minister Erna Soldberg confirmed that assistance to refugees will cost Norway between four and five billion USD over the next five years. The government is deeply worried about the social repercussions this may have. According to an article published in the Barents Observer last Nov 15, 2015 and written by Ariana Ulyanova and Elizaveta Vassilieva entitled "Norway Adopts Stricter Asylum Regulations," almost 5,000 refugee seekers had crossed the Norwegian-Russian border by November 2015. This is why Norway decided to toughen the border regulations against refugee seekers. According to Ulyanova and Vassilieva:

> Anyone crossing the border into Norway must have a visa. Norway will return people who are not entitled to residence in Norway to their country of habitual residence. Applications that appear likely to be denied will be given priority and fast-tracked. People from safe areas of Afghanistan or who have been granted residence in another country will have their application rejected and will be deported.

Furthermore, the Norwegian Ministry of Justice and Public security has reportedly "instructed the Directorate of Immigration (UDI) and the Immigration Appeals Board (UNE) to reject applications from asylum seekers arriving in Norway after having resided in Russia, without considering individual cases in depth."

Why should Norway (or Finland or Sweden for that matter) slow down or stop their immigration process (refugees included) when its own fertility rate is on the decline and well below "replacement" level? Because the rate of immigration is simply too much for them to handle socially and economically. The costs are simply too high and cannot be imposed on the average Norwegian citizen.

It is also important to mention that many Norwegian women now feel insecure and are afraid of walking in their own city streets alone for fear of being harassed or raped, as is happening in Germany and other European countries. Talk about "biting the hand that feeds you!" Furthermore, The New Observer published in Nov 2015 an article entitled "Invaders: Norway Will 'Deport by Force'." They even went to the extent of reprinting this on the front page of the Afghanistan Times on Nov 26, 2015, so everybody could get the message in that country as well. According to the New Observer article:

> The moves come only a day after the Norwegian government also announced the reintroduction of border controls to stop the Angela Merkel-generated Third World invasion from flooding out the Scandinavian nation.

In reaction to the abuse and rapes perpetrated by immigrants and refugees, Germans are starting to fight back. SPEISA is a site that publishes strange but true stories from around the world that are sometimes not published elsewhere for fear of causing social unrest. They do not post satire at all. Speisa.com recently published "Violence, arson and hate speech." These are just some of the things that asylum seekers in Germany increasingly have to put up with.

Now, it is important to mention that according to Bloomberg:

> The number of attacks against asylum centers has increased significantly within the past year. While Germany now has the largest refugee influx since

World War II, from January to July, over 200 cases where refugees and migrants have been subjected to hate crimes such as arson, vandalism and violence have been reported. The waves of attacks against refugee centers in Germany are now so strong that the American search engine Google in July deleted a detailed map that showed information about where the reception centers for asylum seekers were located, for fear that the centers would be subjected to hate crimes.

Russia:

The great country of Russia has not been exempt from the machismo and crazy attitudes of Muslim extremists. There is an article worth quoting for its depth and seriousness, for those who still refuse to believe that accepting people with profoundly different cultures, religion, and ways of treating their own people (especially their own women) are going to cause serious problems. The article was published in *Top Right News* (toprightnews.com) on Feb 4, 2016. It is entitled "Muslim 'Refugees' Molest Women in Russian Nightclub… Russian Men Put Them in the Hospital" and was written by Jason Dewitt who says:

> A large group of Muslims "refugees" who had previously been kicked out of Norway thought it would be a good idea to come to a Russian nightclub and molest and try to rape a bunch of women. But unlike the politically correct Germans in Cologne, the Muslim men found out that Russians are not as "tolerant" of their Islamic "diversity," unleashing a savage beating that put nearly 20 mostly Arab men in a hospital.

The refugees tried to flee but were quickly captured by the Russians. They then took them out to the street and gave them a beating they will always remember. Police arrived to break up the fight, but locals report that they too threw a few punches at the refugees before arresting 33 of them. Eighteen refugees were in such bad condition they had to be taken to the hospital. Local officials said the refugees were immediately deported after being released from the hospital. Kudos to those Russian men — and police — for giving these "rapefugees" the "welcome" they so richly deserved.

To confim the accuracy of the information, I want to quote what Jacob Bojesson wrote in the *Daily Caller News Foundation* on Feb 4, 2016 under the headline "Refugees Go Clubbing in Russia, Harass Girls, Wake Up in Hospital the Next Morning":

> A group of 51 refugees were brutally assaulted outside a nightclub in Murmansk, Russia, after they groped and molested women [on] Saturday, with some [vigilantes] shouting "This is not Cologne!" while hitting them with fists and clubs. The refugees had previously been ordered to leave Norway for "bad behavior" and tried their luck in Russia. What they didn't realize when they went out clubbing in Murmansk is that Russians have less tolerance when it comes to sexual assault on local women than other European countries. The refugees allegedly groped and harassed women in a similar manner as the assaults in Cologne on New Year's Eve. A group of male Russians took them aside to "educate" them that "Cologne is 2,500 kilometers south of here."

It is just a matter of time before the same things happen to any immigrant or refugee who does not abide by the rules and regulations of their adopted country. If any immigrant or refugee, regardless of their background (Christian, Buddhist, Hindu, Jewish, Sikh, Taoist, or any other religious group), fails to behave according to the laws of their adopted country and respect the civil rights of its people, they are risking the same fate, or worse if this escalates. Are the citizens of that country to blame? I dare not comment, because in North America anybody can easily be labeled racist when he or she is not at all racist. Just by presenting real events as factual and bringing to the attention of readers true events and circumstances, a person runs the risk of being called racist even when there is not a drop of racism in his or her body. People sometimes cannot handle the truth, so they lash out with insults and with false accusations, as it used to happen in the time of the inquisition, when a woman could simply be accused of being a "witch" and, without proof, end up being burned to death at the stake. Now, the questions is: What do I really think about what the Russians did?

Well, for me the answer is extremely easy, I take my hat off to those Russians. Kudos to them! You have to be extremely "civilized" or a traitor to your principles not to protect your traditions and the well-being of your own women. We men can only achieve greatness if we have the understanding and support of our women, so our duty and responsibility is to support their goals and dreams while respecting and protecting them at all costs.

Poland:

There was a very interesting but troubling article in the New York Review of Books on January 14, 2016 by Andrew Salomon and the Polish PEN Club. According to this article, Poland does not have a significant Muslim population, so their problems with Muslims are close to none. Nevertheless:

> Anti-Muslim rhetoric emerged as a major feature of the Polish parliamentary election campaign this fall. The victors in the October 25 vote, a populist, nationalist-right party called Law and Justice, promoted xenophobia on a scale unseen in Poland since the fall of communism in 1989. During the campaign, the Law and Justice leader, the former Prime Minister Jarosław Kaczyński, attacked immigrants for carrying "various

parasites and protozoa, which don't affect their organisms, but could be dangerous here." Social media and the far right press also promulgated anti-Muslim slogans and images.

Several massive anti-refugee protests followed. Protesters held marches, burned EU flags, and chanted nationalist slogans. In a number of Polish cities, gangs beat up or taunted dark-skinned "Arab" students or tourists. One victim was a Sikh entrepreneur. On November 18, in the city of Wrocław, a far-right group staged an anti-immigrant demonstration and, moving rapidly from one form of racial intolerance to another, burned an effigy of an Orthodox Jew.

Thus, even in countries that have little or no Muslim presence, people are afraid of a slow and relentless Muslim invasion and the lack of respect and integration that may follow. As much as I can insist on the fact that "not all Muslims are created equal" and that there are also very good, productive, and respectable Muslims, there is very little anybody can do unless people get more informed, educated, and vigilant in these matters.

Greece and Italy:

During my research, I found several articles describing unrest and conflict over the immigration and refugee situation in Greece and Italy. The two following articles caught my attention (among many, many others):

CNN World published an article Jan 25, 2015 by Tim Lister and Ioannis Mantzikos entitled "Add this to Greece's list of problems: It's an emerging hub for terrorism." The article describes how various terrorist suspects were arrested in Greece and confirms what many have been afraid would happen, which is that "Greece's long land and maritime boundaries, its proximity to Turkey, the explosion of illegal migration from Syria and the country's dire financial situation make it an inviting hub for jihadist groups."

The International Business Times published an article on July 29, 2015, by Jess McHugh entitled "Anti-Immigration in Italy: Muslim Prayer Rugs Removed in Turin by Right-Wing Officials, Sparking Anger." The article reported that "two right-wing Italian councilmen sparked outrage Tuesday when they removed prayer rugs from Turin city hall ahead of a Muslim conference." The councilmen were accused of being racists, but they denied this vehemently. They simply argued that City Hall was not a place for people to practice their prayers. Sadly, there was a serious reaction by other politicians:

> The incident was "an arbitrary and violent act," said Michele Paolino of the Democratic Party. Many other democratic leaders have rallied to the sides of Muslims in the community, condemning the actions of these two men.

Scenarios like the one above allow the average citizen to question the presence of other religions in their day-to-day lives and in public places whenever they decide to kneel down, lay down their rugs, and pray. Now, the interesting part is that throughout history the strategy of the military, the politicians, and also private businessmen has often been to "divide and rule." Yes, create confusion and let the opposition fight each other while the instigators play the role of victim and gain strength while sitting on the sidelines, observing and learning. The question arises: Isn't this the strategy of some extremists? Create confusion and divide the country's parties so as to eventually take over and control?

Ireland:

The Mirror website (mirror.co.uk) published an article describing how extremist Muslim groups have blamed the Irish government for allowing American planes to refuel at Shannon Airport before going on to bomb and kill people in Muslim countries. These groups consider the United States to be "the butcher of all time," though they do not speak for hardworking average Muslims who respect freedom and democracy. There is a lawyer called Anjem Choudary, who is the founding member of the banned British Islamist Organization *Al-Muhajiroum*. Reliable sources say this organization was involved in the terrorist attack on *Charley Hebdo* in Paris. Choudary is quoted as saying:

> You know it's not just now that [Ireland has] … become a legitimate target – I believe for a long time that in the eyes of al-Qaeda and others, it is a place which is being used to aid and abet the war. The Irish know their claim of being neutral and not being involved in any kind of war campaign is not something which has been bought by the Irish public or Muslims around the world.

Choudary has also publicly defended Sharia law's nine years age of consent for girls. This is truly amazing. At this age, any girl is still naïve, innocent, and, simply said, very, very young. Choudary has also stated publicly that "if you know this carries capital punishment and there are Muslims who will kill you if you insult the prophet and continue to do it, then you have the blame on your own shoulders." The above are strong reasons why many consider Choudary a serious extremist and somebody to be careful of and to watch on the world stage. Luckily, there are many other people and websites that are more realistic and positive. They also write about the real facts of the lives of millions of Muslims. One of the websites (to some a bit controversial) is that of Mark Humphrys from the UK. He published a statement on March 1, 2016, with which I fully agree:

> Islam in Ireland: As I say on the Islam in the West page, most Muslim immigrants come to the West

precisely *because* they support its freedoms and want to escape failed states ruled by clerics and Islamic dictators. We have a *duty* to let these freedom-loving Muslims in. Western Muslims are the most liberal, tolerant, pro-democracy Muslims in the world. All the dissidents are here – the religious dissidents, the political dissidents, the feminist dissidents, and the gay dissidents. All the dissident works – such as criticism of Islam – are published in the West. This is all much to be celebrated. However, there is a *substantial* minority (10% to 20%) of immigrants who threaten our western freedoms. They are Islamists – essentially religious fascists – who want to impose their religious beliefs on the rest of us. What to do about these aggressors is one of the questions of our time (markhumphrys.com).

Just to clarify, a dissident is a person who goes against an official policy but, most importantly, he or she goes against and strongly opposes any authoritarian state that imposes laws and regulations that go against human rights and freedom.

Ireland is a very neutral country (by our Western definition of neutrality) that does not really want any involvement with Al Qaeda or any other extremist group. Unfortunately, it is already a target of these groups due to their cooperation with the US as narrated above. It appears that if you are not with Al Qaeda, you are then automatically their enemy and on their terrorist hunting list. But it is important to emphasize that this only happens with extremist Muslims, not with every Muslim, regardless of the country in which it takes place.

Great Britain:

An article published on Dec 31, 2015 on the well-known website of the Gastone Institute – International Policy Council (gastoneinstitute.org), and written by Soeren Kern, confirms that in Britain the Muslim population represents 5.5 per cent of the population of 64 million, that is, a total of approximately 3.5 million people. According to Soeren, this is the largest Muslim population in Europe after France and Germany, which, unfortunately, have the most problems with Muslim immigrants and refugees. Among those 3.5 million Muslims in Britain, there is a large number of extremists who represent a continuous challenge to the internal peace and safety of all British citizens.

Soeren quotes Anjem Choudary (lawyer and founder member of the banned British Islamist Organization *Al-Muhajiroum*) as follows:

> Contrary to popular misconception, Islam does not mean peace, but rather means submission to the commands of Allah alone. Therefore, Muslims do not believe in the concept of freedom of expression, as their speech and actions are determined by divine revelation and not based on people's desires. In an increasingly unstable and insecure world, Muslims and non-Muslims alike know the potential consequences of insulting the Messenger Mohammed. So why in this case did the French government allow the magazine *Charlie Hebdo* to continue to provoke Muslims, thereby placing the "sanctity" of its citizens at risk?

Yes, freedom of speech is very important, but more important is to know when not to cross the line between respectful discourse and disrespectful, totally provocative discourse. Of course, nothing justifies violent terrorist action against a person, a group of individuals, or a country. That is a crime that needs to be dealt with by any means available.

Regarding Islam's presence in Britain's social and political life, Soeren wrote:

Islam and Islam-related issues were omnipresent in Britain during 2015, and can be categorized into five broad themes: 1- Islamic extremism and the security implications of British jihadists in Syria and Iraq; 2- the continuing spread of Islamic Sharia law in Britain; 3- the sexual exploitation of British children by Muslim gangs; 4- Muslim integration into British society; and 5- the failures of British multiculturalism.

Joseph Brean from the National Post published on Mar 23, 2017 "Horror Outside the House." He described how a radical lone wolf drove to the other side of the Westminster Bridge in London and mowed down 20 people before crashing into a railing. He got out and stabbed to death a police officer. He was then shot and killed by other officers on the grounds of Parliament. The British born terrorist killed 4 people and left many seriously injured. That happened in broad daylight and in a split second. "We're being attacked," people screamed!

It is well known that many terrorist attacks have been perpetrated on British soil and that the odds for more to come are high. Just the thought of so many categories of Islam-related problems, like those previously described in North America, is alarming and unsettling. We all have to do everything in our power to prevent these problems from growing, though without promoting hate crimes against immigrants and refugees. We need only be friendly, careful, prudent, and vigilant, assisting as much as we can to encourage the full, swift, and friendly integration and assimilation of all immigrants and refugees in a more transparent and efficient way than has happened in Europe.

Netherlands:

This country has long been known as a highly democratic and progressive nation, very keen to preserve the freedoms it has enjoyed. During the late 1960s and early 1970s the economy was booming, and the Dutch allowed more immigrants and refugees into their country, mainly to do jobs many Dutch did not want to do. Immigrants from Muslim and non-Muslim backgrounds were allowed into the country and got jobs in various sectors of the Dutch service and manufacturing industries as "guest workers." The majority came from Turkey and Morocco initially, but their origins diversified later.

When the boom was over, however, many immigrants lost their jobs. Little by little, they started banding together to help each other, creating small, segregated communities cut off socially and culturally from the rest of the country. During the past three decades, these communities have grown in numbers and gotten stronger, but have remained isolated from the rest of the country. Nowadays there seems to be a strong resentment, which started with loss of jobs and unfair market opportunities and ultimately led to a lack of integration and assimilation of many immigrants and refugees. One out of five people in the Netherlands are either immigrants or offspring of immigrants, and one tenth of the Dutch population consists of "visible minorities."

What really happened in the Netherlands with the immigration influx that today represents a national problem? There is a very interesting article posted on a website called Just Landed (justlanded.com) based on a book called Discovering the Dutch, published by the Amsterdam University Press, that discusses the society and general culture of the Netherlands. Released in Nov 2014 and edited by Emmeline Besamusca and Jaap Verheul, the article starts with a very powerful argument worth quoting at length, because what it describes can easily happen in North America, if we do not learn from other's mistakes.

> The prevailing self-image of the Dutch has always been one of strong international orientation and an open mind towards influences from abroad: an open society

with open doors. The Dutch prided themselves on their tolerance for other cultures and religions, and they welcomed immigrants and refugees from all over the world.

In the late twentieth century, the Netherlands had become one of the countries in Europe with the largest share of foreign-born residents. Its generous and respectful policies of multiculturalism served as a shining example for other immigration societies.

Since the turn of the millennium, however, the Dutch mind appears to have been closing at an unprecedented speed. Immigration is now seen as a major problem, as a threat to social stability and to Dutch culture. The murders of politician Pim Fortuyn (2002) and film director Theo van Gogh (2004), both of them outspoken antagonists of immigration, in particular from Muslim countries, shocked the nation. In the 2009 European elections, Geert Wilders' anti-immigration and anti-Islam Freedom Party (PVV) became the second largest party of the country, only three percentage points behind the Christian Democrats (CDA).

In the Netherlands, the situation has turned out very badly, with many extremist immigrants living within Dutch society. The Mayor of Rotterdam, Mr Ahmed Aboutaleb, originally born in Morocco, who immigrated to the Netherlands at age 15 and is a Muslim himself, relayed a harsh and decisive message to the Muslim extremists in his country, as Kayla Ruble reported in Vice News on Feb 13, 2015 under the blunt headline "Mayor of Rotterdam Tells Muslim Extremists in the Netherlands to 'Fuck Off'."

This happened immediately after the Paris attacks. Ruble notes:

the Mayor of Rotterdam made the remark during an appearance on Nieuwsuur, a national television program. Specifically, he said Muslim immigrants who are unable to accept "humorists" creating content for a newspaper could "fuck off" — or *"rot toch op"* in Dutch. He also relayed the message that if any Dutch Muslims are against freedom, then "for heaven's sake pack your bags and leave. There may be a place in the world where you can be yourself, he <u>said,</u> according to the *Telegraph*. Be honest with yourself and do not go and kill innocent journalists."

As of April, of 2018, many Canadians still feel proud to help and assist immigrants, refugees, and asylum seekers (aside from needing their help to strengthen our economy), and can only we hope these people will embrace and integrate into our wonderful country culturally, socially, economically, and politically. We feel satisfied that we are a "tolerant society" because this is not just important, but it is the right thing to do and the right way to be. But what happens if, ten or twenty years from now, the "integration process" turns out to have failed, as is now happening in the Netherlands and all over Europe? What then? Is that what we want for our children's generation and for ourselves when we are old? Our children are naïve and inexperienced. It is easy for them to say "do not worry, it will not happen to us." But when jobs fall short or when opportunities are given to Canadian-born people while very gently and almost invisibly discriminating against immigrants, what will happen then? It is already very difficult for a recent graduate in Canada (immigrant or not) to get a decent paying job in many industry sectors. Canada urgently needs to do something about this.

We certainly want to assist immigrants and refugees as best we can, but we also need their help and cooperation. Let's face it and be honest with ourselves; we need each other for growth, strength, and safety. A multicultural economy is not just extremely interesting, but it can be colorful, beautiful, and fascinating. However, it is important not to allow more people into our country without a proper plan of action, as it happened with PM Trudeau when the availability of housing and government funding for the Syrian refugees fell short.

We urgently require long-term government and private programmes on every aspect of social integration, but most importantly, for the creation of new jobs. As a nation rich in natural resources, we can stop the pure exploitation of these resources for the benefit of the elite few and start promoting manufacturing. The government should implement a fifteen to twenty-year programme to create job opportunities based on industrial expansion and diversification.

Regarding Mexico and Muslim extremists, I am convinced the latter will never be successful due to Mexico's deep cultural roots, which neither the United States nor Canada have yet developed. Some Mexican traditions are thousands of years old. Their food, traditions, and festivals are deeply ingrained in the DNA of every Mexican. They are a very proud, friendly people, but feisty if provoked. In Mexico, immigrants and refugees would never get away with abusing women, because for Mexicans the most important thing is the protection of their women and the Virgin Mary (of Guadalupe). They will make the Russians looked civilized, even after what was done to the immigrants in the Russian nightclub as described above.

The Mexican Catholic population represents about 84 per cent of the total population (as of 2017). Mexicans are very tolerant, but only if the respect goes both ways. They will never allow immigrants and refugees to impose their customs and practices over Mexico's deep traditions. That will simply never happen. An unwritten and invisible law in Mexico is to "adapt or leave." In Mexico, nobody needs to be politically correct; Mexicans respect their flag, their people, background, traditions, and, above all, their women.

Egypt:

About 10 per cent of the Egyptian population is Christian. Muslim extremists have targeted them for a very long time, and on a Sunday morning, Dec 11, 2016, they placed a bomb at St. Peter and St. Paul church, killing 24 innocent people and injuring 49 more. Apparently Mohamoud Shafik Mohamed Mostafa, a 22-year-old, was the perpetrator. He targeted women and young children who were congregated when the blast took place. The Islamic State claimed responsibility for the hideous crime, saying it will continue war against the "apostates" until they adhere to the Muslim faith.

Some Recent Attacks as of June 1, 2017 to March 2018

1. On March 23, 2018, three hostages and a police officer were killed by a French (Moroccan born) Islamic terrorist.
2. On Jan 27, 2018, an ambulance exploded in Kabul, Afghanistan, killing 103 people and injured over 230.
3. On January 31, 2018, four people were killed and 44 injured by suicide bomber in Boko Harm – Nigeria.
4. On Mar 22, 2018, New China posted "15 soldiers killed in suicide bombing at checkpoint in Yemen."
5. On Mar 23, 2018, The Manila Times posted "Army officer killed, 2 soldiers wounded in Davao City clash."
6. On May 31, 2017, CNN World published "Kabul blast: Attack kills 80 near diplomatic area in Afghanistan."
7. On May 26, 2017, Mail Online published "At least 28 people killed, including children, as masked gunmen 'dressed in military uniforms' open fire on a bus carrying Coptic Christians to pray at a monastery in Egypt."
8. On May 22, 2017, BBC News posted "Manchester Arena blast: 19 dead and about 50 hurt."
9. On April 21, 2017, The Globe and Mail published "Gunman targets central Paris, kills officer."

10. On April 7, 2017, BBC News published "Stockholm lorry rams crowds, killing 'at least four people.'"

Conclusion

I could go on forever providing concrete examples of immigration problems and terrorist issues, but it is time to stop. My goal was only to use these examples to underline the following ideas. North America needs to be aware of the likely future social problems due mainly to poor government planning on immigration and refugee policies with an added lack of integration issues in many of the newcomers. We also need to be aware of the likely reaction from locals to the pressures imposed by lax immigration and refugee laws and by the influx of immigrants with completely different values, traditions, and backgrounds to people in North America and competing with them for jobs. We are all aware of terrorism, but the complexity of immigration and refugee problems, added to a potential "immigration phobia" within our own radical and non-radical elements, are still latent, concealed, unseen, and invisible, but with a high potential to create problems that are already springing up. I hope I am wrong, but I highly doubt it. If many countries in Europe have failed, why should we think we are so special that it will not happen here? We need to plan, act, and work hard to avoid these potential future outcomes, beginning "yesterday," and not wait until they start happening.

In North America, we need to take care that no extremists are raised within our societies to become dangerous inside our own territories. To succeed in this, we need to start by accepting our defects and our weaknesses. If we are not aware of them, we will fail. Humility and strength of character are important on an individual basis as much as at national levels. In Canada, we seem to believe that nothing will happen to us if we keep things the way they are and keep working as if nothing has happened in Europe, Asia, and the Middle East, and even as far away as Australia. We all need to be continuously vigilant. We must not cross the line into vigilantism, but we need to take care of our communities and families without expecting only the government to do this for us.

In contrast to Canada, the United States is aware that such things can happen there. This is why they have accepted only a few, and extremely well-scrutinized, refugees from Syria. The US is an amazing country. We Canadians are kind of lucky to have the United States as our neighbours (although some might feel a bit skeptical about this). They are resilient individuals, hard workers, risk takers, freedom lovers, and, above all, they dream big! But again, they are a bit naïve in some national matters. Why? Let me explain.

As I write this (March 2018), the whole world knows that the United States is facing a very difficult and challenging future under President Donald Trump. Some say he is a loose cannon, some say he is brilliant, others say he is a racist and a bigot, and still others insist he is a brilliant businessman who has built sound and profitable businesses around the world. They also say he is a cheater and a liar, and others that he is straightforward and courageous. Regardless of how people see him, he has achieved the presidency of the United States. A large percentage of the US population refuses to recognize him as their President, but he has ended up siting in the oval office of the White House as their Commander in Chief for over a year already. In the meantime, the US economy has done great. Trump will most likely remain there for his full term unless an accident happens or he is impeached. I am certainly not going to judge him now. It is still too early to do so. In fact, who am I to judge him when we all know that the news media there is overwhelmingly against him? The media is so much against him that, regardless of whether their reports are accurate or not, they only end up desensitizing and annoying people after a while. The news can easily be biased, incomplete, and untrue, or it can be very accurate, for that matter. Well-known and brilliant economists and financiers predicted a big market crash if Trump were elected, but the opposite happened. Nobody really knows what is coming, and the truth of the matter is that only time will tell. However, there are a few things I am certain of, which I want to express with absolute respect and admiration for the people of the United States, as follows:

- Everybody in the world knows that the United States has lost international leadership, power, muscle, and economic and military influence over the past few decades. It is also known that people from the United States are often not very welcome and do not feel secure in many other parts of the world. Some even travel with a Canadian flag pin on their knapsacks. But guess what? Canadians are not esteemed as we were in the past. We need to be honest with ourselves, accept this, and learn how to handle the truth, as much as it hurts our pride.

- Hillary Clinton repeated something several times during her campaign that is politically correct but not necessarily the truth: "We have to work not to make America great, because we have never stopped being great." Yes, the United States is still a great country, but far from what it used to be. To my mind, the strength and greatness of the United States needs to be revived with renewed power and vigor. The United States has an amazing population with unmatchable working attitude, guts, vision, and spirit, but they lack strong leadership, like many other countries do.

- In contrast, Donald Trump (as crazy or wild as some consider him to be) accurately and truthfully maintained throughout his campaign that the position of the United States in the international arena needs to be made great again and that he is willing to put in the required effort and professional ethics to achieve it. He has always acknowledged that the greatness of the United States has diminished in manufacturing, international commerce, and even militarily compared to China and Russia. To some, he is a straightforward, down-to-earth style of person. He owes no favors to anybody, and we all hope he has the ability and wisdom to put his proven entrepreneurial track record to work for the benefit of the people of the United States. Let me be clear; I am neither for or against him, but I truly believe people should give any new president a chance and stop criticizing or interpreting out of context every word he says or political move he makes. That does not help anybody; it only antagonizes people, which is obviously the agenda of some individuals or groups.

• Before the election was over, I always thought it took guts and foresight to admit that the United States is not as great as it used to be, but it also took a keen sense of refined vision and a subtle touch of wisdom by Hillary Clinton to boost the pride and spirit of every citizen of the United States by saying that they have always been great. Both were trying to say the correct thing at the time. I still remember when many Americans said that, if Trump won, they would move to Canada. After Trump was elected President of the United States, nothing really happened.

Unfortunately, many refugees have been crossing the border between the United States and Canada almost every day for the past several months, following Trump's decision to return all illegal aliens to their countries of origin. They have crossed the border (and as of April of 2018 are still crossing) mainly through Saskatchewan, Manitoba, Quebec, British Columbia and the Yukon. To the surprise of many Canadians, they are crossing by the thousands, and it can easily get worse. In my personal view, this news is being downplayed for fear of a backlash by Canadians who do not agree with the current Liberal policies and methods on immigration, refugees, and asylum seekers.

By Nov 30, 2017, the border town of Emerson in Manitoba, with about 700 residents, had already received more than 1,000 refugees seeking asylum who were not sent back immediately due to the political arrangements between the US and Canada. According to many Canadians, these refugees jumped the queue and seriously affecting others who have patiently been waiting for their paperwork to go through. Many Canadians consider them illegal aliens challenging the system and its limits. We are simply not prepared for this invasion, which is why Manitoba Premier Brian Pallister asked for federal help to provide the refugees with housing, emergency medical care, food, clothing, shelter and legal and paralegal aid for them to start their refugee claims and be able to settle in Canada.

There is no doubt it is very nice and altruistic to extend a helping hand, but what is alarming is the speed with which the news travels all over the world and, as a result, the speed with which many more refugees and asylum seekers started leaving the US or their countries of origin for their new destination (Canada, not the US anymore) before the window of opportunity closes on them, if it ever does. They are still mainly coming from Nigeria, Somalia, Yemen, Syria, and a few other places. Depending on where they are coming from, they arrive on the American continent through countries that do not require visas, such as Brazil, Guatemala, Mexico, and a few more. Immediately after landing, they start their trek to the great white north, Canada. PM Trudeau has publicly expressed his "open-door" policies in situations like this, without realizing the sensitivity and delicate position of resentment and retaliation from Canadians against people with very different values. Nobody really knows how much of an "open door" his administration has in mind or how refugees are being screened. But it is certainly a concern of many Canadians and for the United States' Homeland Security and National Border Patrol Council among others. The question remains: do these refugees represent just the tip of the iceberg now that across the world we are known to be so "nice and polite?" Is this good for our social balance and peace as well as for the future of Canadians? Again, time will tell!

The Islamic Relief Fund is trying to assist every refugee of Islamic background as much as it can. A noble quest no doubt, but why is it that they cannot help them in their own countries? The answer seems easy to grasp. According to the Islamic Relief Fund, the refugees come mainly because they changed alliances in their country and are now persecuted, or because several groups are fighting for control of their territory, along with the added problem of heavy-duty corruption. But a military intervention is definitely not the answer. Much less a strong financial support, because even in peaceful countries, financial aid alone, does not seem to work. Look for example at what happened in Haiti in 2008. The country went through their worst hurricane disaster, when four storms with strong winds dumped heavy loads of water in that country, killing almost 800 people, leaving over 800,000 others severely affected, and destroying more than 22,000 homes.

International aid poured into that country, but there are still thousands of people living in deplorable conditions, to the extent that Haitian refugees are emigrating to countries like the Bahamas, where they are discriminated against, but where they can get jobs that people from Bahamas do not want to do. On Oct of 2016, Haiti was hit again by hurricane Mathew, so their situation is now even worse.

Message for The Younger Generation

It is worth bringing to the reader's attention the following. On May 24, 2017, Starbucks executive chairman Howard Schultz had a face-to-face presentation and challenged a group of business executives. His main points were: "*I don't need to tell this audience that are all assembled today — whether you're Republican or Democrat or [you] voted for the president or not — we probably can all agree the country is drifting in a* *direction that we all need to be concerned about, and in the interest of being transparent and saying something that might be controversial, I would say the country is in need of an economic, cultural, and moral transformation. We have a government that's dysfunctional and polarized. We're going down a path where many, many people are going to be left behind in this country. And what that means to me is businesses and business leaders are going to have to do a lot more for their people and the communities they serve going forward. <u>Business is a fragile balance between profit and conscience. Social responsibility and making money is going to be more important for business leaders going forward.</u>*"

Then on May 25, 2017, Facebook CEO Mark Zuckerberg said: *"Purpose is that feeling, that you are a part of something bigger than yourself."* Now, if we join the thoughts of Schultz and Zuckerberg to hold hands together, I sincerely hope that the younger generation can innovate, develop, implement, and lead the United States to a more socially responsible and positively motivated society. I also wish and trust Canada follows suit.

Unfortunately, and as a side note, as of Mar 22, 2018, Facebook and their CEO Mark Zuckerberg, are undergoing serious problems regarding the Facebook data breach that has affected over 50 million people's private information.

CHAPTER FIVE: IMMIGRANT AND REFUGEE INTEGRATION AND TRUE LIBERTY

Immigrant Adaptation and Integration

Regardless of the size of our planet in relation to other planets, galaxies, or the universe itself, it is huge in relation to us, with vast oceans and continents where creatures of all kinds live in amazingly complex relationships. We all need to adapt to our surroundings and be happy with what we have, but, above all, we need to take care of what we have for future generations.

From the human perspective, the world we live in is indeed huge, but we have been figuratively shrinking the size of our planet due mainly to amazing new means of communication and transportation. People travel all over the globe very quickly on a daily basis through an intricate network of land, water, and air transportation. As a result of this easy mobility, we all need to adapt to wherever we go. Wouldn't it be wiser to behave as locals out of respect for them and even sometimes for our own safety? In many instances, we are required to modify and synchronize our behaviors and attitudes to fit and belong in the new society, while leaving some behaviors, along with our pride and stubbornness, behind. A flexible attitude needs nurturing, attention, and effort. Nothing good and valuable comes easily, at least not in my world.

The more we travel, the more we meet people from different backgrounds, creeds, traditions, and overall ways of being. We are all the same species regardless of our colour, language, or beliefs. We all need to understand each other or, if we cannot, then at least accept each other the way we are. However, the right attitude has to be taught at home when the individual is still a young child. It needs reinforcing at school, but the key thing is strict guidance, monitoring, and observance by Mom and Dad from the earliest stages of life.

For this to happen, Mom and Dad need to be on the same frequency, that is, have the same boundaries, ethical values, and goals as partners and as parents. If parents have different values and goals, this will make it very difficult, if not impossible, for them to properly guide and provide a good example for their children. An infant needs parents who will give them guidance, rules, and boundaries rather than just being friends who try to satisfy their wants, needs, and desires. Parents need to provide proper protection and mentoring to their children regardless of their situation. Therefore, the integration or assimilation of new immigrants is extremely important in any society, because they then do become an integral part of that new society. This is why it is imperative for immigrant parents to guide and teach their children to integrate into their new society as quickly and smoothly as possible. If there is equality instead of hierarchy between parents and children, this will make the education and integration process more difficult. Integration alone is insufficient, because integration only incorporates people from other cultural backgrounds into their new society as equals. Full integration or assimilation are the key factor to strengthen the cultural values of the recipient society, and this is what Europe has failed to achieve.

Socially and at work, it is an art to properly connect with your peers and others around you. It is not easy, since we are all different and have diverse values. But what it is clear is that with tact, subtleness, determination, and politeness, we can actually achieve a lot more in trying to connect with others. We all know that good manners (or the lack thereof) develop with culture and how people were brought up at home and at school. Depending on your background, the level of politeness varies, but if you go to another country to live, you need to understand the new culture and accept its norms so that you can adapt and act accordingly. None of us wants to be rude or have others act rudely towards us.

When I left Mexico and came to Canada to live, the first thing my parents told me before leaving my old country was:

> If you go to Rome, do like the Romans do. Respect their ways of being and their traditions. Blend in but never forget your roots, your flair, your uniqueness, and your own style. Just treasure it and do it with respect.

That is exactly what I did, and I have never had a problem. In fact, my level of politeness and respect was much more defined than the one I found in my new country, so it was quite easy for me to adapt and outperform the average citizen by far. However, this philosophy is contrary to those of many people coming from various Asian, African, South Asian, and Middle Eastern countries. The cultures and traditions in these countries are very different from those of South America, Central America, and North America. They are also drastically different from those of the European countries, Australia, and New Zealand. Sadly, in almost every country, there are groups that have been granted permission to immigrate and integrate to their new country and culture but are failing to do so. To simplify the integration concept, let's summarize the three main types of integration: full, partial, and non-integrated.

Fully Integrated or Assimilated Immigrants

These are people coming into a country usually with the proper permits and documentation. They are admitted under various categories such as family class, independent, investors, business class, skilled worker class, skilled trade class, experience class, student visa, under a sponsorship program, as a refugee, and others. Every country allowing immigration from abroad has its own set of rules and specific classifications or categories based on the preferences and needs of the country.

Fully integrated or assimilated immigrants bloom in societies that have mechanisms to allow newcomers to be treated equal, and to integrate, develop, and grow within the community while adapting to the new laws, rules, regulations, social etiquette, and overall way of life of their new community. They fully adopt the values and ways of another culture, becoming part of their new society. According to the United States government, full integration is achieved when there is both "social inclusion and economic mobility." Fully integrated newcomers adopt the social behaviors of their host, but also keep their own traditions, creed, language, and their own uniqueness. Fully assimilated newcomers completely adopt the ways of their host and slowly let go the values and traditions of their old country, even their old language. This usually tends to happen to the second, third, or fourth generation of immigrants, though not always to all.

These fully integrated or assimilated immigrants help build strong communities. They increase cultural diversity while strengthening the social fabric and political values of their adopted community. The assimilation of these individuals is very important. They might even still hold hands to specific communities of their own original background, such as the Italian community, the German, the Chinese, the Indian, the Latin American, the Eastern European, etc. As long as those groups work collectively with each other and in harmony with the local communities, everyone will achieve stronger and higher degrees of satisfaction and development, culturally and economically. The overall society grows harmoniously and with almost identical goals and preferences. This will strongly benefit the immigrants themselves, their families, and their new country.

However, this can only be achieved if every culture acts with respect towards other cultures without even thinking of imposing their own traditions, religion, ways of doing business, and philosophical views on others. Exercising mutual respect, tolerance, and social reciprocity among the different groups builds peace, harmony, and a strong progressive society over time.

These types of immigrants deeply integrate into their new society, but their new generations are at high risk of leaving behind and even forgetting some of their own traditions, including their native language. Parents fail to instill these in their children by not practicing them at home, and the children unfortunately sometimes grow up speaking only English, forgetting their parents' native language.

Partially Integrated Immigrants

These are people who still maintain their traditions at home, but have adopted the new country's way of life successfully. They still speak their mother tongue but have also mastered the new country's language. These people try their best to be part of their new society, but also choose to keep their own culture always in mind and go the extra mile to teach their children their mother tongue. They also make a conscious effort to teach their children their own rich traditional heritage.

These immigrants constitute a strong pillar in their new society, because they achieve full adaptation during their process of learning the language, traditions and cultural values of their new adopted country. They work aligned in harmony within their new community socially, politically, and economically, but they do not forget their roots, their traditions, and much less their language and overall customs. They practice whatever traditions and religion they want behind closed doors, but in public they have adapted and act (with their own flair and style) according to the principles and traditions of the society that accepted them with open arms. They also share some of their traditions with pride, respect, and a unique flair, with results that are fascinating to the locals of that new country.

These types of immigrants are very happy in their new country but also feel proud of their roots and where they come from. They never try to impose their own traditions, values, or beliefs on others, however. They share when this is convenient for all, but they never even dream of imposing anything on others, regardless of their religious convictions. They are just happy to share the values, customs, and beliefs of their previous country without expecting others to adopt them. Some cultures may not want to mix as much as others, but they live in peace, with respect and harmony, in their new community while practicing social reciprocity on a continual basis. This group is the ideal bridge between cultures. They promote multicultural societies, which are the future of our planet. Multiculturalism is what makes Canada unique, strong, and gives it enormous potential for the future compared to other countries. But let us be aware, multiculturalism could also be a double edge sword.

Non-Integrated Immigrants

Some immigrants of this type come to their new country of their own free will, but many others have been forced to emigrate by political and economic instability in their home country. They are given the opportunity to arrive as permanent residents (immigrants) and start a new life, but they somehow fail to integrate. Others were granted the opportunity to come to a new country as refugees or asylum seekers, but their desire (or need) to keep practicing their own traditions and style of living, disregarding those of their new country, stays strong. They want to live their lives by behaving and doing business the way they did in the country they came from. They want to treat each other the way their religion dictates even when this goes against local laws and social standards. Their apparently fanatical approach results in unfairness and abuse of others, including even their own women, whom they consider weak and lesser beings, so they tend to keep them subjugated and silent even in their new country.

These immigrants tend not to acknowledge anything else. They insist on practicing their own original traditions and culture in their new country. They even try to influence others to adopt their traditions, their faith, their religion, and their overall way of living within their new community. They lack respect and tolerance and profoundly fail to practice social reciprocity. These types of immigrants do not necessarily want to learn the local language of their new country or eat the local food. Above all, they fail to adapt to the new laws and to the social comportment of that country. They want to enjoy the same privileges while avoiding the responsibilities that all other citizens in their new country have. They believe in a one-way street instead of a two-way street. They demand tolerance from locals but are not willing to tolerate them in return.

There are two types of non-integrated immigrants:

1. Those who live their lives peacefully within their own little worlds. They create their own self-imposed ghettos and live in a small bubble without causing social unrest.

2. Those that want to impose their ways on the new society that embraced them with open arms, regardless of the social consequences. These people, always cause social unrest.

According to various European media sources, the second type of immigrant has been detrimental to their societies. Their adopted countries thought they would integrate and adapt, but they did not. Many people consider them unfit, unstable abusive, and even dangerous. Some of them are even tagged with the labels of extremists or radicals. Not all non-integrated immigrants are extremists or radicals. It seems that the worst non-integrated immigrants in Europe nowadays are the radical Muslims whose faith pushes them to act and behave inhumanely towards non-followers regardless of whether they belong to their own people or not.

Not all radicals act from religious beliefs. Some are social or political radicals who can cause a lot of damage socially. To clarify, radicals or extremists are individuals who have drastic and extremist political, economic, social, and religious ideas or beliefs that seriously conflict the fundamental ideas and nature of the establishment. Radicals are extreme people who think outside the existing framework accepted by their neighbours. They have fundamentally different ideas and values that far exceed the boundaries of logic, fairness, and balance of the society they live in.

Average Immigrant vs. Radical Immigrant

The successful average immigrant arrives as a landed immigrant (with legal status), tries hard to adapt and integrate to the new country, and does so with the best of intentions and a sense of respect and appreciation. These are positive individuals who are eager to belong and some even willing to be assimilated. They are keen and enthusiastic to start a productive new life in a more advantageous political, economic, or social environment than that of the country they left or escaped from. Some fit like a fish in the pond. Others find it difficult but, with time and effort, they succeed. Unfortunately, a few fail to adapt, and because of this, they build up resentment against everything around them.

Immigrants come to North America from all over the world, but the ones that have been in the news almost on a daily basis for the past several years have mostly been Muslims from the Middle East, Africa, and South Asia. There are many types of Muslims, of course, but unfortunately for the average North American they are mainly reduced to two types: the "normal and down-to-earth hardworking Muslim" and the "Muslim fanatics."

Regarding Muslim communities around the world, I want to state clearly that the non-radical or non-fanatic Muslim (that is, the *average* Muslim), like the average member of any other religious group, behaves peacefully, respectfully, and with a pro-active and positive attitude. They do have their own tastes, preferences, and particular ways of practicing their beliefs and performing some daily duties according to their cultural backgrounds. This makes them interesting as colleagues or friends. The average Muslim makes an effort to integrate into the new social environment. Many of these average, non-radical Muslims also tend to stick to their own traditions in a private setting, though they do tend to respect others and will try their best to integrate into their new country nevertheless. They make an effort to blend in, not to stand out. They are just regular people like you and me practicing their own beliefs, traditions, and unique ways of being in private, but in public they make an effort to adapt to the values, traditions, and ways of being of their new country and behave accordingly. They try hard to respect local customs and laws in public life and usually succeed. These are positive people. They enrich and strengthen our country's diverse cultural background and mosaic.

Unfortunately, in every culture or society there are always some extremists who damage the good reputation and image of the majority. This is clearly the case with the radical Muslims who are committing atrocities, not just in other countries against other creeds or faiths, but also within their own Muslim societies. Unfortunately, the mix among different radical religious groups can be dangerous and explosive, as human history has proven in the past many times in various countries. In North America, except for the twin towers, we have not really had serious problems with such radical groups to date. Not to the extent they have had in Europe and Africa.

It is important for me to reiterate that radical Muslims are very different from the average normal Muslim previously described, and even very dangerous, as they have proven themselves to be in several foreign countries. On every tree, not every apple is beautiful, fresh, and edible. Some apples (luckily, only a few) are rotten to the core and need to be weeded out of the healthy tree before they contaminate the rest of it. The same is true in every intricate, wonderful culture in this world of ours.

Shia and Sunni

Islam has two main denominations, Shia and Sunni. Between them, they are by far the fastest growing cultural and religious group in the world. The great majority live in the Middle East, Indonesia, South East Asia, and Africa. However, more and more Muslims (considered now only sizable minorities) have been settling in Europe in recent years, mainly in England, France, Spain, Germany, Netherlands, Belgium, and Norway, as well as in in China, Australia, Russia, and the Americas (mainly in the United States and Canada).

It is well known that some Muslim groups have not integrated into the countries that have allowed them to settle there. Their core values and beliefs are very strong and quite different from others, and this causes some to act irrationally and even aggressively when others do not accept their faith or way of being. These radicals suffer an extreme form of something known as cognitive dissonance. What is cognitive dissonance? According to Frantz Fanon (Martinique-born Afro-Caribbean philosopher, psychiatrist and writer):

> Sometimes people hold a core belief that is very strong. When they are presented with evidence that works against the core belief, the new evidence cannot be accepted. It would create a feeling that is extremely uncomfortable, called cognitive dissonance. And because it is so important to protect the core belief, they will rationalize, ignore and even deny anything that does not fit with the core belief.

Some Muslim immigrants, regardless of the country they go to, have adaptation obstacles that cause serious problems for their new country, problems that can sometimes escalate to dangerous levels. Governments in many countries are not well prepared to solve these issues. Mexico, Canada, and the United States are good examples. Canada in particular seems too trustful and naïve, and observers in other countries sometimes say that Canadians will sooner or later bump into some rough terrain because of this. Countries such as France, Australia, and others have given Muslims a chance to integrate and have tried hard to accommodate them but, on realizing they could no longer do so, invited them to leave their country. Please refer to Appendix 3 for what Australia's prime minister publicly told immigrants who are uncomfortable and do not want to adapt.

In Australia, it has gotten so bad that for a while they have been sending people asking for asylum to the islands of Manus and Nauru. This is another reason some Canadians are seriously concerned. These are considered Australia's offshore detention islands specifically to mitigate their problems in the mainland. The Australian Prime Minister negotiated with the Obama administration to take many of the asylum seekers, but since Trump took over, there has been a political struggle. The US does not really want these people but still needs to honor the original agreement. Similar problems with asylum seekers are happening all over the world, and we need to start developing an international solution or it will just get worse in every country targeted by them.

Leaving Broken Hearts Behind

Refugees and asylum seekers do not always have the luxury of choosing when and where they want to go. They are usually forced out of their country due to political, military, or economic problems. They leave with a great deal of sadness, anxiety, and old memories. They simply have no choice but to leave and escape their homeland, or else they risk being killed, jailed, or dying of starvation. They all leave behind good experiences of earlier years chiseled in their consciousness forever. They leave their homes, family members, friends, and their beloved traditions, style of living, and unique geographical landscape. Not all immigrants can deal with this. As a result, some will have serious integration difficulties, which they may even pass on to their children.

Achieving the American Dream

In general, all immigrants to North America and Europe, including refugees, are searching for a better life and to achieve the "American dream" of success and a happier and safer existence. Not everybody achieves it. For those who don't, frustration starts accumulating until one day some end up misbehaving. Why does this happen? Here are some of the reasons as I see them:

- In North America, we have a very structured and organized society in which we are required to abide by local laws and regulations. In some Middle East or African societies, the social order is much less structured, and when they come here, they feel this as a lack of freedom, which affects their emotions and well-being in the long term.

- Some of their cultural values are quite different from ours. What is important to us is not necessarily the same for them. For example, the typical European or North American couple would like to have two or one or even no children at all. People from Jordan (for example) have extensive families and feel very happy with about eight to 12 children per family.

- With time, refugees and immigrants lose their feeling of identity and belonging to their motherland, but in their adopted country, many will always feel like immigrants. Some of their children born in the new country will adapt, but others will not, as it is happening in Europe. For example, a son of Moroccans born in France does not have the same opportunities as if he had a French last name, lighter skin, or European facial features. There is an invisible discrimination that most people do not openly admit, though it definitely exists. In North America, we are already experiencing the same phenomenon. A good example in Canada is how the Quebecois react against English last names vs. French (Quebecois) last names during job recruitment and in other business and social matters. They clearly favour French (Quebecois) last names. This does not always happen, but enough to create an unacknowledged, invisible discrimination. In recent years, this situation seems to be diminishing.

- The province of Quebec created a law and implemented it to protect their French heritage and language by requiring French on all signs for commercial and industrial purposes and in all public places. Although for many residents this is going overboard and may even seem absurd, Quebecois are proud of their rich heritage. They want to protect their language and are willing to lose business, if need be, to enforce more use of French. Nevertheless, the forced and indiscriminate imposition of French is exaggerated in the view even of many Quebecois, so imagine if people coming from abroad tried to impose their own language while ignoring French and English! Who is to stop them, when Quebecois seem already to be challenging the rest of Canada and the federal government? Now, I completely understand Quebecois and part of me supports them.

- To my mind, our Canadian government has to be less politically correct, tolerant, protective, and over-respectful of new immigrants' traditions and ways of doing business and enforce strict laws regarding this and many other social behaviors and issues. Otherwise, and in the name of "tolerance and multiculturalism," our government will be going against the Canadian way of life and against the interests of Canadian citizens who have been living in Canada for several generations.

- It is important for Canadians to be tolerant, but everything has its reasonable limits. Without these limits, the free reign given to new immigrants will end up creating the same kinds of problems in Canada that caused the immigrants to leave their own countries. It is just a matter of time. We need to evaluate what has been happening in Europe in the past few years. When immigrants leave their mother country's social, political, economic, and environmental disorder and arrive in a new country that has different social values and traditions than their own, they do not necessarily feel comfortable and at home. Many feel uncomfortable and out of place. Many misinterpret our tolerance and with time even learn to demand it and ask for more and more accommodations, thereby placing our social stability at risk.

- For the average European and North American, having a drink Friday or Saturday night is relaxing. For Muslims, it is against their religion, and many do not understand or accept our values. In fact, some repudiate them. Many also consider their women as property and, in their insecurity, try to hide them from the public in various ways. This is contrary to what Western men and women are used to or should accept.

- Refugees going to North America or Europe receive free transportation to their adopted country, legal papers, shelter, food, clothes, medical coverage, driver's licenses, child benefits, electricity, gas, water, and a monthly income, among many other benefits. The average immigrant to North American or to Europe has to earn his or her daily living with hard work if they want to stay and make a decent living. They also have to pay their taxes and interest on their loans, thereby contributing to the local economy. Immigrants that are not in the category of refugees have to work extremely hard because they get nothing for free after their arrival. They are risking their future without guarantees or any kind of initial assistance. But for many refugees and asylum seekers, it is sometimes easy come easy go. History has proven that people who are given everything for free end up not necessarily appreciating what they receive compared to those who have earned what they have. In fact, they demand more and more. A good recentm example is that of Uruguayan Muslims complaining that the many things that Uruguay has given them are still not enough. They want more free assistance, and now some even want to go back to their homeland. For more information, please refer to an article in BBC-Mundo, Cono Sur (Sept 8, 2015) written by Ignacio de los Reyes and entitled "Los refugiados Sirios que se quieren ir de Uruguay: -Nuestro futuro aquí es muy negro." ("The Syrian Refugees that want to leave Uruguay: - Our future here is very dark") The following site has the details: bbc.com/mundo/noticias/2015/09/150908_refugiados_sirio s_uruguay_irm

- The average European or North American believes women should have the same opportunities as men, at least under the law, and that is what we are all trying hard to achieve. Many Muslims, however, think women should be kept ignorant and suppressed. In many instances, women are prohibited from showing their faces and have to wear the famous burka (all covered), or the niqab (only the eyes uncovered). An alternative, the hijab, allows women to show their faces but not their hair. Muslims do not necessarily want to understand how Westerners and Europeans can hug and kiss their women in public, which is against Islamic cultural and religious values. Now, if refugee women in North America start demanding their freedom from these old traditions, as their new country promotes and supports, this will certainly cause resentment and confrontation in the future.

Three Examples of Failed Integration

The Globe and Mail (November 21, 2015) published an article entitled "Integration: A New Strategy" by Doug Saunders, an international affairs columnist, in which he provides three good examples that should definitely make us think.

1. Belgium has accepted many immigrants and refugees and, among them, many Moroccan families. Some settled along a canal known as Molenbeek on the western side of Brussels. Before this, Molenbeek was a place of "lively scenes of bustling commerce and street life." But the Moroccan newcomers have scared away and pushed out all the local Belgian businesses, and Molenbeek now stands separate from the rest of the city. Saunder reports that "Moroccan gangs have pressured [the locals] and made life too dangerous for [their] employees." According to Saunders, the local government acknowledges that these gangs are a threat and a serious problem in modern Belgium society, but for every gain the government achieves, there is an immediate setback caused by young non-adapted Belgian Moroccans. Saunder asks: "What turns these young European-born men and many of their neighbours – who generally came from non-religious, educated backgrounds – into violent extremists?" To me his question must go unanswered…for now. It is very difficult to know how that younger generation got derailed from mainstream Belgium society.

2. In the same issue of the Globe and Mail, an article by Joanna Slater explains how three Syrian brothers survived civil war in Syria, threats from the Islamic State, and a 3,400-km voyage to emigrate to Germany. Even though life was not

perfect for them in Germany, it must have been better than where they came from. However, their reactions were mixed, causing concerns and confusion in many, as Slater reports:

> Some things the three brothers found baffling: Why do families here have so few children? Others they found pleasantly different: the orderly traffic, the punctual trains and the ability to hug women friends in greetings, for instance.

However, the anxiety and idleness at the refugee camp where the brothers were housed were corrosive. One of the brothers said: "Germany is good, but this place is bad. Better to go back home and die in peace than live in a barn like animals." Reading this, I reflect that nothing comes easily in life, but the expectation of immediate gratification is one of our modern diseases. Many immigrants went through a lot worse to get established in North America in search of a better future for their children. Why not accept what Germany is offering and hold your head high with honor and appreciation, while trying to be patient and working from within the German system for a better future and full integration in your new society?

3. According to an article in the National Post (November 16, 2015) entitled "Associate of Jihadi John held over suspect terrorism plot," Aine Leslie Davis, who was born in Hammersmith west of London, is accused of being a British follower of Islamic State. He is married to Amal El-Wahabi who was jailed for two years for funding Jihadi fighters in Syria and allegedly was involved in attacks in Istanbul with ties to the infamous "Jihadi John" (Mohammed Emwasi) who has slaughtered countless people. These are all people with British passports who had either turned against their own country or failed to adapt.

Similar situations are happening in all the other European countries that have accepted refugees and immigrants in large numbers. If this is happening in these experienced European countries, what makes us think it will not happen in North America? It is hard to believe that the American melting pot will melt these types of people into their society, or the friendly Canadian diplomacy strategies and approach, will integrate and fully assimilate all newcomers, instilling an unbreakable harmony and balance. The truth is that problems have already started. The US has experienced "internal" terrorist attacks already. One example is the Ohio State University rampage in November 2016, in which a Somali-born student, Abdul Razak Ali Artan, drove his car into a group of people and then attacked others with a knife before a university security guard shot him dead. The Islamic State claimed responsibility.

Meanwhile, in Canada, Mercedes Stephenson (a well-known Canadian journalist) reported the following on CTV News on August 10, 2016: "A suspected ISIS sympathizer believed to be the lone suspect in a suicide bomb plot on a major Canadian city was killed Wednesday during a dramatic police takedown in a southern Ontario town." Regardless of how tolerant and friendly we are, every citizen needs to be alert and report anything suspicious to the local police, though we fervently hope that nothing will happen.

I believe that Canada is among the world's least discriminatory countries. If a person is qualified and well behaved, our doors will be open to them. However, I truly hope that our politicians will practice due diligence and meticulously screen everyone wanting to enter Canada and monitor, support, and guide them after they arrive until they are on their feet again.

Proven Techniques for Integration

It is easy for the average immigrant to develop a romanticized view of the past and forget what really pushed them to leave their mother country. When things turn difficult in their new country, the old country is remembered through rose-tinted glasses and the new country is often criticized. Therefore, techniques for integration on part of government programs and incentives are crucial for a smooth transition. However, the immigrants themselves need to cooperate and fully trust the new system. They need to work hard and, above all, learn how to let go of the past, though without forgetting their roots.

Also in the Globe and Mail of November 21, 2015, an article by Doug Saunders entitled "Integration: A New Strategy" provides some valuable advice on what the government should focus on to help integrate refugees and break down barriers during the resettlement process. His research is based on studies and evaluations done by Germany's Bertelsmann Foundation, the Global Diversity Exchange at Ryerson University, and the Brussels-based Cities Alliance, among other institutions. According to Saunders, the main four strategies for successful integration are:

1- Remove physical barriers in housing, transportation, and neighborhood location. According to various studies, isolation brings alienation and resentment, while placing the new immigrants close to people of their own background promotes a friendlier integration, because people around them with similar backgrounds can guide them and assist them during the process. According to Saunders, scattered newcomers need to get closer to people of similar or identical backgrounds. An important factor here is home ownership, which allows the immigrant to feel a sense of ownership and pride, promoting a more integrated community. Saunders suggests that, to achieve ownership of their own houses, cars, or anything else, immigrants need targeted, flexible bank financing that addresses their specific needs. If the new immigrant feels welcome and has an ownership feeling in everything they possess, they will work harder and their integration will take care of itself simultaneously.

2- Address barriers at the institutional level by issuing and efficiently matching landed status file numbers with other documents such as driver's licenses, healthcare IDs, school IDs, social insurance numbers, tax numbers, etc. Immediate access for the children to good schooling systems that are tolerant of newcomers is also very important. Tolerance goes both ways, so the school system should have a proper method of teaching tolerance to every student, while reminding them that almost everybody has an immigrant background. According to Saunders, in Zurich a magnet-school program known as QUIMS (Quality in Multi-Ethnic Schools) was so successful it is now being expanded to over 100 schools in the region.

3- Create government incentives or grants to promote the entrepreneurial spirit in immigrants by enabling them to be financially assisted to get a business established at a very low cost. The lack of such incentives is something every immigrant faces when trying to establish a new business. According to Saunders, the costs of complying with all the local bylaws, rules, and regulations in Canada are very high for a small or medium-sized business, discouraging would-be entrepreneurs. He suggests:

> It would be worth emulating Boston's Back Street program, which relaxes business and licensing regulations in low income areas in order to allow dense, informal and more improvised markets that appeal to visitors and give migrants an easy entry point to the world of commerce.

Another good example is happening in Vancouver. Not long ago, people were not allowed to operate food stands or restaurant trucks on the street due to strict sanitation regulations. Eventually, however, Vancouver had to adapt to the less strict ways of doing business that immigrants brought from their mother countries. Another example is the large number of restaurants in Vancouver that do not accept credit or debit cards. We all know that tax evasion is rampant, but I guess that tax-free money ends up back in circulation when people spend it to cover personal, business, and family needs. Sooner or later, the government will get their money back from a different venue. But tax evasion definitely takes place. It would be ideal for all those restaurants to pay their fair share of taxes, but hey, we guess it is the cost of integration, expansion, and progress in the short and medium term, and it promotes higher population density, which will expand the government tax base.

Another example is all those mainly Korean and Chinese grocery stores and supermarkets where more than half of products on the shelves have stickers and labels only in their own native languages. The average Canadian cannot understand what that product is, much less how to use it. But those places have a fascinating taste and flair of their own due to the culture they come from, which we all enjoy, and we feel proud of what other cultures bring to Canada. We need to try harder with better and more refined levels of tolerance and understanding, though going both ways.

Small successful business environments are key to enabling immigrants (like the new Syrian influx PM Trudeau has promoted) to get established with a sense of pride and strength in numbers within their community and continue to make Canada a great country with the most diversified mosaic of people in the world.

4- Another very important factor that Saunders brings to the table concerns citizenship. Making immigrants wait years for citizenship (and the sense of strong and permanent belonging that goes with it) can bring tragic results. Citizenship is critical for integration, according to Saunders. He cites one very interesting example:

Germany learned this the hard way, when two million Turks went for 40 years without access to citizenship, and became an isolated, lost generation who could not invest in their communities or futures. In recent years, German Turks have become citizens in greater numbers, and now are becoming a success story.

The more quickly immigrants are integrated into the economy of their adopted country and get access to housing, banking, schooling, professional credentials, medical insurance, and other essentials, the more quickly they will integrate socially, culturally, and politically, and come to love their new country. However, it remains important to maintain strict mechanisms of observation, re-evaluation, coordination, and supervision of immigrant communities, using specially trained government agents, in order to detect any extremists with, of course, the help and cooperation of the immigrant communities themselves. As Saunders says, "prevention is better than cure." Indeed, monitoring and policing should not be targeted at immigrants only but applied to everyone in our country for the sake of security and for peaceful and productive lives.

Policing and monitoring is required in all communities, including non-immigrant ones. As much as the average Canadian (immigrant or not, refugee or not, Canadian or not) might accept with open arms the new Syrian families, there are always people who will not accept them due to fear, lack of self-confidence, ignorance, economic concerns, personal background, or religious views. In fact, in reaction to PM Trudeau's acceptance of the first 25,000 refugee Syrian families (mostly Muslim) aggressive incidents have already taken place in British Columbia and Ontario. For example:

- In Toronto, a Muslim woman was attacked when she went to pick up her children at school. The assailants robbed her of money and her cellphone and hurled racial slurs. They called her a "terrorist" and told her to "go back to her country." According to police, the men tore her hijab and punched her. (Source: Global News in an article by Kevin Nielsen on Nov 16, 2015 entitled "Muslim Woman Attacked in Toronto.")

- In Peterborough, Ontario, police and firefighters responded to an emergency call at the only mosque in the city, Masjid Al-Salaam. According to police, it was a hate crime against the mosque and its followers. Al-Salaam is a mosque with over 200 members who tend to keep to themselves, but some locals hate them and decided to attack when over 70 people were celebrating the birth of a child inside. Police say that, during the day, the mosque is used as a school, and it would have been disastrous if the attack had happened then.

- Erika Stark reported in the *Calgary Herald* on December 3, 2015 on a racist graffiti attack at the Tuscany LRT station in the city. The graffiti threatened and insulted Syrians coming to Canada at Prime Minister Trudeau's invitation. Stark describes how a man called Parneet (from a Muslim background) even stopped to take pictures of the graffiti for posting on social media for his friends. Parneet commented that "clearly these people are not thinking straight and are highly misinformed about Islam." The people that assaulted the station with racist graffiti did not even write English properly. They wrote "F_ _ k Syrea," for example. It is sad to see that all the effort made by Calgary to welcome 500 Syrian families was tarnished by an event of this kind. The more racist attacks that take place in Calgary (or anywhere else in Canada), the more antagonism there will be on both sides. Certainly, the Syrians will not just take it quietly. It is human nature to defend ourselves. I understand why Parneet posted pictures on social media, but personally I think it was a mistake. It will just make more people angry, and I am concerned that, slowly but surely, sentiments will escalate to the level they are in Europe. I truly hope I am wrong, but only time will tell.

Burka, Niqab, and Hijab

Women who wear a hijab only cover their hair. They are not hiding their faces or their identity, and we need to respect their wishes, just as we respect someone wearing a cowboy hat or a baseball cap. What's better: to see a woman with a scarf covering her hair with proper makeup (if she so wishes), discreetly and elegantly, or a trashy woman (regardless of skin colour) with uncombed, messy hair, anti-makeup, and a defeated attitude towards herself and others regarding the way she portrays herself in public?

The niqab (covering the face but not the eyes) and the burka (covering the face including the eyes) are more controversial, and there are conflicting accounts of why they are worn. There are many mixed feelings behind the real reason to wear them and their interpretations along with the potential and imminent repercussions in more modern societies. Unfortunately, not every native-born Canadian or immigrant is tolerant and most likely never will be. Some critics insist we need to closely monitor intolerance using trained officers and specialized units with the cooperation of average citizens who are also responsible for their security and that of their neighborhoods. Other critics (the majority in North America) insist the niqab and burka should not be allowed and that immigrants and refugees should comply with our values, our way of life, and even our dress code, or leave our country. One thing is very clear; nobody should ever act as a vigilante, although everybody should be vigilant and observant of what is going on around them. Again, tolerance is a virtue, but it has to come from both sides. It is not just a one-way street. Both native-born citizens and immigrants need to be tolerant of each other and respect the laws and traditions of the country. Respect and courtesy promote good understanding among cultures during the adaptation and integration process for both.

Every immigrant needs to adapt and integrate to our way of life. If they fail to do so, they are only creating a nest of vipers around themselves that "might" one day attack their communities with mortal accuracy. In Canada we are very tolerant, but like any other country, don't we also have our limits? Most Canadians do not feel comfortable with the burka or the niqab. The great majority do not like them or feel at ease around them. The same applies in Mexico and the United States. Obviously, it bothers most people not to be able to see who is behind the covered head and body. They may not even be able to tell whether they are looking at a man or woman, or if the person is concealing a weapon. Most people just step aside or leave the area, feeling uncomfortable. They would never attack and insult anyone, but, in silence, they feel invaded in their peaceful personal space in public. However, there are others who will attack or insult. From their perspective, immigrants have to respect and adhere to North American ways of life and leave behind the oppression they used to live in, which is not accepted here.

Let me explain. Prime Minister Justin Trudeau dropped the controversial "niqab appeal" in order to allow women to wear it during the citizenship ceremony. Conservatives are against this and for good reason. One of our fundamental Canadian values is to accept and acknowledge everybody's identity for the sake of honesty, peace, comfort, security, transparency, and friendship. This requires being able to look at each other eye to eye. When a woman (or a man) hides behind a robe or piece of cloth, using archaic and discriminatory religious excuses, they are affecting the fundamental value that Canadians place on acknowledging and seeing others eye to eye. To many people, hiding their identity is unhealthy in North

America and in their mind, should not be allowed. For many Canadians, when some Muslim women (or men) hide themselves behind their burka or niqab, they must know that the average Canadian will not feel comfortable and at ease to peacefully and calmly acknowledge their existence, their rights, their freedom, and grant them the respect that a normal friendly person deserves. In the eyes of many Canadians, and people all over the world, the burka and niqab represent the repression of women and are a barrier to connecting with others in society. Some people see them as an act of disrespect and aggression against normal and average people in the adopted country. Let's face it, many cafés, restaurants, and other public places in Europe have been blown away by people covered either with a burka or a niqab, killing men, women, and children without remorse. The locals do not see it coming because the attackers are completely covered and nobody can know if they are hiding explosives or any other kind of weapon.

Prime Minister Trudeau, as a good politician, said: "In our policy as a government, we will ensure that we respect the values that make us Canadians, those of diversity, inclusion and respect for those fundamental values." But what about the fundamental values of other Canadians? What about trying to avoid conflict among Canadians who feel very uncomfortable with burkas and niqabs? There have to be limits to people's freedom to practice their religious and cultural traditions when these promote discrimination and oppression, in this case, the oppression of women. That should not be allowed in Canada. When Prime Minister Trudeau said "let us respect … fundamental values," he forgot to add … "the real Canadian values based on freedom and fairness to all."

When immigrants are allowed to wear the burka and niqab in public, we are promoting their lack of integration as well as the distrust of many Canadians towards them, whether we like it or not. It is very sad to see, in their country of origin, even on a hot summer day, many women completely covered in black without even exposing their eyes, while the males are usually in long white robes, and in many cases, with white or light colored shorts and t-shirts. There is no way those women are not suffering and sweating inside their black "walking tents," regardless of any type of light lingerie they may be wearing underneath. While men wear cool white robes, their women in black wear the symbol of oppression, and most probably are afraid of admitting they feel oppressed. Many therefore believe that we must do what we can in North America to protect women from being forced to wear the niqab or burka. Their male counterparts just show their primitive and insecure attitudes when they use "religious beliefs" as an excuse. Why don't they wear the niqab or burka themselves? The niqab and burka should be banned in North America, as in France, Belgium, Netherlands, Denmark, Italy, and even Syria. Imagine if we allow the use of the niqab or burka against the wishes of the average person in North America? This will be a recipe for problems, aggression, and social unrest. Niqabs and burkas are strong hindrances for assimilation.

The following quote has circulated widely on Facebook:

> The women in Islamic states are very afraid of Sharia law, because most of Sharia law (written by men) deals with the subjugation and punishment of their women, i.e. Sharia law gives the Muslim men the means to punish their women even if they are innocent. Therefore, the women in Islamic states try very hard not to anger the Muslim men.

In the minds of the great majority, that attitude and behavior should simply never be allowed in North America. Let's face it. Not even in the Canadian north are people are allowed to go and shop wearing a balaclava. The reason is security. Regardless of how cold the weather may be, as soon as the person enters a shop, they uncover their face out of respect for other clients and the storeowners. Many believe the same situation should apply to any immigrant who wants to cover their face, regardless of their cultural background or religious beliefs.

CBC News – Toronto carried a report on Nov 19, 2014 entitled "Burka worn by robbers in $500K Toronto jewelry store heist." It described how two robbers armed with guns and wearing burkas had held up Mona Clara Jewelers on York Mills Road on the morning of October 14, 2014. The only information the police officers had was a surveillance video showing the two individuals in burkas. No facial features of any kind were visible. Mike Earl, the police inspector in charge of the investigation, confirmed this was "not the first-time robbers have used burkas as a disguise." Burkas have been used in the past in bank robberies and have left the police force clueless. The only hope of catching the robbers was to keep a keen eye out for people trying to sell the stolen jewelry to pawn shops, retailers, or to individuals on-line. The police ended up having to ask for help from the public, publishing a phone number where they could be contacted by anyone with information.

If somebody enters an average store in North America with a mask covering their face, everyone else will naturally feel uncomfortable or even fear for their safety. What is the difference with the burka or niqab when nobody knows if it is a man or a woman underneath? Why the discrimination against us locals? Okay, probably because it is not normal for us to walk around in masks. In North America, it seems people are asked to modify their behavior to allow immigrants to walk among us without even having a clue of who really is under those garments or what their intentions are and to tolerate the obvious indication that they do not want to integrate and socialize with the rest of us. Their burka and niqab are perceived strongly, though in silence, as an integration barrier by the great majority of North Americans, though the hijab is definitely widely accepted. But everybody is afraid to talk.

Invisible Minefield

The average North American feels discriminated against, angry, uncomfortable, or even intimidated by women in a burka or a niqab. Some people ask: isn't this reverse discrimination? Should we accept it? How can an average North American socialize and mingle with somebody whose face, expressions, and, in the case of the burka, whose eyes they cannot even see? Are we supposed to recognize and interact with them only by their tone of voice? After miraculously identifying them (if they ever speak), are we supposed to approach them in a friendly and sociable manner and say, "I think I recognize your voice, are you Amal, Nahala or Karima? Ahhh, you are Karima! Well, it is so good to 'hear you' again!"

Come on, isn't this ridiculous? Let's face it, for the majority of human beings, the eyes (and to many also our facial expressions) are considered to be the reflections of the soul. Weren't we all taught in our culture to give a firm handshake and look people straight in the eye when introduced? And now they call us racists. How twisted is that? Many Canadians, in the spirit of being tolerant, are allowing people to come to our land to discriminate against us. Is that going to promote proper integration among people in the future? Is it not going to slowly but surely build an invisible resentment that sooner or later will explode?

Incidents have already started to happen across Canada and the US. In Montreal, a man has already posted threats against Muslims, saying he will kill one a week. Yes, that is very wrong and irrational, but it is also very real. I truly hope it does not get worse. I am crossing my fingers as I write these lines. But wait, I am wrong. It already started to happen in Canada only a few weeks ago (Jan 29, 2017) in the form of a deadly internal terrorist attack that took place at the "Centre Culturel Islamique de Québec" (Islamic Cultural Centre of Quebec) in the Sainte-Foy neighborhood of Quebec City. Six lost their lives and many others were seriously injured by a local Canadian radical. Is he the only one throughout Canada? For more information on both of the above cases, please refer to:

1. "Jesse Pelletier, 24, has been charged with uttering threats, inciting hatred and using a fake firearm" (CBC News, November 18, 2015): cbc.ca/news/canada/montreal/montreal-police-arrest-man-mask-joker-muslims-1.3324089.

2. "Suspect in Quebec City mosque attack charged with six counts of murder" (Globe and Mail – Jan 31 2017): http://www.theglobeandmail.com/news/national/quebec-city-mosque-shooting/article33822092/

How can businesses and individuals feel secure when other cultures are allowed to wear, for "religious reasons", the burka niqab, or even to carry the kirpan (ceremonial Sikh dagger), potentially putting at risk the average, good-spirited, naïve, and tolerant Canadian? Now regarding the kirpan, "kirpa" means mercy and "Aan" (or aanaa) means honor. The kirpan is originally meant to prevent violence and protect the weak from tyranny and dishonor. But the questions still remain: Can a weapon of "defence" turn suddenly into a weapon of "offence"? Shouldn't we all be allowed to carry a switchblade knife to protect the weak as well, regardless of religion? This would have saved the two men stabbed to death on May 28, 2017, in a commuter train in Portland (Oregon) by an anti-Muslim man (Jeremy Joseph). Joseph was verbally harassing two ladies wearing a hijab. If the two dead Samaritans were Sikhs instead of regular people, would Joseph be dead instead? Would that be an accepted better outcome in society? In the minds of many, it appears that religion is so powerful that supersedes the rights of non-religious people to protect themselves. It might also indicate it provides a minority religious group an edge to protect themselves over others.

Regarding the kirpan, its use was initially deemed delinquent or criminal in Canada and other parts of the world, but things have changed over time, and in Canada it is now allowed as long as it is a dull blade less than three inches long. Unfortunately to many, the Supreme Court of Canada has ruled that even children can bring their kirpan to school, although it is regarded by most Canadians as a weapon, not a religious item. This ruling was made on March 2, 2006, overturning a Quebec Court of Appeal ruling that the kirpan should be considered a weapon and be prohibited from any school in the province. In an article on Boreal.ca (March 6, 2006) entitled "KIRPAN I - Court Okays Children Bringing Concealed Weapons to School," Bernard Payeur commented:

> This decision brings a whole new unwelcome dynamic to schoolyard bullying. A bully may think twice about bullying someone with a concealed weapon unless it's the bully who is legally allowed a concealed weapon. If that's the case, don't argue when you are asked for your lunch money or anything else for that matter."

Many Canadians admire Payeur for this. Why? Because the average Canadian citizen is afraid of speaking out and clearly expressing their true thoughts and feelings regarding these kinds of issues. They are afraid of being called racists when their views have nothing to do with racism but everything to do with security, rejecting women's oppression, and insisting on the right to be respected by immigrants. Why do we have to respect and tolerate them if they do not return the favour? "Gimme, gimme" is the natural selfish way of many humans, and we Canadians are going to have to learn how to deal with this. Ignorant or aggressive people who lack the knowledge, patience, intelligence, or common sense to have an intelligent and constructive debate often use the word "racist" to attack or counter-attack others.

Regardless, here are only four brief examples in relation to the use the kirpan:

1. "Sikh who stabbed woman with ceremonial dagger in neighbour dispute is jailed for six years." The victim, Kalli-Rae Lavin, almost lost a leg after being knifed twice. (Express & Star, July 1, 2016).

2. "Manjit Mangat, 53, a prominent lawyer and President of the temple, was stabbed in the abdomen with a kirpan, resulting in a 12-centimetre wound ("Kirpan attack in Brampton renews concerns," CBC News, April 7, 2010).

3. "Police say a 13-year-old Sikh boy last week used a religious dagger to threaten another student outside a school in Montreal. Police say the knife was wrapped in cloth at the time" (*Montreal Gazette*, September 16, 2008).

4. A man named Gursant Singh was called for jury duty in California. When he was not allowed to step into court with his kirpan (or any other weapon for that matter. It's the law!), he got upset and started making a big fuss about the religious connotations of carrying the kirpan. In an article entitled "Sikh man up in arms against court in California over his kirpan" (April 24, 2014): https://www.americanbazaaronline.com/ Deepak Chitnis reported:

> County law specifically forbids any kind of weaponry to be brought into the courthouse. Under normal protocol, all banned items are checked in with security at the front, but Singh is apparently unwilling to do this.

Singh had to face the fact of being barred from jury duty, which is mandatory in US law. If he would have simply failed to show up for his jury duty, he would have faced stiff fines and possibly even jail time. In an effort to rally support to his cause at the time, Singh launched a campaign on YouTube to spread awareness of Sikh teachings and show that his kirpan is a required tenet of the religion and not a weapon. In fact, Sikh scripture forbids the use of the kirpan as an offensive weapon, saying it is only to be used in self-defense.

A Personal Note on the History of the Veil

According to the *Economist* (December 10-16, 2016) German Chancellor Angela Merkel has said that her efforts to ban the burka were a mistake. She cited European values on sexual equality and religious tolerance, but we all know that to take religious practices to extremes will only allow the abuse of women in public as a "religious right." Her about-face has made many Germans uncomfortable.

In reality, history shows that Islam did not introduce the tradition of wearing the veil. An ancient Assyrian tablet contains the first known law on wearing a veil, according to Dr. Amanda Foreman, who became famous through a documentary series entitled "The Ascent of Women." She asserts that the veil was first adopted in middle-eastern cultures 2,000 years before Islam. History has shown how Islam adopted it as a religious excuse to continue the segregation and oppression of women and still enforces it for the same reason. Alexandra Kinias in "The History of the Veil" is worth quoting at length on this topic:

> With the passionate cries for wearing the veil, the controversy it is causing in the West and since it only shrouds the bodies, heads and faces of Muslim women, it left no shred of doubt that it is an Islamic dress code. And how can one dare argue that when clerics, based on their interpretations of the holy scripts, left everything else behind and are condensing their efforts to preach, direct and scare Muslim women to comply with it after reaching puberty. However, researchers who have tracked the history of veil proved that it was not introduced by Islam. But as it became today the

symbol of the most zealous fanatical regimes, Islam is wrongly blamed for that. The status of the women in Afghanistan also confirms that Islam practiced segregation and seclusion of women, even though these practices were common in several ancient civilizations that existed in lands far away from Arabia, thousands of years prior to the rise of Islam: The Sumerian, Assyria, Babylonian and Persian.

According to Kinias and Foreman, veils were introduced to distinguish respectable and honorable women from prostitutes and other "low-class" women. The latter were forbidden from wearing a veil to distinguish them from the elite women who in public had to comply. The Assyrian tablet confirms five categories of women: the wives and daughters of the upper class, concubines, temple prostitutes, harlots, and slave girls. The veil was mandated for the first two categories and forbidden for the rest.

In any case, the true purpose of mandating the veil has always been to hide, dominate, and subjugate women and guarantee men's absolute power and control over their women. The Persian Empire imposed its traditions and values on every new country they conquered, but as Persian social, economic, and military power weakened, the Muslim conquest of Persia slowly took place. Muslims adopted many of the ancient traditions of the lands they conquered, and this is the case with the use of the veil, which originally had nothing to do with any religion. It is simply a symbol of the oppression of women, and we should not allow it in modern society. It has nothing to do with religion, but Muslim extremists want to navigate the seven seas waving the religious flag and demanding religious tolerance. In my mind, that should be unacceptable.

Going back to Germany, if Merkel allows the niqab and burka in public places, she might be encouraging the creation of a "parallel society" for the benefit of a small minority of religious fanatics. In Europe and other western countries, religious freedom is not absolute. Imagine a social worker, teacher, border patrol officer, doctor, or another essential public service provider wearing a burka or a niqab. Somebody once asked me: Would you feel comfortable if a "woman" wearing a niqab or burka suddenly showed up in the school bus to take your child to school? His question caught me by surprise and initially I did not know how to answer. After a few seconds, I said: most likely not. I felt bad because I believe in tolerance and multiculturalism, but my gut feeling and immediate reaction was a strong no. A person I cannot recognize driving my children to school. I do not think so! I might be wrong, but it is hard to believe that anyone would tolerate or accept this.

Kinias' article ends by stating something extremely important:

> Those who want to ban veils are not worried about security but about immigration and integration. To them, limited bans confirm only that mainstream politicians are too timid to embrace the real thing. Some of them worry legitimately that Muslim immigrants do not share Europe's liberal norms. But the best way to preserve those freedoms is to let women dress as modestly as they please.

Many people have serious trouble trying to understand how all the allied forces go abroad and interfere or invade countries in the name of freedom and equality. But for the sake of political correctness, they are afraid of banning the use of the burka and niqab, which clearly represent a culture of women's oppression and are now also opening a window to lack of integration of new immigrants. This goes against the same principles of fairness, freedom, and democracy that current citizens and their ancestors fought for or were born with. It goes against fundamental local values and ideals and privileges immigrants who are not willing to respect the local laws and customs of the country that amicably allowed them in. For some North American politicians, the valuable and true concept of patriotism is being weakened, but in other countries they are willing to fight for it. This is one of the reasons Donald Trump was elected in the United States. We cannot and should not tolerate male oppression of "their" women.

It is amazing that, for religious reasons, some people can wear the burka and or carry the kirpan while others are not allowed to even wish somebody Merry Christmas and a Happy New Year for fear of offending somebody else. It is like prohibiting Jewish people from wishing each other Happy Hanukkah. Many Canadians feel their rights are being invaded when they are not allowed to freely say Merry Christmas because they might offend others. Even politicians avoid saying those two words, which represent a longstanding tradition and express a feeling of belonging. Instead they say "Happy Holiday Season; rather than, have a Merry Christmas (*Felíz Navidad*)!

This is crazy, unfair, and unacceptable. Where is the concept of tolerance that every politician is so quick to mention when wanting to seem in harmony with our "celebrity" Prime Minister Justin Trudeau? Respect and tolerance go both ways, but the average politician plays with tradition and tolerance like the wind plays with our flag's wavy contours, one way today, another way the next day, depending on whom they want their votes from. Immigrants need to be tolerant with us as well and stop playing the crybaby game, stop feeling offended, and stop trying to impose their own ways on Canadians on our own soil in the name of religion or anti-racism. Grow up, adapt, and go to work to keep your mind busy and your level of respect for others at an intelligent and human level.

Paris Terrorist Attack vs. French Reaction

On the evening of November 13, 2015, the Islamic State perpetrated the worst terrorist attack that France has suffered to date. A suicide bombing, mass shootings, and hostage taking took place simultaneously in Paris. By the next morning, over 130 people were dead and many more injured. Only seven perpetrators executed that powerful and painful damage, but they had the determination, efficiency, and deadly force of a lot more men and women. They acted in the name of Allah, who is considered by a great number of Muslims to be "all-merciful and omnipotent."

The immediate French reaction was one of fear, confusion, fury, and desire for revenge, but one young man gave the world a lesson about strength of character in his personal reaction to these hideous attacks against the French people, and against his personal family. This self-controlled, brave, and intelligent young man's name is Antoine Leiris. Here in full is his message (in English translation) as quoted by Jessica Durando in *USA Today* on November 3, 2015 (for the original French version, please refer to Appendix 3):

> Friday night, you took an exceptional life – the love of my life, the mother of my son – but you will not have my hatred. I don't know who you are and I don't want to know, you are dead souls. If this God, for whom you kill blindly, made us in his image, every bullet in the body of my wife would have been one more wound in his heart. So, no, I will not grant you the gift of my hatred. You're asking for it, but responding to hatred with anger is falling victim to the same ignorance that has made you what you are. You want me to be scared, to view my countrymen with mistrust, to sacrifice my liberty for my security. You lost.
>
> I saw her this morning. Finally, after nights and days of waiting. She was just as beautiful as when she left on Friday night, just as beautiful as when I fell hopelessly in love over 12 years ago. Of course, I am devastated by this pain, I give you this little victory, but the pain will be short-lived. I know that she will be with us every day

and that we will find ourselves again in this paradise of free love to which you have no access.

We are just two, my son and me, but we are stronger than all the armies in the world. I don't have any more time to devote to you. I have to join Melvil who is waking up from his nap. He is barely 17 months old. He will eat his meals as usual, and then we are going to play as usual, and for his whole life this little boy will threaten you by being happy and free. Because no, you will not have his hatred either.

For some odd reason, the French attack brought to my mind another case, very different but also lethal and related to the same issue of radical Muslim immigrants and terrorists. Although to some, this might be stretching it, I offer it as food for thought. I refer to the 2011 attacks in Norway by a very different radical terrorist, who said he acted out of loyalty to his country. He was a vigilante who considered himself a loyal citizen and a real patriot, though some still wonder about the real reason he acted as he did. His first attack was a car bomb in the executive government quarter of Oslo. Eight people died and over 200 were injured. Immediately thereafter, Anders Behring Breivik ("the lone wolf" as they called him) attacked a summer camp on the island of Utoya, where the Norwegian Labor Party had organized a Workers Youth League summer session. There he shot 69 to death and injured over 100. The majority of the victims were very young with bright futures ahead of them.

There are radicals in many religions and political parties, as well as many radicals trying to stop them, as in the case of this Norwegian right winger, who denied his guilt, arguing that he killed out of "necessity" in defence of his country. According to justia.com, the defence of necessity applies "when an individual commits a criminal act during an emergency situation in order to prevent a greater harm from happening."

According to various sources, Breivik was known as "the lone wolf" and claimed that the greater damage he was trying to prevent was the "invasion" of Norway by radical Muslims. He said he was defending Norway from liberals, Muslims, and multiculturalism. In his view, immigration was destroying the identity of Norway, its culture, traditions, lifestyle, and Christian religion.

Breivik's actions were horrible and wrong, but in his own mind he was trying to warn his country that unregulated, uncontrolled, and overly accommodating immigration could end up destroying the Norwegian identity. I do not have all the information to explain his reasoning, but the fact remains that he did what he did, which is extremely disturbing. Every country has its own right-wing and left-wing radicals, and any spark among them can trigger a deadly outburst.

To my mind, multiculturalism is inevitable, and we need to embrace it. Europe needs to do the same, or they will succumb in the long term. But better government integration programmes should be implemented during the formation of a new society. In the specific case of Canada, we Canadians should all feel proud of the fact that at least the Quebecois in all their relentless language enforcement, and even in their "misunderstood" separation movement, have always been non-violent while trying to protect their culture.

Public Dissonance in the Syrian Immigration Process

A great number of Canadians have been silent, though skeptical and concerned, about allowing the initial 25,000 Syrians into Canada before the end of 2015, as PM Trudeau promised to do. This action will remain in the history books as either an amazing humanitarian act or as a reckless stunt placing national security at risk. Only time will tell. The skepticism in Canadians comes from the fact that the government had to really speed up the immigration process and most likely, sacrificed due diligence, regardless of their guarantees to carry out proper investigations of the background and health of each Syrian immigrant. Why do I bring this up? Because this has been brought up by the media as something that did happen. Therefore, as an example of potential mistakes or omissions, we all need to keep in mind the case of Mr Jaspal Atwal, who was convicted in 1986 B.C. terrorist shooting and was a one-time member of what used to be the International Sikh Youth Federation. Mr Atwal was invited to a dinner with PM Trudeau and his wife at the Canadian High Commission in Delhi on February of 2018, by what many called, "a big mistake." This event raised concern with Canadians and with Indian Prime Minister Narendra Modi by having Prime Minister Trudeau ashamed for "being lenient" or "making a mistake", on handling Sikh separatism. Even with proper timing in background checks mistakes or omissions happen, imagine when you speed up matters.

Regardless of the above, the refugees come from holding camps where they have been waiting, sometimes for two or three years, and often lack proper documentation even to prove they are who they say they are. Meanwhile, the Canadian media has failed to show the whole truth and the overall picture of all recruited immigrants. They only show what they want us to see, images of children and women with very sad faces, as if to convince us that all the refugees are innocent victims of the Syrian civil war. Whether this is true or not, for the sake of national security we need to act with caution and practice due diligence through adequate and comprehensive background checks along with complete immigration paperwork for all applicants. Everybody seems afraid to say this publicly. They do not want to be seen as unfair, cruel, or racist. The government, the media, and many citizens have known what has been happening in Syria for at least the past six years. Nobody really cared or did anything about it, until suddenly our government decided to go overboard and rush into a situation that might come back to haunt us. What triggered all this good-hearted commotion was the extremely sad picture of a little Syrian boy who drowned in the Mediterranean and was washed to shore by the tide. His name was Alan Kurdi. He was found (and photographed) face down in the sand, and his tragic death broke the heart of humanity. After this, many countries suddenly decided to accept thousands of refugees from Syria.

Some people fear that when we decide to accommodate immigrants (refugees or not) without proper background checks we are opening the doors for dangerous terrorists to enter our country in disguise. Some also insist that we could be promoting the rise of *internal* terrorists who, in their own minds, are trying to protect this country and the rights of their people from a foreign threat. People are afraid of expressing their true thoughts, but some already believe it is detrimental and dangerous to allow immigrants to come and disturb our society or show disrespect for our culture by challenging or avoiding our laws and imposing their behavior and styles of doing business. When we accommodate immigrants (refugees or not) without doing proper background checks, we increase the possibility that terrorists in disguise will enter our country. That will be the day that we turn our back on all those Canadian soldiers who fought for our liberty and sacrificed their lives for our democracy and our freedom. That is the day we will betray our own values and our own history. Hopefully, that will never ever happen.

As Canadians, we need to celebrate Remembrance Day with honor and acknowledge and treasure our freedom, equality, and democracy under a free and elected government. It would be a disgrace and an insult to previous generations to allow our rights, freedoms, lifestyle, privileges, and advantages, which people fought and gave their lives for, to disappear into thin air in front of our eyes while we do nothing about it. We should never take things for granted. That includes our right to defend and preserve ourselves by protecting our borders and being selective about who crosses those borders. We cannot hold hands with everybody, accommodate everyone, and even give them special privileges. By doing this, we are disrespecting our own citizens and our own values. Canadian laws are meant to be respected. People have to abide by them whether they agree with them or not.

On Nov 28, 2015, I received an e-mail from a friend of mine. The message seems to have gone viral across North America and beyond. It quotes an article written by a retired firefighter from Cold Lake, Alberta, Scott Wilcox, and is entitled "Security Background Check." The article concerns Prime Minister Trudeau's political decision to allow thousands of Syrian immigrants to enter Canada through the fast lane against the interests of Canadian national security. Most people in Canada are in favour of humanitarian assistance, but believe that it needs to be accompanied by rational, viable, and proven security procedures. This matter is of such crucial importance that I want to quote the entire letter. It goes like this:

Letter to Prime Minister Trudeau

On Nov 16, 2015, a retired firefighter wrote:

To the Honorable Justin Trudeau, Members of Parliament, and Provincial Premiers… Will We Learn Nothing From Paris?" [referring to the Paris terrorist attacks of Nov 13, 2015 in which over 130 people were killed.)

I am a proud Canadian, and proud of our heritage of being a true global leader in Humanitarian efforts. Given the events of recent years and more importantly the recent week, however, I believe prudence requires a pause in our assistance package for Syrian refugees, and indeed all refugees and asylum seekers. I say this not in a tone of political partisanship, but one of Citizenship. Any Parliament, be it Liberal, Conservative, or NDP has as its first mandate the protection of our country and its citizens. This must take precedence over all other considerations and activities.

As a Retired Firefighter/Fire Officer of the City of Calgary, I have an experience I believe is timely and valuable. In my final assignment at the end of my career, I asked for and received a transfer to work on the Airport Crash Rescue Unit at the Calgary International Airport. A requirement for all staff working at the Airport is to undergo a police background check. In between the time the background check is initiated, and the time it is competed, an employee must be accompanied by another employee who has the appropriate screening and credentials. I can't remember precisely how long it took for the RCMP to conduct my check, but it was several months. Bear in mind that this is for a person who was born in Calgary; completed primary, secondary and post-secondary education in Calgary/Lethbridge; had passed a security clearance to gain employment as a Calgary Firefighter, and had worked in this civic institution for 18 years at the time. I had also been vetted by the Provincial Government's Lieutenant Governor Norman (Normie) Kwong to sit as a long-term member of the Alberta Labor Relations Board. In short, it would not be difficult to find information on me. I was also required to be finger printed as part of the process.

When the day arrived and I was notified that I had passed the security clearance, I was escorted to the terminal building by a colleague to pick up my coveted airport pass. While in the waiting room, I met and visited with what seemed to be a very nice man of Arab descent, who if memory served was from Jordan. During our discussion, he indicated that his pass had only taken two weeks to get, as opposed to the months mine had taken. He left after receiving his pass, and so when my turn came I asked the RCMP Sargent why on earth it would take so long for me to acquire a clearance when this person who indicated he was a recent arrival to Canada received his in two weeks or less. The answer I received haunts me to this day. The answer: "We can't really do that much of a search on these people. They often arrive without even a passport or Birth Certificate, and unless they appear on an INTERPOL watch list, we generally let them pass. Often the police departments from these fractured countries are unable or unwilling to provide information or detailed data, and we simply have to go with what we can learn. We also make sure they have no criminal record while in Canada, which for many of these folks is a very short period of time," or words to that effect.

In the couple of years, I spent at the airport, I never stopped thinking about that. These people were everywhere: loading aircraft luggage, cleaning the airport with access to virtually all areas right up to the jet ways, acting as security guards and everything in between. It was then and there that I realized that the issue of security was truly an illusion in our country. I do not say these things lightly. I represented Calgary and its 1500 members as the President of the Calgary Firefighter's Association in New York in 2002 at the 911 Memorial, which was attended by 77,000 firefighters from all over the world. The hole at ground zero was still a testament a year later as to the impact of what can happen when a country lets its guard down. So, my questions to the Current Government and to the two opposition parties, and to our provincial leaders, in light of the recent events in France are:

1. "Who are the refugees"? How can you possibly screen 25,000 people adequately in such a short period of time to ensure that none of these people pose a threat to me and my country in the future?

2. What specific process(es) is/are engaged to determine the identity of who these people are?

3. What agency is tasked with performing the background checks, and has the capacity to conduct appropriate checks on what amounts mathematically to about 800 people per day

if they are all to arrive by Christmas. I note that in the USA., the head of the Department of Homeland Security, Jeh Johnson, admitted that "we don't know a whole lot about these people" and that we have "no real protocol for screening refugees" – My guess and fear is if they can't do it between the DHS, FBI, and CIA, there is no reasonable hope that Canada can possibly have any credible system. I believe Canadian citizens are entitled to know this. I would commend to you the words of Governor Greg Abbot of Texas who today said: "Given the tragic attacks in Paris and the threats we have already seen, Texas cannot participate in any program that will result in Syrian refugees — any one of whom could be connected to terrorism — being resettled in Texas." That seems like a very reasoned approach at the moment.

4. Bill C-45 (2003), which became an amendment to the Criminal Code of Canada after the Westray Mine accident, allowed the courts to find officers of corporations criminally negligent if their actions either willfully or by gross negligence contribute to the preventable death of an employee. Does this legislation reach to the political elite if, in the future, an innocent citizen is harmed or killed by a refugee because the sitting government failed to properly screen them? If not, we need to amend it. As I read the Act, Clause 1(1) extends the reach of Bill C-45 to "all organizations", which I assume includes political parties. Would you concur with this view?

5. What is the projected, long-term cost per refugee and what current, existing benefits will suffer because of this for existing citizens?

6. What is the demographic make-up of the refugees being allowed into the country? What percentages are women, children, married men accompanying a family, and single men?

7. Will refugees be required to undergo a polygraph test, be finger printed, and be drug tested as is required of several types of employment for Canadian Citizens such as the Calgary Fire Department?

8. Will Refugees be screened for infectious diseases including TB, HIV, hepatitis, leishmaniosis, meningitis, and the host of other physiological problems, which have been identified with these disadvantaged people?

9. Why are neighboring, wealthy countries of Syria with similar cultures such as Qatar, Saudi Arabia and Kuwait not accepting ANY refugees?

10. There are reportedly 19 million refugees globally from places as diverse as Libya to Myanmar. Are we to take them all? In the case of Syria, is it not better to spend our money pushing for a UN peacekeeping force to be deployed and contributing our resources in that fashion so that these people can have the opportunity to stay put and rebuild their own country? How we managed the war in Cyprus comes to mind. Is that not the road we should be following instead of pretending that we are blind to what the USA and Russia are doing there?

11. Terror attacks appear to be occurring in random places with high civilian populations with little if any police or military presence. I have never been that concerned with gun restrictions, however like our brothers and sisters in France; we Canadians live a country with severe gun restrictions. Can you comment on how Section 7 of the Canadian Charter of Rights and Freedoms squares with my inability to carry or possess (without significant restrictions) a weapon for self-defense? Put another way, how can I possibly have the right to Security of Person where I don't have a reasonable ability of self-defense? Do you intend on travelling anywhere (inside or outside of the country) without armed guards? While you will no doubt have me look to the south (USA) for reasons not to re-consider this, I would point you east, to Switzerland, which is one of the most heavily armed, yet peaceful nations on earth.

In all of this, I am not suggesting that as a nation we turn a blind eye to those in need. We do have an enviable reputation in the world that each of us is proud of. Having said that, we unfortunately live in an ever-changing world. For all of the forgoing reasons, I would ask that the sitting government halt the refugee program until it can be demonstrated to all Canadians that every single refugee being allowed access to our country, and being offered benefits that most of us have worked a lifetime to fund, have been thoroughly vetted. I would also argue that it is time to re-open the debate on gun legislation from a constitutional perspective. We don't have a "second amendment" as our US brothers, but without the right to meaningful self-protection, the Canadian Charter guarantee of "Security of Person" is starting to ring very hollow. In closing, are we going to learn anything from Paris? While social media is replete with people stating "we are Paris", my suggestion is we make immediate alterations to the issues noted above, before that Facebook slogan changes from an echo of support to a prophesy. Respectfully,

D. S. (Scott) Wilcox / Cold Lake, Canada"

Refugee vs. Immigrant

In relation to the initial 25,000 Syrian immigrants offered entry to Canada by the Liberal government of Canada, Mr Ian Gillepsie, the CEO of a development company in Vancouver, B.C., Westbank Projects, asked "Why are we not thinking of these refugees as a wonderful thing? This is how we build our country" (Globe and Mail, Nov 21, 2015). To my mind, what Mr Gillepsie failed to consider is that, with few exceptions, Canadian immigrants and refugees have traditionally come mainly from European countries, which have similar values and cultures to Canada and do not harbor religious extremists and radicals. Now ask the First Nations, would they feel the same way about Europeans? Times have drastically changed since the first immigrants and refugees arrived on the North

American continent. History has evolved. The rules of the immigration game have changed and are changing daily at lightning speed. We should be in favour of immigration (refugees included), but at a decent pace and only after effective background checks before we let them walk free in our country. For security reasons, we need to be 100 per cent sure of their backgrounds. Immigrants and refugees should not mind this at all, considering what we are, in good faith, doing for them. I truly believe accepting all kinds of immigrants is the right thing to do. Let's open our doors but only after proper evaluation of everybody's background and without rushing the process.

Unlike a typical refugee or asylum seeker, when I chose to come to Canada and proceeded to apply, I knew that I would need to integrate and respect the laws and ways of life of Canadians. I needed to at least learn English thoroughly, honor the flag and national anthem, and respect and learn about Canadian history, art, religions, sports, and overall lifestyle and social behavior. I was the one who chose to come. Nobody pushed me out of my old country, nor did anybody recruit me. After an exhaustive and difficult evaluation, I decided on my own accord to come to this new and wonderful land, not to change it but to respect it and adapt to it. I consider myself fully integrated, though not assimilated. As Canadians, we are all required to enrich our rich and diverse mosaic of cultures. When we hold hands together with this common goal, we create this amazing and fantastic country called Canada, envied by many beyond our frontiers. As simple as that!

When I left Mexico City 30 years ago, I wanted to achieve a better quality of life for my family and myself. Mexico is a beautiful country with amazing and fascinating traditions, and above all, it has very friendly, hard working, and altruistic people. Their music and their food is to die for, and their flag is recognized and respected all around the world. Yes, I have

Mexico in my heart and always will until I die, but now I am a Canadian first and proud of this. I left behind a city that was a concrete jungle with the highest population density in the world after Tokyo and poor quality air at the time, due to serious pollution problems from industry and an extremely high density of vehicles in the city streets. Kidnapping for ransom was common and getting worse. Overall, it was not a city in which you could live safely and healthily to bring up a family.

I chose Canada for many wonderful and positive reasons, the most important of which were its amazing multicultural diversity and tolerance, its fair legal system, its openness, sense of community, and pride, its respect for other cultures, and its friendly and clean international reputation. But every country has its problems, and you need to be willing to sacrifice, work hard, and adapt as best you can. Yes, there is also corruption in Canada, but not as much and as open as in other countries. The beautiful, positive aspects of Canada completely outweigh the negative aspects by far. In the eyes of many, there is no better country than Canada, and we should never take it for granted. But above all, we should protect it from negative influences. It is our most basic civic duty and responsibility. I have brought a lot of my traditions, foods, music, art, and overall way of being from Mexico, but I invite my fellow Canadians to share and experience these with me if they want. I would never think of imposing my habits and lifestyle on others. Why rub them the wrong way? They have their own beautiful culture already highly developed, though we are still searching for our own identity. We just need to coexist in peace, harmony, and good will and enrich our new country's diversity with respect, camaraderie, and flair. I could and would have adapted to Chinese culture had I immigrated to China or to the Finnish culture had I gone there.

Now that I have adapted to Canada and call it my home, I am willing to fight for it even more strongly and enthusiastically than some of those born here. Why? The answer is simple. I know what is out there. I have been lucky to have travelled extensively. The average Canadian has not experienced in person the crude realities of abroad that I have seen. The average Canadian has mainly lived in a protected bubble in their own country, which works almost like a Swiss clock in many cities. I will continue to work hard to protect our Canadian values and traditions and to protect our country against any alien interference or imposition. I certainly do not want radicals of any sect or political belief to come here and disturb our peace, our security, and our relentless development, growth, and expansion. The same goes for internally born radicals and extremists, whom we also have to protect ourselves from.

The most valuable asset a human being has is to be born and remain free. But equally important is to keep our freedom of expression, as long as it is practiced with respect. We Canadians have both freedom and freedom of expression. Yes, we need to abide by rules and regulations (as in any other society), but we have the opportunity to dream and dream big. If we put in the time, effort, hard work, faith, and the right attitude, the chance to succeed is within everybody's reach. This is contrary to many other countries such as Syria, Libya, Iraq, Afghanistan, Sierra Leona, Uganda, Somalia, and so on, in which people are suffering due to corrupt or incompetent governments, armed opposition and rebel groups, or the interference of foreign forces. Many countries have rebel groups fighting against each other. Some even recruit rebels from neighboring countries to come and fight for their cause in a war in which the foreign recruits have no interest, but fight merely for money or perhaps religious beliefs.

The Syrian civil war started as early as January 2011 and was still going strong throughout March of 2018, when I was writing this chapter. Just imagine: eight years of brutal civil war in which houses, government buildings, schools, bridges, mosques, roads, ancient archeological sites, and more have been bombed and destroyed on a daily basis, and the basic means of survival – clean water, gas, electricity, food, medical services, police assistance, etc. – are simply unavailable. I cannot fathom this, nor do I want to. We definitely need to extend a helping hand to legitimate refugees from such a place. But we need to do it properly, keeping our national security in mind first, not just in the naïve altruistic Canadian spirit to make us feel and look good. Unfortunately, this has not happened under the new Liberal government, which seems to have decided otherwise. We need to keep in mind that Islamic radicals have the US and Canada as a target? Are they not perhaps infiltrating future terrorists among the regular innocent people being pushed out of Syria? Is this part of their strategy for which Canadian immigration does not know anything about, yet?

Again, I am not against accepting more refugees and asylum seekers, but we definitely require more diligence in our background checks. For now, we want to believe and hope that the background checks for all those Syrian refugees that have been done to date, have been done properly and with sufficient documentation. Yet, history always repeats itself. I hope I am wrong and that the selection process for those initial (and subsequent) 25,000 Syrians has been and will be done diligently. I trust the government is not misleading the average Canadian by saying that the process has been professional, exhaustive, and fully supported by intelligence methods and procedures more accurate than those of some other countries. However, it was initially done at the speed of light, while it can still take a very long time for a regular Canadian firefighter, RCMP officer, and others seeking "sensitive" positions to get security clearance even with full and reliable documentation on hand. This "red tape" is exactly what retired firefighter Scott Wilcox encountered, which he explained in his letter to PM Trudeau quoted previously.

Real Life Example

CNN has a news section called "Impact Your World - Make A Difference Now." Here they published an excellent article about a young, but very mature, British man who has gained respect and admiration from almost everyone who has read his story. The article, "Amputee soldier's heartfelt Muslim Facebook post goes viral," (Dec 10, 2015) by James Masters describes how the young man, Chris Herbert, lost his right leg during military service in Basra, Iraq, when a bomb severed his lower right leg. This happened in 2007 when he was 19 years old, while he was driving his military Land Rover with Private Luke Simpson, who lost his life in the incident.

Luckily for everyone, Chris Herbert decided to share what happened to him through social media. His post was so down to earth and logical that I want to quote it in full:

> Getting frustrated by some people expecting racism from me, because I got blown away. Here it is:
> Yes. A Muslim man blew me up, and I lost my leg .....
> A Muslim man also lost his arm that day wearing a British Uniform. A Muslim medic was in the helicopter that took me from the field. A Muslim surgeon performed the surgery that saved my life. A Muslim Nurse was part of the team that helped me when I returned to the UK. A Muslim Healthcare Assistant was part of the team that sorted out my day to day needs in rehabilitation when I was learning to walk. A Muslim taxi driver gave me a free ride the first time I went for a beer with my Dad after I came home. A Muslim doctor offered my Dad comfort and advice in a pub, when he didn't know how to deal with my medicines and side effects.

I hope people around the world will understand and internalize Herbert's wise thoughts, as he observes, "blaming all Muslims for the actions of groups like Daesh [Islamic State] and the Taliban is like blaming all Christians for the actions of the KKK, the Inquisition or Westboro Baptist Church." The post concludes: "Get a grip of your lives, hug your family and get back to work."

The Birth of Vigilantism

Vigilantes have existed throughout human history in two main categories: loners and groups. In the United States, both types of vigilantes are currently "protecting" their border with Mexico. According to the MailOnline (Oct 3, 2015), there is a veteran known as the "Nailer" leading a group that, with camouflaged uniforms and heavy machine guns, is guarding certain sections of the border against an "immigrant invasion." Their efforts are well regarded by millions of Americans concerned about illegal immigration, human trafficking, and drug smuggling. An article by David Sim in International Business Times (Nov 17, 2016) entitled "Heavily armed civilian vigilantes patrol US-Mexico border for illegal immigrants" describes how one typical group operates:

> Formed in 2011, the armed group is made up of former US military and law enforcement servicemen and women, as well as private security guards. Led by US Army veteran and former meth user Tim "Nailer" Foley, the group – which claims up to 200 volunteers – does not consider itself a militia, but rather a group of citizens supplementing US Border Patrol efforts to counter illegal border activity.

This group seems to be well organized, but nobody really knows how far they may have gone while trying to stop illegal immigrants. Do they operate strictly within the law? According to Foley, they describe themselves as "vigilantes upholding the law where there is no law." That is a scary thought and opens the possibility for all kinds of abuse and criminal acts by a small group of people enforcing what they believe is right from their own point of view. More worrisome is the fact that there are also many vigilante *loners* who commit atrocious criminal acts in the name of justice and patriotism, giving all vigilantes a bad image and reputation.

However, the vigilante syndrome is intensifying all over the world. The International New York Times (June 11-12, 2016) published an article by M. Germanova, B. Dzhambazova, and H. Bienvenue entitled "Taking a vigilante approach to Europe's migrant problem." It reports that, in Slovakia, people against asylum seekers have taken vigilante-style measures to protect themselves. Desperate immigrants are crossing borders in many places throughout Europe and, on the way to their final destinations, are assaulting people in train stations, metros, stores, back alleys, etc. Locals have had enough and are starting to fight back through determined groups of vigilantes who protect their streets and their borders but create serious illegal problems. Some of these vigilante groups are more civilized than others, especially those organized by political parties like the People's Party Our Slovakia. Nevertheless, the vigilante phenomenon is very dangerous. In Hungary, a certain Mr Vass and more than 300 of his peers were agitating through social media about what they see as the threat of immigration. Mr Vass has lead a group called Hyundai Border-Guard Unit, which also represents a serious threat of potential social unrest.

According to the *International New York Times* article, in Bulgaria:

> Petar Nizamov said he was proud of starting an informal group called Civil Squad for the Protection of Women and Faith, which a few months ago began hunting for migrants along the country's borders, pushing them back into neighboring Turkey.

These type of vigilante groups may be trying to do their best under their existing laws, but many cases get completely out of hand and go unreported. Mr Vass from Hungary was quoted saying "we are Christians and they are Muslims," implying that they are from opposite poles and that Muslims can never integrate with or respect Hungarian values. Now let us face it, nothing can guarantee that this will never happen in North America. Governments, especially in Canada, do not see that they need to assist their own people before assisting refugees and asylum seekers with utterly different value systems, some of whom lack a sincere desire to integrate. There are many Canadian citizens in real economic and social need who require our help. We should help them first to get them back on their feet and provide them with real job opportunities, social housing, and better education.

The Chinese have generally added value to our economy and our culture across Canada. The majority have integrated, and those that have failed to assimilate do not represent a terrorist threat to anybody. But unfortunately, though understandably, our government has allowed the Chinese community's demand for housing to displace the purchasing power of the average Canadian working person, who can no longer afford to buy a house in cities such as Vancouver and Toronto. They have allowed the Chinese with high incomes and savings to push the price of houses to exorbitant and unrealistic levels. Real estate is now too costly for Canadians who are not yet in the real estate market. They can no longer purchase their own home and start building a patrimony. The government recently imposed a tax on empty houses used for speculation, which is having a slight positive impact, but still not enough. This has become so bad that vigilante groups have started to show signs of discontent. They call themselves the "Alt-Right" and are inviting people to join them across Canada. In mid-November 2016, for example, they placed racist flyers in public places promoting their efforts to "save our cities from Chinese people."

Personally, I like the Chinese culture, its entrepreneurial spirit, and family values. I fully agree with those who see anti-Chinese activism as a horrible thing. Racism of any kind is not welcome in Canada. Unfortunately, however, it has started already, and my fear is that, if we do not fight for respect and reciprocity in unison, we are going to endure the same pain as in Europe, but now with the added threat of the "potential terrorist" from Muslim backgrounds or "potential internal terrorist" from our own country. For more information on the anti-Chinese flyers, please refer to the article posted on Nov 18, 2016 in Nextshark-Asia entitled "Racist Anti-Chinese Flyers Are Popping Up in Mailboxes Around Canada."

Immigration - Open Door Policy and Reciprocity

Even though I personally feel quite comfortable extending a helping hand to the new refugees (or asylum seekers), and or any other immigrant that wants to come to Canada under our established immigration and refugee programmes, I also want to express my reservations. PM Trudeau, in Nov 2015, promised to bring 25,000 refugees from Syria before the end of that year. A noble thought, but was it a rational one? Wasn't PM Trudeau risking our national security by pushing the Syrians through the system at lightning speed, using shortcuts that invited errors and omissions just to keep his word? Wasn't he supposed to look out for our welfare as Canadians first and only then turn his attention beyond our frontiers to assist other people in need? It is not a matter of whether errors were made; we all now know they did. Again, we need to show compassion for people in need, but we should never do this by putting our own peace and security at risk. How do we know there is not a long-term terrorist strategy by Islamic radical groups to infiltrate Europe and North America using so-called refugees, mostly legitimate refugees but including some terrorists in disguise? We will only know after years go by.

Immigrants, refugees, and asylum seekers need to adapt as much as we require to accept them the way they are. We all need to leave racial concerns behind. But it is a two-way street. The average North American knows and is willing to leave racial issues in the past, but there needs to be a sense of reciprocity in the new comer's behavior. They should not try to impose in public places their traditions and should make a sincere effort to let go of some old and conflicting religious taboos. Some of these continue to subjugate and oppress women, then, regardless if it is right or wrong, they are instigating a backlash of aggressive racial reactions towards them sooner or later by the locals. Why? Because their lack of reciprocity goes against the identity and values of the average North American individual, but above all, it goes against their social sense of openness, integration and sense of security. With this attitude, newcomers automatically promote social exclusion and segregation, which can have a nefarious impact on their future society.

We need to act in harmony with the goals, efforts, and sacrifices of all the fallen Canadian soldiers during the First and Second World Wars. Remembrance Day celebrates all those Canadian soldiers who sacrificed their lives during the First World War to keep Canada safe and free from foreign threats while protecting their families and their nation, our nation! In the section below, I want to briefly explain why the Remembrance Day is so important to us and what it means, as well as what the Commonwealth really represents and what its relation to our "free" country and our future is.

Remembrance Day

The 11th of November of every year, Canadians celebrate Remembrance Day. Also, known as Poppy Day, it commemorates members of the armed forces since the end of the First World War. Every year, an important ceremony takes place in memory of all the soldiers who died in the line of duty for their country and for other international interests, and we all make an effort to pay our respects. The red poppy has become a well-known emblem during the commemoration of this important day. In many other countries, they also celebrate the end of World War I, which formally ended on the 11th hour of the 11th day of the 11th month, 1918. Canadians of all ages, social classes, and races went to fight for the Allied Forces in Europe during World War I. Why commemorate? According to Veterans Affairs Canada:

> We must remember. If we do not, the sacrifice of those one hundred thousand Canadian lives will be meaningless. They died for us, for their homes and families and friends, for a collection of traditions they cherished and a future they believed in; they died for Canada. The meaning of their sacrifice rests with our collective national consciousness; our future is their monument.

We pay our respects because they fought and died to ensure that future generations could enjoy a free, peaceful, and secure country. The world beyond our frontiers is unstable, risky, and dangerous. Other countries envy deeply the way we live, what we have, our standard of living, our opportunities, our level of organization as a country, our justice system, our modern communication networks, our medical system, our abundance of natural resources, our discipline and strength as a country, our future. We require protecting from threats coming from other countries, especially from countries that, sadly and regrettably, we are sometimes bombing to assist our allies in their own deep secret interests, though in the name of freedom and justice.

Do we really believe that our military interventions in foreign countries will benefit those countries and that everybody there will be happy, loving, and appreciative after we leave? I sincerely hope I am wrong, but we should think again and be prepared to embrace a strong reaction from extremist and radical groups against Canadians abroad. Let us hope we can stop foreign threats from infiltrating and establishing secret networks of extremists in our country. Look at what happened to the Twin Towers in New York, at least according to what the press released at the time. Something similar could cause serious damage, grief, and pain to Canadians, just as various terrorist groups have done to the people of Great Britain, Netherlands, France, Belgium, Spain, and many others.

The following image has always impressed me, because even though it was taken during the Second World War, the same thing happened in the First World War. In both world wars, many soldiers left their homes and families to fight a war for the political and military interests of the British Empire and its allies at the time. Their sacrifice was not directly related to defending our Canadian sovereignty or interests. They were not wars in which Canadians fought to defend Canadian soil and their people and families from direct, immediate threats.

Canadians departing for active service in Europe during the WWII, 1940. *(Source: Library and Archives Canada C-38723)*

The Commonwealth

The Commonwealth has existed for over 60 years as a worldwide organization. It is a voluntary association of 54 countries, including Canada. On the official website of the British monarchy (royal.gov.uk), my attention was caught by the following description, which I quote at length because I find difficult to believe that a country that fought for its sovereignty, which should mean autonomy and independence; would then join the Commonwealth and tie itself to foreign interests regardless of the benefits that it might represent, when we still have the Queen (or upcoming King) as Canada's "head of state":

> After achieving independence, India was the first of a number of countries which decided that, although they wished to become republics, they still wanted to remain within the Commonwealth. To reconcile these aims, the 1949 London Declaration recognized King George VI as Head of the Commonwealth. After his death, the Commonwealth leaders recognized Queen Elizabeth II in that capacity. Canada is a parliamentary democracy and a constitutional monarchy with The Queen as Sovereign. As a constitutional monarch, The Queen abides by the decisions of the Canadian Government, but she continues to play important ceremonial and symbolic roles. Over the course of more than 60 years and over 20 Royal Tours, Her Majesty's Canadian tours have included stops in each of the 13 provinces and territories, often playing a key role in national celebrations and recognizing achievement in all walks of life.

After researching what Canada really is as a country and what is understood by the average Canadian as well as the average foreigner, I found a page at the website of the Parliament of Canada that explains the situation simply and clearly. (http://www.parl.gc.ca/About/Senate/Monarchy/senmonarchy_ 00-e.htm)

> Since 1534, when the King of France claimed possession of what is now Canada, the history of our country (Canada) has been marked by reigns of an uninterrupted succession of monarchs, both French and

British, who have had a significant influence on our country's development. Under the Crown, Canada developed first as a colony of two empires, originally the French and subsequently the British, then as an independent dominion, and now as an entirely sovereign nation. The Crown occupies a central place in our Parliament and our democracy, founded on the rule of law and respect for rights and freedoms; the Crown embodies the continuity of the state and is the underlying principle of its institutional unity. The Crown heads all three branches of government, the Executive, where the Prime Minister is the principal advisor; the Legislative, which recognizes the Crown as one of three constituents of Parliament, acting with the consent of the Senate and the House of Commons; and the Judiciary, since all decisions made by the courts are given in the name of the Queen.

On one hand, we are considered a sovereign country. On the other hand, the British Crown still occupies a central and crucial place in our parliament and in our democracy. A sovereign country is one that controls its own affairs, but history has shown us that we have not, and perhaps still do not, control our own affairs. It is also important to mention that, in Dec 1931, Canada signed the Statute of Westminster, which basically is an act of Parliament of the United Kingdom. Even though it makes the Dominions (such as Canada) sovereign countries, it also confirms a strong relationship between the Commonwealth nations (such as Canada) and the British Crown.

Unit 10 – Commonwealth of Nations says:

The Commonwealth of Nations, formerly known as the British Commonwealth, is an intergovernmental organization of fifty-four independent member states. All but two of these countries (Mozambique and Rwanda) were formerly part of the British Empire, out of which it developed. The member states cooperate within a framework of common values and goals as outlined in the Singapore Declaration. These include the promotion of democracy, human rights, good governance, the rule of law, individual liberty, egalitarianism, free trade, multilateralism, and world peace The Commonwealth is not a political union, but an intergovernmental organization through which countries with diverse social, political, and economic backgrounds are regarded as equal in status. Activities of the Commonwealth are carried out through the permanent Commonwealth Secretariat, headed by the Secretary-General, and biennial meetings between Commonwealth Heads of Government. The symbol of their free association is the Head of the Commonwealth, which is a ceremonial position currently held (*as of Oct 2017*) by Queen Elizabeth II. Elizabeth II is also monarch, separately and independently, of sixteen Commonwealth members, which are known as the "Commonwealth realms."

In my view, the Queen still has a strong cultural power and influence in our country, which is blocking Canada from developing its own identity as an independent country away from the shadow of the British. If we were to develop our own national identity and uniqueness, any immigrant (including all refugees) would adapt and fully integrate faster and more easily, but many resent the idea of being loyal to the Queen due to what the British Empire meant to their colonized country of origin in the past. Without going too far, many native people in Canada were seriously affected by British colonization and resent the British influence and the influence of the Royal family when they come for their "social tours."

It was not until 1982 that Canada repatriated its constitution from the British Parliament. This constitution contained the addition of a Charter of Rights. Repatriation succeeded only after lengthy negotiations between the federal government and the provinces, especially Quebec, and a decision by the Supreme Court in September 1981 that: (per *Historica Canada – Patriation of the Constitution*)

> Ottawa was legally allowed to make this request [for repatriation] of the British Parliament but ... the resolution offended the constitutional "conventions" developed in Canada over the years, referring to practices that were important but not legally enforceable. The court held by a 7-2 majority that no legal limit "to the power of the Houses [the House of Commons and the Senate] to pass resolutions" existed.... By a 6-3 majority, however, the court also ruled that whenever amendments were proposed that would reduce provincial powers, the presentation of a joint resolution by Ottawa without a "consensus" of the provinces would be a breach of constitutional convention. Although such practice was a matter of convention rather than law, the court argued that such conventions are of great significance. In the words of the court, "Constitutional convention plus constitutional law equal the total constitution of the country." (*Historica Canada – Patriation of the Constitution. For more information refer to:* thecanadianencyclopedia.ca/en/article/patriation-of-the-constitution/).

It proved extremely difficult to have every province accept the Charter of Rights, but, in the end, the new constitution was proclaimed on the 17 April, 1982 without Quebec's agreement. Years later, Quebec's then-prime minister Robert Bourassa and Canada's then-prime minister Brian Mulroney tried to have Quebec sign the agreement via the Meech Lake Accord, but failed again. Québec remains estranged from the Canadian "constitutional family." However, during the Meech Lake negotiations, something very interesting happened that changed the events to come:

The accord recognized the Province of Québec as a distinct society within Canada. At the same time, it recognized, as fundamental characteristics of Canada, both the Anglophone minority in Québec and the francophone minority elsewhere.

After this, the provinces were allowed to nominate their people to sit on the Senate and the Supreme Court of Canada. Meech Lake changed the method for amending our constitution. It now needed consent of Parliament and the legislatures of all the provinces, but it was not well received and, if the Accord did not become law, a backlash from Quebec was feared that could threaten national unity. It is important to mention that "to become law the Accord had to be ratified within three years by Parliament and the legislatures of all 10 provinces in accordance with section 41 of the Constitution Act of 1982."

The political consensus fell apart. It started with Manitoba, which could not collect all the required signatures. Then Quebec followed suit by forming the Bloc Quebecois, dedicated to pursuing Quebec's interests in the House of Commons. The Charlottetown Accord of 1992 failed when Prime Minister Mulroney and nine provincial premiers once again tried to obtain Quebec's acceptance of the Constitution Act of 1982. By then, Canadians were fed up with all the political mumbo-jumbo and total lack of integrity by some political parties. The process no longer seemed worth pursuing. The only thing that has transpired since then is that in 2006 the House of Commons passed a motion acknowledging francophone Quebecers as a nation within a united Canada. As of 2014 there have been no further efforts to obtain Quebec's official acceptance of the Constitution of 1982. According to the entry "Constitutional History" at the Canadian Encyclopedia:

In 2006, Prime Minister Stephen Harper introduced a

motion in the House of Commons that recognized the Québécois people "as a nation within a united Canada." The motion was overwhelmingly supported in the House; however, it prompted the resignation of Harper's intergovernmental affairs minister Michael Chong, who said the motion could be interpreted as promoting ethnic nationalism in Canada.

Wouldn't Mr Chong be better by saying that in Canada we are tolerant and accept differences within our own country, leaving the door open for other minority groups in the future to demand the same? How can we say no and stop them instead of promoting national unity and true identity?

The Court's nine justices ruled unanimously in 2014 that any substantial change to the Senate – including imposing term limits on senators and creating an elected Senate – required a constitutional amendment covered by the 7/50 rule (consent of 7 provinces with 50 per cent of Canada's population). Also in response to the government's query, the Court said abolishing the Senate required a constitutional amendment unanimously endorsed by all 10 provincial legislatures and the federal Parliament. (For more information see http://www.thecanadianencyclopedia.ca/en/article/const itutional-history/)

First World War: Canadian War or British War?

Queen Elizabeth II is known to be the Sovereign of the constitutional monarchy and parliamentary democracy of Canada and therefore of all Canadians. To many immigrants like myself, it seems we are not considered an independent nation and are still a constitutional monarchy owing allegiance to Her Majesty. In this regard, please refer to a site called "Citizens for a Canadian Republic" ((canadian-republic.ca/goals.html), which states:

Presently, Canada is a constitutional monarchy. It shares its unelected, hereditary head of state, Queen Elizabeth II of the United Kingdom, with that country and fourteen other former British colonies. In Canada, the Governor General is the representative of the Queen and acts in her name on the advice of Parliament. Therefore, in practice, the Queen is Canada's 'official' head of state, while the Governor General is our 'acting' head of state.

I found a summary from Wikipedia, which I corroborated with further research and is worth quoting as follows:

Constitutionally, Canada's head of state is Queen Elizabeth II (*as of Oct 2017*). She is represented by a governor general at the federal level and by 10 lieutenant governors, one per province. The three territories each have a commissioner representing the Queen. Canada is a parliamentary democracy and constitutional monarchy with The Queen as Sovereign. As a constitutional monarch, The Queen abides by the decisions of the Canadian Government, but she continues to play important ceremonial and symbolic roles.

The Canadian War Museum (warmuseum.ca) says the following on Canada's participation in the First World War:

Britain's War:
Great Britain, which had long pledged to defend Belgium's sovereignty, issued an ultimatum to Germany on 4 August 1914 demanding the withdrawal of German troops. When the ultimatum expired at midnight, without a German retreat, Great Britain and Germany were at war. So too was the British Empire,

including Canada and the independent colony of Newfoundland.

Canada's War:
In 1914, Canada was a self-governing dominion of the British Empire, but it did not control its own foreign affairs. As during the South African War (1899-1902), the Canadian government would decide the nature and extent of Canada's war effort, but legally the country was at war the instant Britain declared one. In 1914, most, but by no means all, Canadians would have agreed with the 1910 statement of Prime Minister Sir Wilfrid Laurier that "when Britain is at war, Canada is at war. There is no distinction." They nevertheless debated vigorously the size and nature of Canada's war effort and, increasingly, its relationship with Britain.

The Canadian War Museum states that 619,000 Canadians enlisted with the armed forces out of a total population at the time of under 8 million people. In other words, 7.5 per cent of the population enlisted to go and fight a war that we did not start or have anything to do with, except for our allegiance to the British Empire and its monarch.

It has always been difficult for many to understand why Canada went to war when war had not knocked directly at our door in a hostile manner. In my research, I bumped into a very interesting site whose account of Canada's entry into the First World War is worth quoting:

> On August 1st, three days before Great Britain entered the war, the Canadian Government became so concerned over the danger threatening the Mother Country that this message was sent to the British Government through the acting Governor-General: "My advisers...wish to convey to His Majesty's Government

the firm assurance that, if unhappily war should ensue, the Canadian people will be united in a common resolve to put forth every effort, and to make every sacrifice necessary to insure the integrity and maintenance of <u>the honor of our Empire</u>." In reply, the British Government sent the following message: "With reference to your telegram…His Majesty's Government gratefully welcomes the assurance that in the present crisis they may rely on the whole-hearted co-operation of the people of Canada."

Preparations were at once made by the Canadian Government to support the Mother Country and, within six weeks of the outbreak of war, an army of 33,000 men was enrolled, trained, and embarked – the largest single force that had ever crossed the Atlantic. Since then Canada has continued to give her men, her women, and her treasure, and on the bloody fields of France and Flanders Canadians have won undying fame in the greatest struggle of the ages.

Sadly, all Canadians, regardless of whether or not they had a British background, were sent to the front lines, along with soldiers from Africa, Australia, India, the West Indies, and other countries that owed allegiance to the British at the time, and were slaughtered in the hundreds of thousands for a cause that did not serve their interests.

Second World War: Canadian War or British War?

Canada joined the Second World War on a different basis than the First World War. This time it was the result of a decision by the Canadian parliament that, by joining Great Britain and its allies, we would help stop the continued expansion of threats to North American capitalism and our democratic and free way of life. Once again, however, the British Crown held a central place in parliament and our democracy. Parliament was far from free to ignore the desires and interests of the Crown, which put it in a very difficult position when it came to making decisions with Canadian interests at heart.

International Allies

We have to keep in mind that Canada belongs to a team of international players called allies, with Great Britain and the United States being the most important. Therefore, we need to support them in many international affairs, whether we like it or not. Between freedom and capitalism versus communism and loss of freedom, the majority of Canadians would choose (myself included) freedom and capitalism. Also, between choosing our own religion or having one imposed on us, Canadians, we would rather choose our own, without a doubt. The average Canadian does not really know why Canada went to WWI and WWII. Of the people that I approached, the great majority could not believe that we needed to send our sons and daughters to fight our "motherland's" battles only because the British government or King George asked us, as it actually happened. This would not happen today, but if a similar conflict arose, we would most likely end up backing our allies. Aside from protecting our sovereignty, that is what allies are for, correct? We must back-up each other.

Citizenship and True Freedom

As an immigrant, I was not well versed in Canadian history. I had a general idea of Canada's overall history and of the social background and economic situation at the time (late 1980s). I did study for my citizenship exam with devotion, but there was not a lot of detailed information in the materials provided by the government or in the other historical materials I laid my hands on to prepare for the citizenship test. When the time came to be sworn in as a new Canadian citizen, I was told during the ceremony to repeat out loud my allegiance to Queen Elizabeth II. I felt very uncomfortable. Under absolute duress, I was forced to swear something that was against my ideals, desires, hopes, commitments, and principles. But since my citizenship was at risk, I did not say a word, I just kept quiet. Since then a new law has been passed that enables new citizens to avoid swearing allegiance to the monarch.

Many Canadians have told me in past conversations that they acknowledge and even envy the sense of pride and the strong sense of belonging of people from Mexico and the United States. When Mexicans and US citizens are asked about their nationality, they immediately step forward and state their nationality with obvious pride and satisfaction. Unfortunately, Canadians grew up singing "God Save The Queen" along with "O Canada." That might be the reason so many Canadians lack the enthusiasm, pride, conviction, and devotion to say out loud, with their chest forward and high, "I am Canadian." We certainly do not yet have the necessary level of pride and conviction concerning our identity and our gorgeous national flag and national anthem. A good example was when the Canadian tenor Remigio Pereira changed the lyrics of the Canadian anthem in the middle of a public event. While it was an insult to many of us, other Canadians just did not care. Now, do not take me wrong. Canadians feel proud of being Canadians, but their pride falls short compared to other nations that would feel insulted if somebody were to change the lyrics of their national anthem. I personally felt infuriated and offended when Pereira changed the lyrics. But that is me.

Since I first came to Canada, the situation has improved, but we are still behind the sense of belonging and pride that people from Mexico and the United States have. I sincerely hope the day will come when Canadians feel as proud as people from Mexico and the United States, because there are many other Canadians like me who really do feel very proud of our land, our culture, our flag, and are proud of being Canadians, regardless of our origins or the province we live in. Yes, we are a young country made by immigrants, and it sometimes takes a generation or two before that pride kicks in, unless we are playing hockey against another country, where I have seen the true devotion and spirit of Canadians.

Allegiance to Canada or the Queen

A high and increasing number of Canadians would like to have this monarchy abolished and make Canada a full-fledged republic, that is, a totally independent country free from any kind of foreign allegiance. We would then make our own decisions in Parliament in relation to the future of our nation and the future benefit of all Canadians without forceful foreign influence. In the minds of many Canadians, the government should be free of any judicial, executive, and legislative influence or interference from the Crown.

What does it mean to search and, if need be, to even fight for absolute freedom? It means doing what the United States did when they cut all ties to Great Britain or what the Republic of Mexico did when they cut all ties with Spain and went in search of total and absolute independence. For Canadians, cutting all ties, will also mean no more governor general, lieutenant governors, and commissioners representing the Queen, who in the minds of a considerable number of Canadians, are superfluous for our country.

Why belong to the Commonwealth, when many members do not even fight for the essential human rights of their own people, being this one of the main goals of such an organization? Do we really need to be in the Commonwealth to improve economic cooperation and encourage democracy among members when many fail to do so? The United States, Japan, China, Germany, and many more do not belong to the Commonwealth, nor need to.

British people have a complex history and a fascinating culture. They have contributed greatly to human civilization.

Except in a few minor matters such as fox hunting, I admire and respect their society, their traditions, their art, their food, their scientific and technological contributions, their architecture, and much more. Many have immigrated to Canada not to swear allegiance to the Queen but to swear allegiance to an independent Canada.

Canadians need to swear allegiance to their flag and to an independent country not influenced by the Commonwealth, and much less, to swear allegiance to the Queen. We need to fight common goals regarding human rights, freedom, privacy, security and the ability for everybody to bring their dreams to fruition. We require stepping away from obstacles that impede us from reaching those goals. A previous Prime Minister, Stephen Harper, provided a good example on Oct 7, 2013. In an article for CBC News entitled "Harper's Sri Lankan boycott includes swipe at Commonwealth; PM denounces lack of accountability for meeting host's human rights abuses," Terry Milewski noted that Commonwealth member states have no legal ties with each other but fight for common goals that include democracy and the protection of human rights. However, some members are not practicing what they preach, and this was the main reason that then Prime Minister Stephen Harper did not want to participate in the Commonwealth meeting taking place in Sri Lanka. His reason, Harper said, was "the absence of accountability for the serious violations of human rights and international humanitarian standards during and after the [Sri Lankan] civil war." According to Milewski, Harper cited "intimidation and incarceration of political leaders and journalists, harassment of minorities, reported disappearances, and allegations of extra-judicial killings."

Why belong to the Commonwealth when many of their members turn a blind eye towards what other members are doing (or not doing), and hypocrisy and lies do not seem to be considered contrary to the Commonwealth mission, goals, and objectives. Why should we belong to this organization, when we profess the opposite in our immigration law and in our overall commitment to human and constitutional rights? Do not take me wrong. I sincerely like Queen Elizabeth II. What bothers me is only her undeniably strong influence on our parliament and overall society. As Canadians, are we really free? I truly doubt it. What bothers many Canadians the most is that our governments (federal and provincial) are willing to spend exorbitant amounts of our tax dollars on every Royal family visit, while many indigenous people and other Canadians live below the poverty line and are being helped by no one. Many of these people require our help as much or more than any refugee or asylum seeker in the world. That, to my mind, is a real insult to our national pride.

I have had the opportunity to talk with many other immigrants about this matter in the past. A great majority seem also to regret having had to swear allegiance to the Queen. In their view, Canada's connection to the Crown stops us from developing our true set of values and identity as Canadians and prevent us from being a truly independent country. To make matters worse, many immigrants come from countries that were conquered and abused by the British Empire, so the last thing they want is to swear allegiance to the Queen. What would happen if we were to ask every Quebecois to swear allegiance to the Queen in defiance of their French language and heritage?

To many Canadians, we appear to be independent, but are we really? We only need to look at our currency, which has the Queen's image on some bills and all coins. If we go to any Canada Post office, we will find the Queen's image on our stamps and even on the minted silver and gold coin collections. Even our passports are issued in the name of the Queen. I have always asked myself how much we pay in royalties to use the Queen's image? How much does it cost the average Canadian to play the game of having the Queen of Great Britain (and her family and heirs) visit us for various reasons, along with the large staff she brings with her?

I truly hope that one day Prime Minister Trudeau (or one of his successors) makes a statement similar to the one President Charles de Gaulle of France "mistakenly" once made regarding Quebec and its liberty, but in this case accurately declaring in favor of an independent and free Canada from coast to coast, by saying "Long Live A Free Canada." We should never again have to swear allegiance or have any kind of political ties to anyone but ourselves as a free independent republic, while also keeping deep and strong social and economic ties with our allies and beyond.

British Royalty vs. Canadian Freedom

Every time I hear about British royalty coming to Canada for "royal tours," I feel sad for the average Canadian who may not realize how many of their hard-earned tax dollars are used to pay for the so-called strategic alliance with the British royal family. What I am about to write might be politically incorrect, but it is a conviction I have arrived at after a lot of research. To swear allegiance to the Queen (or future King) during citizenship ceremonies or even to sing "God Save the Queen" is not just unfair but insulting to many Canadians and Canadians-to-be, and certainly to a great percentage of new immigrants and citizens. It is absolutely irrelevant, annoying, and, to some, even offensive and hurtful. I truly hope the day arrives when the government will listen and do something about the silent uproar and agony of many Canadians concerning this issue.

Apparently, the media in Canada is ignoring the deafening silence of the great majority of Canadians and forcing a false admiration of the Royal Family on us. How can people respect Prince Charles when Lady Diana Spencer passes away in a "suspicious" accident inside a tunnel with no cameras or witnesses, and shortly thereafter, he marries his long-time lover Camilla? Many ask themselves: how moral and ethical can that be in the eyes of his people and those of the rest of the world? It is amazing how Camilla was accepted (or forced upon) by the British people (including Prince William and Prince Harry) and Lady Diana seemed to have been forgotten with such ease and speed, though I am sure William and Harry have suffered in silence. Personally, I respect it and is not my business, but what is my business is when they come to Canada flashing their aura of royalty and nobility while dazzling many Canadians and blurring our logical thinking, common sense, overall sense of reality and down-to-earth economic facts.

Is the Royalty an Economic Burden on Canadians?

Absolutely yes, and a lot more than most people realize. Here are seven examples to enable the reader to understand my frustration with how royal visits suck money from our system and, therefore, from the pockets of every Canadian.

1. Giuseppe Valiante reported in the *Toronto Sun* (May 4, 2014) that "the price to taxpayers for the whirlwind Canadian tour [by Prince Charles and Camilla] is $721,000 – minimum, according to the documents released under federal Access and Information laws." According to Valiante, this does not include the cost of security services during the visit. The Canadian Tax Heritage department has always said they are proud to show what Canada has to offer to the world through those visits, but are such visits really the best way to show our rich heritage to the world?

2. Royalty costs Canadians a lot more than it does the British themselves. Katie Engelhart brought this to our attention in July 2009 in an article in Maclean's magazine. Unfortunately, this fact seems to have fallen on deaf ears, because since

then the burden has just gotten worse, with more and more visits whose real purposes and benefits we never accurately know. Engelhart explained that, over the previous ten years, the cost of supporting the monarchy had doubled. Imagine how they are by now, especially with our devalued Canadian dollar and increased visits by the royals. Engelhart noted that it costs Canadians more per capita for these trips than it does the British. This includes expenses for what she calls "the royal clan" running the office of the Governor-General and ten provincial Lieutenant-Governors. And with more trips by the royals to Canada, costs are skyrocketing. Engelhart wrote:

> Tom Freda, national director of Citizens for a Canadian Republic [said] ……. "Ah, the Monarchists. They love to break it down to per capita and make it sound all nice and rosy," he says. "But $40 million or $50 million [a year] sure sounds like a lot to me." The Monarchist League supports that figure, estimating that about $50,147,000 was spent during the 2006-07 year. The problem, Freda says, is that Canada effectively has two heads of state: The Queen and the Governor General, as well as a band of provincial reps, and that overlap creates "redundant and obsolete positions" that end up costing Canadian taxpayers' big bucks. The Queen's agents need to learn a lesson in frugality during these tough times, he argues, especially since most of the work done by lieutenant-governors is already handled by deputy premiers and other officials.

I could not agree more with this statement by Engelhart: "*According to a Canada Day poll by Strategic Council, only 30 per cent of Canadians feel a connection to the Queen or Governor General. And 65 per cent think ties to the monarchy should be cut once the Queen dies.*" I am convinced these percentages have moved even more against the monarchy since Englehart wrote her article.

3. On Apr 30, 2012, the *Globe and Mail* published an article by Steven Chase entitled "Tories blasted over $1 million 'bread and circus' royal tour." It reported how New Democrat Member of Parliament Pat Martin had complained about Harper's government spending money on superfluous but flashy royal trips. Chase quotes the following very accurate statements Martin made:

- It's "Let's keep the country impressed with some glitter and flash while we are cutting and hacking and slashing at public services and jobs."
- What an appalling contradiction. On the day they are announcing public service staff cuts!
- It's an insult to families that are reeling with shock from another pink slip. I care more about Canadian families than the Royal family.

Again, here we are with serious problems of unemployment, poverty, and inadequate health services, but we are bowing to a royalty that is thousands of years old and absolutely obsolete. Chase brings to our attention that, at the time these royal trips were taking place, the Conservative government was cutting $5.2 billion dollars from Ottawa's budget and more than 12,000 public service jobs. Does this make social, economic, and overall business sense?

4. Michael Bolen, news editor at HuffPost Canada, wrote an article on Jan 31, 2014 entitled "It's Time for Canada to Cut Off the Queen." One of his key points was this: "There's no reason Canadians should indulge in the curious human habit of celebrating the rich and powerful people who oppress us. The case is even stronger when it comes to the royals because they've done nothing to earn their status." This might be a bit exaggerated, but it definitely contains some truth. The royal family has done many positive things during their trips for good humanitarian causes. Travelling sounds nice, but as a job it is not easy, regardless of how well you are treated and

attended to. However, I agree with Bolen that we do not need to celebrate royals whose ancestors conquered, abused, robbed, and inflicted so much pain and suffering for the sake of the British Empire's expansion. This is like adding insult to injury. I do not see any Latin American country revering and celebrating Spanish royalty. Perhaps this is because there are more British people in Canada per capita than Spaniards in Latin America, and it is understandable that they want to keep their traditions. In any case, the royals should be able to pay for their own trips. It is a matter of principle and decency to place your own citizens first, and our people certainly need the money more than the royals do. A few brief examples include: lack of proper funding for our police force (RCMP), insufficient social housing for our people and new refugees, better improvements in healthcare in communities up north, more support for anti-suicide programmes for indigenous people, etc. The list can go on and on.

5. According to those in favour of the monarchy, royal visits promote the devotion and dedication the royalty has shown towards Canadians throughout the years. Every time I read comments like that, I feel frustrated but hesitant to say anything, because, if I do, people living in ignorance will accuse me of being negative and ungrateful. Therefore, I decided that instead of commenting myself, I would simply quote a well-known writer, Alhia Raj, who published this statement of one Canadian citizen's feelings about the Queen's "dedicated service to our country" on Mar 22, 2013 in Huffpost Canada:

> Dedicated service???? What a heap of absolute nonsense. Your government makes me so damned angry with your kowtowing to British monarchy that you keep shoving down our throats…when the majority of Canadians have very little interest in this most undemocratic of institutions that is in direct violation of our Charter of Rights and Freedoms."

6. David E. Smith is the author of *The Invisible Crown: The First Principle of Canadian Government*. In this book, he describes how the monarchy works in Canada and he says, "if you are not puzzled by quantum mechanics you will never understand it". This sounds smart and intriguing, but to me it is just shallow. The fact is that the Canadian relationship to monarchy is such a tangled and convoluted issue that only a handful of people can properly understand its real impact on our country. Every time I ask an average Canadian what kind of country we are, or specifically what they understand about Canada being a Constitutional Monarchy, the majority do not have any real understanding.

In an article in Yahoo-Insight-Finance (April 20, 2016), Andrew Seale reports that the Monarchist League of Canada concluded, after research, that the cost of the royals to Canadians (from 2011 to 2012) was about $1.63 per capita. They compared this to medium-size cup of coffee from Tim Horton's. However, that cost, totaling about $56.9 million dollars, did not take into account many other expenses such as hosting the Queen and the Royal Family, minting coins, printing bills, and printing stamps, for example. Nobody knows the real hidden cost of the monarchy to Canadians, but it is certainly well over $100 million dollars today. Can you imagine being given just 2 per cent of that budget as a gift? How fortunate would you feel? Even better, imagine investing that money in reducing university tuition fees for many Canadians? That would have a truly positive impact on our future as a country! And if that is not enough, multiply that minuscule cost of a Tim Horton's cup of coffee by including the costs per capita in other countries such as Australia, New Zealand, Pakistan, Ceylon, and South Africa, among many others. Aren't we talking about billions of dollars for the British royalty?

Seale quotes Nathan Tidridge, a high school teacher who was awarded the Queen's Golden Jubilee Medal for educating Canadians on the role of the Crown:

The queen is the personification of the state; our whole parliamentary democracy is fused onto this idea of us as a constitutional monarchy. Everything from the relationship between the provinces and the federal government to how laws are made to our court system and – something that's really coming to the forefront – our treaty relationships with First Nations are all attached to the Crown. It's really fundamental to the whole Canadian state.

If that is true, it merely shows dependency and a lack of the independence we have been taught to believe we have. But wait, let's consider what constitutional monarchy means according to Encyclopedia Britannica:

> the system of government in which a monarch shares power with a constitutionally organized government. The monarch may be de facto head of state or purely a ceremonial leader. The constitution allocates the rest of the government's power to the legislature and judiciary.

The expression "de facto head of state" is a tricky, confusing, and murky phrase and, to some, "a slippery slope." A head of state is the highest-ranking position in a sovereign country, and it is always vested with specific powers to act as the chief public representative of that country or state.

7. Not too long ago, the Duke and Duchess of Cambridge visited Canada from Sep 24 to Oct 1, 2016. Their itinerary included Victoria (Sept 24), Vancouver (Sept 25), Bella Bella (Sept 25), Victoria and Kelowna (Sept 27), Whitehorse and Carcross (Sept 28), Victoria (Sept 29), Haida-Gwaii (Sept 30), and Victoria (Oct 1). Nobody really knows the actual cost of their visit, and we will never be given the real figures, but it is interesting to note that not everybody was happy with their "imposed" visit. Grand Chief Stewart Phillip, the leader of the Union of B.C. Indian Chiefs, did not participate in the

reconciliation ceremony known as the Ring of Reconciliation upon the Black Rod. The chief stated that his absence was not from a lack of respect, but was rather a matter of principle. He said that he could not in good conscience attend:

> when he remembers the deepening poverty in First Nation communities, the missing and murdered indigenous women and girls, and the ongoing negligence of indigenous child welfare policies. Our people on the ground that are in the midst of dealing with these tragedies on a daily basis will appreciate us standing up and acknowledging their plight and not blindly participating in yet another grandiose pomp and ceremony that would create the illusion that things in our communities are progressing....

In the minds of most Canadians the question is: why are we not investing our dollars in serious social issues in our own country instead of in these kinds of trips from (and for) royalty? Is this what we call democracy? It would be very interesting if the government stated in detail the tangible benefits to the Canadian economy or society of every royal visit. I would really love to be proven wrong in this matter, but the media and government are so overwhelmingly pro-royalty that we seem to be suffering from the same syndrome people in the United States suffered from in the last election, which I call "media alienation and allergic reaction." Is our Canadian government going to ignore its people's voice as the Democrats did in the United States in this last election, which caused them to lose the presidency?

Populism vs. Establishment

Populism is getting more and more popular around the world. People in many countries have started to react by breaking their silence and going full steam ahead to vote for populism. In essence, this movement is a mobilization against the political establishment, which is controlled by a closed elite insensitive to the real needs of the country. Many consider this elite anti-patriotic, unscrupulous, greedy, prepared to put its interests above and beyond those of its country, and only interested in their bottom line. Populism is not a right or left movement. Its goal is just to confront the elite group controlling the country in favour of the less sophisticated and average citizen. It wants to tackle the corruption of the elite head-on.

The media and most governments use the word populism in a derogatory way that demeans the concept of the people – the masses – and of public participation in democracy. Populism has taken off mainly in democratic nations without military oppression and with a certain degree of freedom and liberty. In *What is Populism*, Jan-Werner Müller, a writer and a political scientist at Princeton University, argues that "populism is not just antiliberal, it is antidemocratic – the permanent shadow of representative politics." Müller questions whether populism really puts people closer to their government or is actually a threat to democracy. He asks: who are the people and who speaks for them? He maintains that populism is the breeding ground for an authoritarian state, which goes against democracy itself.

Populism: A Relentless Movement

Populism is a serious movement that merits the attention of governments all over the world because of its promise to work for the real people, the people in need and the silent majority. Well before Trump's rise, the movement had attracted worldwide attention. A few places where populism has had a major impact include:

- Italy, where Silvio Berlusconi secured himself a resounding majority for his centre-right political party in 2001. His goal was to get rid of red tape, reduce taxes, and promote economic growth. During the elections of March 4, 2018, the populism movement gained more terrain.

- Venezuela, where Hugo Chavez was elected as President in 1998. Chavez stated that he was a modern-day Simon Bolivar (the "Libertador" of South America from Spanish colonization) leading the fight against what he called "the empire" (the United States). He started a movement based on populism called "Chavismo", which gained amazing momentum and won a series of elections by landslides.

- The Philippines, where Rodrigo Duterte was sworn in as President in June 2016. He launched himself to victory by promising people he would kill all drug traffickers and addicts and dump their bodies "until the fish will grow fat." He also promised to instil discipline in a "graft-infested" society.

- Centrist, Emmanuel Macron beat Marine Le Pen, in the Presidential elections in France on May 7, 2017. Le Pen, leader of the National Front (FN), vowed to pull France out of the European Community (EC), which ultimately caused her defeat. Le Pen still won 34 per cent of the votes, proving there is a strong populist movement in that country, which is also in favour of stricter and more selective controls on immigration.

- The United Kingdom, where Nigel Farage is considered a heavyweight populist who pushed Britain to "Brexit." He has always been against the political elites and promised to guide Britain out of the EC. Farage's popularity defies what many say has been a "centuries-long streak of moderation and pragmatism" in British politics.

- Brazil, where Joao Doria (former host of Apprentice Brazil) in October, 2016 won 53 per cent of votes in the Sao Paulo municipal elections with a slogan that resonated in all

Brazil: "I am not a politician, I am a businessman." He was elected Mayor of the largest South American City and belongs to the right-leaning Brazilian Social Democratic Party.

According to an article by Griffe Witte in The Vancouver Sun (Nov 19, 2016) entitled "World on Fire," a "populist tide was rolling worldwide well before Trump's ascension. People feel they need a champion to blow the establishment to smithereens." He suggests that Austria may be the first country to vote for a far-right head of state since 1945. A similar situation will most likely happen in Brazilian elections in 2018 after Doria's win in Sao Paulo and the strong movement of Jair Bolsonaro (a far-right lawmaker with presidential ambitions). According to Witte, the wave of populism can be attributed to:

> Anxiety over economic gains that accrue to the few and leave the rest stagnant or sinking; unease with the cultural implications of an increasingly interconnected world; and alienation from a self-serving political class that aligns with the wealthy at the expense of the working class.

The above goes to show that the Democratic Party in the United States profoundly failed to tackle with determination and professionalism a populism movement that has been growing internationally and that they certainly knew about, but failed to recognise the strength of this discontent. They never considered it strong or important enough to launch Trump to victory. They rested on their laurels and did not listen to the people, while alienating them with sneering and inflammatory attacks on Trump.

The media too failed to see (and still fails to accept) that they were helping the Republican Party to place Trump as the next President with their relentless and excessive daily attacks on him, both nationally and internationally. Their arrogant attitude and relentless pit-bull style of attack alienated many people who decided to go and vote against the "insensitive establishment." According to Witte, "voters across the western world want nation state democracy, proper border controls, and to be in charge of their own lives." In Germany, populists have also managed to "get some more moderate and less moderate people supporting them who feel threatened … by refugees, by Islam." And the Democratic Party could not see all this? Why didn't they counterattack and address the issues that were important for the average citizen in the United States? Part of the nation now worries that Donald Trump will be either impeached or perhaps his plane might have a sudden "mechanical failure" to protect the United States from a potential "authoritarian White House". Time will tell, won't it?

FINAL THOUGHTS AND RECOMMENDATIONS

Introduction

The main goal of the human species is simply to survive, as every other species on the planet strives to do. However, humans have been gifted with a capacity for reasoning and learning far beyond that of any other species. All species reason and learn, whether we acknowledge this or not. The main difference between animals and humans is that our species can make the same mistake over and over regardless of the consequences. Animals usually avoid making the same mistake twice. It is not that humans cannot realize we are making the same mistake again, but we humans have a "dark side" in our soul called "uncontrollable greed." Our unquenchable desire for wealth and power has spun out of control and now completely surpasses our capacity for critical and logical thinking, common sense, objective reasoning, and even our humanity itself.

This *rapacity* driven by greed is a disease we generally either overlook or find ways to justify, but it causes immense suffering. Rapacious people and groups have existed throughout human history and will never disappear. Unfortunately, they are products of our human nature, which no human or divine effort can correct. We all need to smarten up, play the game, and make as much of a difference in our own small worlds as we can. Making a living and avoiding trouble are the rules of the game. When you see a storm approaching, look for cover, close your eyes, huddle tight, cover your ears, say nothing, and when the sun shines again, go back to your regular business and your regular self.

According to the Merriam Webster dictionary, rapacious people are "excessively grasping and covetous." That is, they are individuals who are desperate to possess more and more things, typically things belonging to others. Rapacious people or groups are the main cause of wars, poverty, injustice, disasters, mass killings, and almost every other man-made disaster that has tortured humankind throughout history. Is there any way to control or at least minimize rapaciousness either on a personal basis, as a community, as a society, as a country, or as a species? Probably not. But we have to keep trying. We have failed profoundly for thousands of years, and no solution is in sight. To my mind, there is only one "hope": if artificial intelligence one day replaces human decision-making and creates one world without borders and without the most cancerous evil, which is human greed.

Regardless of what fate has in store for us, it is a fact that our privacy and our freedom are a thing of the past. They have slipped through our fingers and are now an illusion even in the most democratic countries in the world. For many, eliminating privacy and freedom is the only way to achieve security for the future. In any case, we all have to do the best we can to take care of what we have, make a decent living for ourselves and our families, and live in harmony with our neighbours.

If privacy and freedom are an illusion, and if you have achieved a decent level of living, what is next? The last words of Steve Jobs, a founder of Apple along with Steve Wozniak and Ronald Wayne, may provide a clue. His last thoughts and words before he died were to acknowledge that, in the world's eyes, he had achieved a successful life. He had accumulated riches beyond his imagination and had grown accustomed to unending success. Then suddenly, there he was, lying in a hospital bed, realizing that all those things he was so proud of were insignificant in comparison to his approaching death. He realized there was more to wealth than accumulating money. There was art, memories, family, and love.

With his dying breath, Jobs declared that we should stop pursuing wealth, which we only have to leave behind. He said: "I can only take away the memories that were strengthened by love." This is the only wealth that will follow you and give you the strength and light to face your death. Jobs realized that he could hire anybody to do anything he wanted, except carry his illness for him, despite having the most expensive bed with the most expensive medical care in the most expensive hospital in the world. Material things, he realized, are lost and found, but life, when it is gone, is gone forever. Before he died, he urged people to treasure their families, their spouses, their children, and their friends while they still had time to do so. He insisted we should treat everyone with decency and respect while staying friendly with our neighbours. His last words can be found at various websites including rojakpot.com, belimitless.com, foreverfulfilled.com, and many more.

Action vs. Passive Aggression

When someone sees a bully or criminal in action and has the means to interfere but does nothing, he or she is almost as guilty as the aggressor. This applies to our daily lives, but even more so in business and in government, where decisions and policies can negatively affect the lives and environments of millions of people. As Bronwyn Fryer says in "The Ethical Mind" (Harvard Business Review, March 2007), people have a duty to monitor their peers and leaders and hold them accountable, as long as they have experience and authority to do so. Fryer quotes the seventeenth century French composer Jean-Baptiste Lully: "It is not only for what we do that we are held responsible but for what we do not do".

We are all responsible for what happens or does not happen around us. In my experience, the average person tries hard to avoid any kind of responsibility, but if we love our country, we need to be responsible and act like patriots. I consider myself a patriot of our beautiful and great Canadian country as well as patriot for the North American values, interests and well-being we share with the United States and Mexico. A patriot is an individual who loves his or her country and is willing to prove this by going against the government and private or public institutions when these act against the best interests of the country. True patriots are willing to risk their own future due to their high sense of responsibility and loyalty, but they act peacefully, with respect, and with critical thinking backed by researched facts. The best weapons are knowledge, commitment, peaceful approach, and tenacity, which can now be amplified through social media and the World Wide Web.

An average citizen lives passively, but a patriot acts on behalf the country against any kind of threat, internal or external. For a patriot, actions are stronger than words. Some say that patriots protect our land while a nationalist protects the way we live. I certainly consider myself both. Canada is a diverse and multicultural country but, because of its young age, falls short in its sense of national identity compared to Mexico and the United States. But patriots and nationalists love our diverse cultural background and our equality and tolerance, while acknowledging our deficiencies and making an effort to improve and protect our existing values and beliefs. We embrace our languages and our increasingly diverse heritage.

Allowing things to happen that risk our future security or diminish our democracy shows a lack of love for the country. Internationally, Canadians are known as "nice" people, but also as conformist, passive, and even complacent. If true, this is a national problem, not the solution we are seeking.

Hard Facts and Initial Solutions

Throughout history, the ruling class has divided the middle and lower classes from each other and within each class in order to "divide and rule." They have done this very successfully. They accentuate any differences through all the different means of communications they control in cahoots with the government, and as a result, the middle and poorer classes are never able to join forces. The strategy of "divide and rule" or "divide and conquer" has been implemented since primitive times. It was mastered by the Romans under Julius Caesar, the French under Napoleon and the British in India, where they managed to drive a murderous wedge between Muslims and Hindus that, sadly, still exists today.

The ruling class stokes differences among people using race, religion, gender, sexuality, income, social status, education, job opportunities, and a myriad of other factors. At the same time, they provide pacifiers in the shape of national events, holidays, festivals, television, movies, celebrities, sports, selective news coverage, social media monitoring, advertising, technological gadgets, etc. It is well known that the ruling classes purchase excellent legal advice and use whatever loopholes their expensive lawyers can find to avoid paying taxes while the middle class and working class pay the brunt. The more educated people are, the harder they are to distract and control, which is why in many countries education is only accessible to the elite, especially opportunities to go and study abroad. The masses swim in a pool of disinformation and ignorance. Many feel comfortable because of a distorted sense of security. They fail to see the reality, or if they do see it, they refuse to accept it. We are also absorbed in trying to survive, provide for our families, and, if possible, save for a dignified retirement after our energy has been drained dry.

The average person is smothered with superficial truths and misleading or incomplete data about our economy and social issues. The media echo the messages and strategies of the government and ruling class like a synchronized group of beating drums, bombarding people's minds and numbing their understanding and reasoning. This makes people believe the media's hypnotizing melody about "long-lasting progress." Canada is now undergoing serious economic and financial changes. As of March, of 2018, the main symptoms are high government and personal debt, high trade deficits, increasing interest rates, high unemployment, steep inflation, and a devaluated Canadian dollar. By Feb 27, 2018, PM Trudeau's Liberal party revealed its 2018 federal budget, which details an $18.1 billion deficit. Unfortunately, PM Trudeau insists that spending borrowed money is still good for Canadians. In the United States, two other serious symptoms are afflicting factors, an overvalued dollar and the fact that over half of the US debt is in foreign markets, puts its economy, at the mercy of external variables and decision makers the US cannot control. If the petrodollar collapses, so does the United States, and the odds for this to happen, are high.

Some analysists believe the Canadian economy is in deeper trouble, especially since PM Trudeau got into power. According to Ashley Csanady in the National Post (Jan 5, 2017), government debt in Canada now tops 1.3 trillion dollars. The government will have to pay $25.9 billon in interest payments in 2017 alone. Infrastructure maintenance and improvements are desperately required throughout the country, so the debt is expected to spike. In the meantime, our gross domestic product (GDP) has experienced the steepest decline since 2009, augmented by the impact of the Fort

McMurray fire that destroyed the city and disrupted tar sands production. When GDP decreases, government debt increases, the international trade balance goes further into the red, and pressures on the dollar increase. Meanwhile, the price of our most valuable commodity, oil, remains low and our unemployment rate is still too high. What can we logically expect in the near future?

I cannot avoid asking myself the following: Is Prime Minister Trudeau the celebrity we want him to be or the businessman and politician the country needs? He is certainly very charismatic, and many people love him for this. But he is definitely no businessman, and when the economy comes crashing down and the personal financial situation of the average Canadian family deteriorates, I wonder if people are still going to love those charismatic looks or demand more business and political acumen. We all truly and sincerely hope he does step up to the plate and transcend his experience as an elementary math teacher, his traditional political upbringing, and his limited entrepreneurial experience.

Initially, waiting in the wings was Kevin O'Leary, a self-made businessman and billionaire who fully understands long-term economics, finance, manufacturing, and international balance of trade and how to promote Canada's GDP while reducing government debt and getting a grip on a steep downward-sliding economy, which was barely noticeable by many.

Many Canadians seriously question many of PM Trudeau's liberal party decisions, like donating $2.65 billion "over the next five years to help developing countries fight climate change" (Rosemary Barton, *CBC News*, Nov 27, 2015). At the same time, Prime Minister Trudeau broke several promises by allowing the Trans Mountain pipeline expansion project to increase transportation of 300,000 to 890,000 barrels of oil per day. He also allowed the expansion of Enbridge Line 3 pipeline from 390,000 to 915,000 barrels of oil per day. As Carol Linnitt (desmog.ca, Nov 9, 2016) reports:

> According to Environment and Climate Change Canada, the two pipelines combined represent an increase of 23 to 28 megatons of carbon dioxide equivalent released into the atmosphere. Under the Paris Agreement Canada pledged to reduce emissions 30 per cent below 2005 levels by 2030. Canada's current policies aren't expected to meet those targets. According to a recent analysis by Climate Action Network, Canada is expected to miss those targets by 91 megatons.

Security is not limited to external and internal terrorist attacks only, which in fact represent a drop in the bucket compared to environmental threats and a state of economic and financial disarray. Is national security enhanced when governments donate billions of dollars to causes abroad while millions of their own citizens are discriminated against or live in poverty? Is that the kind of security people vote for and aspire to?

Now guess what? All of the above may actually be irrelevant to most people. The average cultured and educated person knows many of these problems already, but the great majority seem not to take an interest nor have the time to learn or do anything about these issues. Even to the educated, what does a 1.3 trillion-dollar deficit really mean? How can we truly know if this is too much or too little or assess its potential negative impact on our future? It seems we live in a dormant state. Perhaps, that is the best way to live nowadays. If we make sense of our reality and try to confront it head on, we will most certainly be accused of being ignorant, exaggerated, pessimist, and who knows what else? Should we simply be quiet and happy with what we have and hope nothing will happen?

An alarming additional obstacle is that an overwhelming number of Canadians also prefer economic growth to the protection of their environment. As mentioned earlier, a good example is the support that Prime Minister Trudeau gave to the Province of Alberta by approving the Kinder Morgan's Trans Mountain Pipeline, against his original promises to protect the environment and our ecosystem, regardless of the carbon tax. Trudeau just seeded the thought in every Canadian's mind that growth and development are more important than diversification, new initiatives, new technologies, less exploitation of our natural resources vs. increasing value-added activities with more manufacturing and a stronger commercial approach. Again, to my mind, it is about greed and power in preference to protecting our land and environment. I wonder why Albertans do not go and build residential areas close to the tar sands, while having their children grow up and "enjoy" that area as their backyard and playground? Is it perhaps because it is a toxic wasteland?

There is a famous book, "The Secret," by Rhonda Byrne, which has sold over 19 million copies worldwide. It is a wonderful book to apply to our daily lives, keep us hopeful, and encourage us to do our best to bring about life-changing results on the basis of positive thinking and the law of attraction. It will certainly help bring health, wealth, and happiness to some, but what Byrne appears to have left out of her book is that all these goals are cyclical. For example, in the crash of 2008, many lost everything they had previously achieved perhaps by applying "The Secret." Regardless, many ended up committing suicide. There is no doubt Byrne is much smarter from a marketing and sales point of view than many other writers. She limits herself to positive thinking, while other writers, like myself, go beyond this into actual facts, including the hard-core facts that many people prefer to avoid, but do happen and need to be handled head-on with courage and determination.

This reminds me of a small story that makes for an interesting comparison. Death asked Life why everybody loved her and hated him? Life answered, "because I am a beautiful lie and you are a sad reality." I certainly do not want to portray a sad reality, but the truth is undeniable, and as a resilient species, we need to open our eyes and acknowledge what is happening around us in a constructive manner. Jane Fonda visited Fort McMurray in early January 2017 to promote cleaner energy alternatives to the tar sands of Alberta, but the locals irrationally lashed out at her instead of focusing on winding down the oil extraction and supporting emerging clean energy programmes as their only hope for the future. The same thing happened when PM Trudeau accurately answered questions during his tour on Jan 13, 2017. He said that nobody can expect the oil extraction to cease immediately, but said it needed to be slowly wound down. Albertans reacted with outrage. Premier Rachel Notley declared that "the job of Albertans, and the job of Canadians, is to make sure that that world market looks to the oil sands, as they should, as the first choice for where they get that product from" (BBC News, Jan 13, 2017). However, regardless of the fact that Albertans are hurting from the low price of oil, they need to think about the future, because in matters of our environment, they are also in debt to the world, not just to themselves. To my mind, there are three main options people can choose from:

1. Don't we need to "take the bull by the horns" and avoid negative propaganda, subversive groups, anti-patriotic sites, unrealistic and extremist groups, pessimistic people, etc.? What we need is to expand our horizons and understanding by watching less television and fewer sporting events, caring less about celebrities, giving our mobile devices a break, avoiding phubbing, etc. We need to join the human elite that loves reading, information, education, and research and that, in a low and peaceful voice, seeks to protect their environment, their human rights and their security.

2. Shouldn't we reconsider what is really important? If people are comfortable the way they are, so be it, but at least we should all try to care about our environment and the economy by reducing consumerism, ending our accumulation of more and more "gadgets and things", avoiding trying to match or outshine our neighbours, controlling our expenses, increasing our savings, improving our patience, avoiding the distorted need for immediate gratification, focusing on real-life relationships, cherishing our families, and treasuring our friends.

3. Keep being who we are. Be happy and do not worry about anything. Just coast along and whatever happens, happens! Who cares about the future? We are not going to be around too long anyway. So simply let it be, covering our eyes and ears while keeping our mouths shut. They say silence is golden, don't they? Personally, I consider these types of people mediocre, lazy, and passively destructive, but I hope *The Runaway Trilogy* will help to change their attitude for the better.

Tragic Defects Versus Delightful Traits

It is ironic that, throughout history, humans have kept pushing the boundaries of hypocrisy, abuse, treachery, self-interest, discrimination, destruction, infidelity, mass murder, slavery, etc., but at the same time the human species is unique and sincerely admirable. We also possess the ability to be grateful, creative, inventive, caring, protective, helpful, respectful, honest, loyal, artistic, proactive, inventive, etc.

In the past, we have survived through a balance between our negative and our positive traits. Unfortunately, these traits resemble the tides and waves. They come and go as they please and at their own natural and uncontrollable rhythm. Forces outside of our planet control the ocean tides, but human actions are controlled by four main forces: survival instinct, greed, faith, and sometimes by plain stupidity. I will bring to the table three brief examples of what I am trying to explain. These three examples are known worldwide, so I expect the reader will see clearly what I am trying to illustrate.

1. On December 28, 2016, the US Secretary of State, John Kerry, gave a speech on the two-state solution for a long-lasting peace between the Palestinian and Israeli people. Kerry said Israel could be either Jewish or democratic but not both. The United Nations Security Council had voted 14 to 0 in favour of Israel ceasing further settlement expansion into Palestinian territory, which started in 1967 and has been increasing ever since. According to the Security Council, the settlements are a "flagrant violation of international law and of the Geneva Convention." For once, the United States did not veto the resolution, and Israeli Prime Minister Benjamin Netanyahu lashed back, accusing Kerry of "false moral equivalence" between construction of settlements and Palestinian terrorism. Surprisingly, in the autumn of 2016, the US government had agreed to a $38 billion memorandum of understanding that allotted more than 50 per cent of total US foreign military aid to Israel in order to "sustain Israel's qualitative military edge for years to come." In 1947, only roughly 10 per cent of Palestine was occupied by Jewish residents and 90 per cent by Arab Palestinians. By 2000, the proportion was reversed, and Palestinians continue to lose more land by the day due to non-stop Israeli settlement within Palestinian's territory.

    According to various sources (i.e.: jweishvirtuallibrary.org) the population of Muslims and Christians in Palestine represented 68.63 per cent and the Jews only 31.37 per cent. By 2013 the Jewish population grew exponentially due to continued expansion of settlements in Palestine representing and astonishing 75.83 per cent of the total population, while Muslims and Christian represented the remaining 24.17 per cent. Many countries around the world are very worried about this, but Israel's politicians disregard their concerns and continue expanding their settlements.

2. In India, the population was brutally exploited both socially and economically, murdered, executed, and heartlessly starved by the British Empire during 200 years of British colonization. Millions and millions of Indians died. Dr. Shashi Tharoor (Congress MP and former cabinet minister), author of *An Era of Darkness – The British Empire in India*, among many other books, became famous overnight after the tape of a speech he gave at the Oxford Union Society went viral through Youtube. In his speech, Tharoor proved that British colonization brought misery and suffering to the Indian people, pointing out that India's share of the world economy plummeted 23 per cent to less than four per cent under British rule. While the British economy rose on the shoulders of India's counterparts, the Indian people fell into a subhuman existence in many areas of their country. Tharoor destroys the "myth" of all those "British gifts" such as railways, bridges, highways, ports, and other infrastructure, as well as democracy and political unity.

Dr. Tharoor shows that all these "advances" were brought to India only to facilitate the exploitation of the colony for the benefit of the British and other Europeans. The British built up India exclusively for the sake of their own trade and power, not for altruistic purposes:

> The British industrial revolution was built on the premise of the de-industrialization of India. In the 19th century, India was Britain's best cash cow, the world's biggest importer and exporter of British goods and the source of highly paid employment for British civil servants. Indians literally paid for their own oppression.

He estimates that close to 29 million people died of starvation in British-induced famines during the colonization. He gives the example of the Great Bengal Famine that took place between 1769 and 1773 in the lower Gangetic plain of India, when over four million people died. Another of his examples example concerns Winston Churchill:

> As a matter of British ... policy [Churchill] diverted essential supplies from civilians in Bengal to ... Europeans as reserve stockpiles. For Churchill, the starvation of underfed Bengalis mattered much less than the sturdy Greeks – Churchill's actual quote. When conscious British officials wrote to him pointing out that people were dying because of this decision, he peevishly wrote in the margins of the file: "Why hasn't Gandhi died yet?"

Violence and racism was at the core of the colonial experience. As Tharoor quips, "no wonder the sun never set on the British Empire, because even God could not trust the British in the dark." While Churchill is a hero to most British people, for Indians he is a symbol of torture, abuse, and a murderer of millions of their compatriots.

Now, everybody knows that the Spanish conquered America and brought unforgettable terror, along with the horrors of the Spanish Inquisition, from the southern tip of Chile and Argentina to northern California, and from Haiti to Cuba to Florida and almost everything in between. They were ruthless conquerors who humiliated, enslaved, and massacred the native Americans, regardless of the country they set foot in. They completely destroyed beautiful, advanced, and mainly peaceful cultures such as the Aztecs in Mexico and the Incas in South America. With this in mind, I will now use Cuba as my third example.

3. Cubans have always battled for their independence, but Spanish colonialism lasted close to 500 years, from when Christopher Columbus (Cristobal Colón in Spanish) "discovered" America, landing in Cuba on Oct 28, 1492, until the War of Independence from 1895 to 1898. Did Columbus really *discover* America and Cuba? Of course not; they had always been there, and native Cubans had occupied their island for at least 4,000 years.

After Columbus' arrival, the Spaniards began the biggest and bloodiest colonial conquest that any nation has ever perpetrated. To some historians, their atrocities were worse than those committed by the Greeks, Romans, British, Germans, Mongols or any other colonial culture. After 10 years of Spanish colonization in Cuba, over 92 per cent of the native population had been exterminated, either by direct murder or by diseases brought from Spain that they had no immunity for. This is the reason why the Spanish started enslaving and importing Africans to Cuba and other parts of the Americas. Over 12 million Africans were brought as slave laborers, an estimated 1.4 million of whom died during their trip due to subhuman conditions.

In the nineteenth century, various other Spanish colonies in South and Central America all the way north including Mexico, succeeded in winning their independence from Spain, except Cuba. The Spanish had enormous economic interests in Cuba through the tobacco and sugar industries, which were so lucrative that Spain resisted until the very end of the century. It was not until Valeriano Weyler, a Spanish general, constructed concentration camps to quell the independence movement that Cubans turned for help to the United States. Then President William McKinley sent the USS Maine battleship to Cuba, but it was blown to pieces in Havana harbor. The perpetrators have never been identified, but many believe the US engineered the explosion in which 261 sailors (out of 355) lost their lives as a pretext for war with Spain. The next day, US newspapers began whipping up support for war with headlines such as "Bloodthirsty Spaniards Blow Up US Man-Of-War Maine in Havana Harbor."

The US government quickly declared war on Spain and, thanks in large part to a commando group called the "Rough Riders" led by Theodore Roosevelt, the US and Cuban rebels drove the Spanish out. The US Navy then destroyed the Spanish fleet as it tried to escape back to Spain, freeing Cuba from Spanish power at last. However, although Spanish colonization ended in 1898, it was replaced by US friendly "domination." As typical American "democratic" practice shows, nothing comes easy and much less free. It was time for the Cubans to pay back the assistance they had received from the US. From a colony of Spain, they turned into a US client state run in the interests of American corporations, even after the new Republic of Cuba gained formal independence on May 20, 1902. Unfortunately, this "independence" came at a very high cost. They had to sign the Platt Amendment, part of the 1901 Army Appropriation Bill, which imposed strict conditions on Cuban independence. The two main conditions were to allow the United States to establish military bases in Cuba, the most known at Guantanamo Bay, in order to ensure US control of the Caribbean and the Panama Canal, then under construction, and to assert the US right to intervene in Cuba whenever it wanted for the benefit of the United States' government as much as their private companies established in Cuba at the time.

Some Fundamental Questions

The Jewish people have fought for their rights throughout the world on a daily basis since the Holocaust, and with absolute justification. About 5.5 million Jews were horribly murdered in that genocide. I have never heard or seen elsewhere of such a successfully coordinated campaign. It continuously presents the Holocaust as a uniquely terrible event, and they have the right to do so, but we rarely hear about the 29 million people who died in India as a result of the British invasion or the tens of millions of native Americans massacred by the Spanish conquistadores in South, Central and North America. This makes me want to ask two questions:

1. Is it time for the Indians and the Native Americans to ask for apologies and compensation from the British and Spaniards respectively? Should they demand all the gold, silver, and art stolen from them to be paid back or returned? Should they repossess those lands that are currently in the hands of the descendants of the British and Spanish invaders?

2. Should we keep holding current and future generations of Germans hostage without also opening the doors for other nations to hold current and future generations of the British and Spanish hostage as well?

   I certainly do not have an answer to these questions, but the discrepancy is obviously unfair. Democracy implies equality, but this situation certainly does not honor that definition. What is fair for one has to be fair for the other, unless we live in a dictatorship or a monarchy, correct? We should never forget the past, but we should either let it go, or all claim in unison what is rightfully ours. However, the past is past, and we should learn from it by not making the same mistakes again while focusing in the future only. We need to learn to let go, but we should do this unanimously and with equality for all parties concerned, without exceptions. What do you think?

   But if we are not going to try and achieve the above, then we need to develop the unity, pride and very strong identity the Jewish people have, above and beyond many other nations. They have an amazingly strong sense and consciousness of their origins, their freedom, their land, their flag, national anthem, their language, their memories throughout history, etc. to mention a few. That alone, is to be admired and serve as an example to follow by other nations.

Do Humans Change?

Faith, trust, understanding, and positive change are the basis of my personal philosophy and of my hopes. However, I have to admit that every day those principles are tested by events somewhere on our planet fueled by greed, oppressive political power, or selfish economic and financial interests. I also fear that technology is rapidly becoming a means to control people in a network of surveillance, shattering our individuality, privacy, freedom, and other rights. Against all my values, I have to admit that as a species, humans will probably not change. To prove this one last time, I invite readers to read the following declaration that Charlie Chaplin once made:

> I'm sorry, but I don't want to be an emperor. That's not my business. I don't want to rule or conquer anyone. I should like to help everyone if possible- Jew, Gentile, black men, white…
>
> We all want to help one another. Human beings are like that. We want to live by each other's happiness, not by each other's misery. We don't want to hate and despise one another. In this world, there is room for everyone. And the good earth is rich and can provide for everyone. The way of life can be free and beautiful, but we have lost the way.
>
> Greed has poisoned men's souls; has barricaded the world with hate; has goose-stepped us into misery and bloodshed. We have developed speed, but we have shut ourselves in. Machinery that gives abundance has

left us in want. Our knowledge has made us cynical; our cleverness, hard and unkind.

We think too much and feel too little. More than machinery, we need humanity. More than cleverness, we need kindness and gentleness. Without these qualities, life will be violent and all will be lost. The aero plane and the radio have brought us closer together. The very nature of these inventions cries out for the goodness in man; cries out for universal brotherhood; for the unity of us all.

Charles Chaplin wrote this in 1940 at the beginning of the Second World War nearly 80 years ago, but we have not changed one iota since then. If anything, we have gotten worse thanks to much more sophisticated weaponry and other technologies. What makes the reader believe we will ever change? Hope, promises, trust, desires, dreams, etc. are all beautiful lies when compared to humanity's instinctive inner nature. I am not being negative but only realistic. I am not being hypocritical but honest. Do not crucify me; I am just a humble messenger. By the way, I am not stating that change is impossible or that no one is capable of changing as an individual. Such change is happening. But as a species, I doubt we can ever change even in the face of climate change and its consequences. We have too many opposing cultures, traditions, beliefs, ideologies, financial and economic interests, and, above all, our stone-cold uncontrollable human greed.

The Greek philosopher Plato (fl. 428 B.C.), who was the student of Socrates and later the teacher of Aristotle, said that four virtues needed to be followed and treasured: wisdom, courage, self-control, and justice. Have humans learned that lesson yet? Have we applied those virtues to our daily lives? Will we ever learn them or ultimately abide by them? I do not think so. Perhaps artificial intelligence is the only long-term solution, but it could easily turn out to be the cause of our own demise. This reminds me of what Dr. Cornel West, Professor Emeritus at Princeton University, has always tried to inculcate. His formula for happiness is "live, love, and laugh," but only a minority of humans are truly conscious of the deep significance of this and actually try to apply it responsibly in their daily lives.

Self-Segregation

On Feb 20, 2017, Stephen Fuhr of The Daily Courier, published "Muslim MP doesn't deserve torrent of insults". Ultimately, this was a direct result of the mosque attack on Jan 29, 2017 in Quebec City where more than 50 people were at the "Grande Mosquée de Québec" for a Sunday evening prayer, when a local Canadian terrorist attacked and killed six people and injured many more. Even though many people across Canada, like myself, had seen this coming, we never expected it to happen that soon. Why? Unfortunately, when minority groups start portraying themselves as exclusive and unique, like Quebec has done in comparison to the rest of the Canadian provinces, problems are bound to happen. Yes, Quebec is certainly a distinct society, but constantly insisting on this has caused serious problems for our nation and is the main reason the 1982 Constitution has still not been 100 per cent approved. Regardless, I fully understand and respect Quebec's position, so we require finding a better solution.

Let me give you a small example of what happened after the mosque attack, though before I do this, I want to send my sincere sympathy to all Muslims across Canada for their loss. My thoughts are with you, and I mean this from my heart. Having said that, allow me to bring to your attention, with due respect, what many people across Canada saw when Boufeldja Benabdallah (co-founder of the Islamic Cultural Centre of Quebec and the representative of the Muslim community in Quebec) said when interviewed by the media (CBC News). Benabdallah was speaking fluently in English about his personal sentiments and experience regarding what happened and how the Muslim community felt, when he suddenly stopped and said, "sorry for my English, but I am French." Like many other Canadians, I was surprised to hear him say publicly that he was French, instead of saying he was Canadian. Where is our identity as a country and as true and unique Canadians?

If Benabdallah does not want to be seen and treated differently by people across Canada, why did he separate and mark his community as a different society, which only angers others in Canada, even perhaps to the extent of contributing to the creation of internal terrorism, not just external terrorism? Again, I am trying hard to say this from a neutral point of view and with absolute respect, but aren't Benabdallah and all the Muslims in Quebec Canadian first and then Quebecois? Where does the "French" come from? Aren't they already segregating themselves from the rest of Canada? In my case, I am Canadian first and then British Columbian, then Mexican and then North American. Quebec is a province that accepts integration, multiculturalism, and tolerance, but at the same time, they separate themselves from the rest of Canada as a nation within our nation. This idea is quite confusing to many Canadians. If we Canadians cannot put our act together and end the distinctions that cause divisions among our provinces, how can we expect peace, quiet, and respect among immigrants, refugees, and asylum seekers?

In Fuhr's article in the Daily Courier, he mentions that the Liberal politician Ms. Iqra Khalid has endured a "torrent of insults" from the public and politicians because of her private member's motion 103 before the House of Commons to "quell the increasing public climate of hate and fear, and condemn Islamophobia and all forms of systemic racism and religious discrimination." To many Canadians, however, she is singling out Islam and putting it above other religions. According to Fuhr, many Canadians immediately expressed their outrage that Parliament would consider supporting the motion. Isn't this like trying to put out a burning frying pan with water?

The above reminds me of the controversial issue of Quebec nationhood, when ex-Premier Stephen Harper entered into the debate by saying he would introduce a motion recognizing that Quebecers form a nation "within a united Canada." First, they demanded the title of Quebecois instead of "French Canadians," then the concept of "distinct society" kicked in, and now they insist on the idea of a "nation within a 'united' Canada." If this is granted, they will most likely be asking, from a position of strength compared to the past, for their independence and complete separation from Canada. Who knows? That might end up being the best thing. Quebec has something very valuable that the rest of Canada seems to lack, deep values and stronger identity. This reminds me of the margarine ad where there is a tiny innocent girl with freckles on her cheeks looking shy and timid, but when a hand shows up offering a cracker with margarine, she strikes with an amazing dinosaur-style bite that almost rips off the helping hand of the other person. The more you give people, the more they want. That, unfortunately, is human nature, and we cannot change it. Let's be honest with ourselves; it is in our DNA. So, the question remains: shouldn't the government draw a strict line and say enough to uniqueness, distinctiveness, and self-segregation when these cause conflict? Is that the tolerance and multicultural society we want to live in, where there is plethora of distinctiveness and exclusivity to the extent of curtailing our rights to speak freely, and respectfully use words like Islam, Muslim, Judaism, Christian, Catholic, etc. without being called bigot, racist and anti …. whatever?

In the eyes of many, the inclusion of the word Islamophobic is not required and could be inflammatory. It should not be viewed separately from "all forms of systematic racism and religious discrimination" and is very wrong, regardless of the fact that it was voted for 165-126 in the House of Commons, where Prime Minister Trudeau voted in favour of including the word Islamophobia. It seems to me that Trudeau himself is pushing for future social problems by dividing and acknowledging condemnation of Islamophobia rather than condemning all forms of systematic racism and religious discrimination. In the past, the term anti-Semitic was also included and acknowledged separately.

Unfortunately, Trudeau and the majority of the House of Commons did not learn from that mistake. In my mind, this puts at risk people's social views towards Muslims and Islam. The rights of many Canadians are being squashed to uphold the rights of the minority, in this case the rights of Muslims, who are already creating social waves of unrest not just in Europe, but now in North America too. I hope I am wrong, but I am afraid that by acknowledging the Liberal's motion 103, we are giving the Muslims strength as a unique religion in our society in comparison to others, creating fear, and angering people who might one day lash back with aggressive actions similar to the Quebec City mosque attack of Jan 29, 2017.

In the edition of January 28, 2017, the National Post (reprinted in the Vancouver Sun) published an article entitled "Is Kellie Leitch for real?" in which former Conservative MP, Ms. Kelly Leitch, was quoted as stating that "the elites are out of touch with the average Canadian. Along with the insiders and the left-wing media, they are pushing their open border and globalist agenda." Well, many Canadians strongly agree with Leitch. They also believe immigrants, refugees, and asylum seekers should be tested for anti-Canadian values not just to keep our country safe, but to promote a quick and proper integration. This is why many Canadians liked Kelly Leitch and would have voted for her is she would have remained as a candidate for the Conservative party. In the same article, there is a comment by a worried Canadian named Don Link, who grew up in Calgary and says:

I see things changing for the worse. I envision – looking at what is happening in Europe at the moment, in Germany, France, Belgium, England – that Canada is going the same direction. I think Canadian Muslims are trying to impose Sharia Law in Canada. It is happening already.

Unfortunately, that same feeling is already in millions of Canadians and growing. They fear for their children's peaceful future. We do not really know if things will get worse or not, but look at the European example and to a wise saying in Spanish that goes, "If you hear the river roar, it is because it's carrying lots of water". Another saying is, "Where there is smoke, there is fire." But one thing is definitely sure, if our government fails to provide a fertile land for a smooth and proper assimilation, then multiculturalism and parallel societies will prevail, darkening the future of our young Canadians, whom now, cannot see the difference, and much less foresee the future.

Personally, I am confused by all this and very uncomfortable. It is pulling us away from unity and inclusiveness and the goal of achieving our own solid identity. It is like putting dry wood in the fire and expecting it to put the fire out. Now, let me tell you a little story. An Arab Muslim friend of my brother once stated, "Westerners should not force their values upon immigrants. They should provide the venues for our education and righteousness." Personally, I found that absurd, because to me the term "righteousness" already has a religious tone. Behind that religious tone there are moral beliefs supporting that righteousness. Whose moral beliefs are we to follow, ours or theirs? Which are correct and which are wrong? Aren't they supposed to follow ours, which we have had for hundreds of years in our own North American land? In the eyes and understanding of many North Americans, they are the ones coming from faraway lands and need to adapt. In my personal view, each individual should be free to practice his or her own moral values in an absolute private and intimate setting, and the rest have to respect that. But publicly, all religious symbols, expressions, and actions should be absolutely banned. Quebec is working on this already through the Charter of Quebec Values. I find some points of the charter very smart and practical, in fact absolutely necessary to keep peace and harmony among the Canadian people, which is a mosaic of nationalities (totally multicultural) from all over the world. The points I agree with are as follows:

- Establish a duty of neutrality and reserve for all state personnel.
- Limit the wearing of conspicuous religious symbols.
- Make it mandatory to have one's face uncovered when providing or receiving a state service.
- Amend the Quebec Charter of Human Rights and Freedoms.

Whatever will go through, the spirit of avoiding division and segregation has to be there for the benefit of all Canadians and not just Quebecois. Other provinces should follow suit. The Canadian government should truly make an effort to integrate Canadians first, put aside completely any religious individual acknowledgments and religious connotations, and stop pretending to be multicultural and tolerant when we are only multicultural but not tolerant, as falsely marketed abroad. That might be why the Conservative candidate at the time, Kevin O'Leary, referred to Trudeau as a "surfer dude" who is having a wonderful adventure, but "killing the country." Many Canadians just see him as a celebrity with charisma, a nice smile, but no business substance, that is, no real knowledge of economics, finance, and national security. Before withdrawing, O'Leary said: "if I am chosen as the Conservative leader, I will go against PM Trudeau immediately and that is going to get ugly". He stated "2019 is not an election, it is an exorcism."

In modern societies, nobody should ever single out their own values or beliefs as better than others if they are in search of cooperation, understanding, and integration. With this in mind, I once read something on the sign of a protester in a women's rights event that got stuck in my mind. Since then I have seen it stamped on T-shirts as well. It goes like this: "Men of Quality do not Fear Equality." I fully agree that both quality men and women with substance and education should not fear equality. Equality is a two-way street. Men and women of quality should not fear values different from theirs, as long as their values are also treated the same way by others, that is, with complete reciprocity. This is the only way a country can grow strong and remain at peace, by enabling integration and assimilation to come smoothly in future generations.

Placing women's and LGBTQ2 rights aside for a moment, a good example of perfect harmony to my understanding is how the Limburgish language in Holland has been existing in coordination and harmony within the Dutch population with pride since the sixteenth century. They have not tried to distinguish Limburgish as a distinct language from Dutch "within their nation." No doubt Europeans are more civilized and ahead of us in knowing how to handle some social affairs. They have kept their language in a non-confrontational way and have never imposed the Limburgish language above the Dutch language in areas of Holland where it is mostly spoken, contrary to what has happened in the province of Quebec, for example. The Dutch people, especially those that speak the Limburgish language, have diligently tried through centuries to preserve it and pass it along to the next generation, and in many areas, it is generally used as the colloquial language in daily conversations.

Inclusiveness and diversity sound very nice, but if we just talk about it and do not fully practice it, what is the point? We are portrayed to the world as a bilingual country, but it is embarrassing that not every Canadian speaks English and

French or is tolerant of the other. An average European speaks several languages quite fluently and has a big competitive edge over the average Canadian as a result.

Many people believe that before we brag about being multicultural and tolerant, we are in urgent need of teaching our kids to be true Canadians, and creating an identity and a pride throughout our country for our own style of music, food, sport activities, art, inventions, literature, poetry, two legal languages, etc. For example, Mexicans are very defined in who they are, their background, their values, their traditions, etc., but they also have their own identities state by state. However, their sense of Mexican unity is so strong that no immigrant can impose their values and traditions on Mexicans.

Immigrants in Mexico end up totally integrated while still enjoying their own subtle and non-imposing communities where they share their traditions and beautiful art, literature, food, and overall way of being. The majority keep their language, but Spanish and English are a must in the schooling system. Very similar phenomena happened in the rest of Latin America. In Brazil for example, the joy and honor of being Brazilian, by completely integrating and assimilating, has always been a matter of pride and is particularly strong. They are a good example to the world.

Critical Path

The United States and Canada have suddenly taken first place positions in the eyes of the rest of the world regarding issues of immigration and refugees. On March 6, 2017, the Trump administration proposed for the second time their new policy to eliminate security vulnerabilities by targeting countries that have been compromised by Islamic and other radical terrorists. The banned countries included Iran, Somalia, Yemen, Syria, Sudan and Libya. This time, Iraq was not included in the list. The overall reasoning behind the

Trump administration's strategy is to "keep America safe." At the same time, however, Prime Minister Trudeau has challenged the United States. Trudeau has famously pursued his "open door" policy. To some Canadians, this endangers the average citizen in the long term, and to the surprise of many, more than bombs, killings, cultural clashes in society, and abusive family relationships amongst the newcomers, the real threat is the negative economic and financial impact it has and will still have on the back of all Canadians.

While every other country in the world has started closing their doors to the excessive influx of refugees from various parts of the world, Canada is giving them easier access. As of February 2017, Canada is the destination, and the US is the main passage to that destination. Let us analyze a few matters briefly to provide the right perspective on the potential problems being seeded by Trudeau's Liberal government, and to the eyes of many, a mistaken open door approach.

There is a detailed and powerful article published by James Traub in the Foreign Policy Group on Feb 10, 2016 entitled "The Death of the Most Generous Nation on Earth: Little Sweden has taken in far more refugees per capita than any country in Europe. But in doing so, it's tearing itself apart." Sweden has been the most friendly and welcoming country in the world than any other country in the past, but even they have started to close their doors to refugees. This is not due to selective immigration, racism, or anti-refugee politics. It is strictly an economic survival strategy. Sweden simply cannot afford to continue providing immigrants and refugees with the assistance they need, until they become independent enough to care for themselves and their families. During the first quarter of 2018, most of the refugees come from countries like Somalia, Syria, Yemen, and Egypt for example. Compared to many refugees in the past, they are poorly educated, but adhere strongly to very different values than the Swedes. This is contrary to the influx from Bosnia that in the early 1930's arrived to Sweden with better education levels and similar moral and social values overall ("more moderate version of Islam"). It has been said that "accepting refugees is what means to be Swedish", but no more. Even Denmark has taken out ads in Arabic newspapers warning potential refugees that they will not be welcome and will be returned home. It has also passed a law to allow officials to seize the assets of immigrants who are already in Denmark to pay for their stay and care.

Swedes have stopped helping their own Swedish citizens as they ought to and, instead they have been helping refugees. This is ripping their society apart. Some Swedes say their government has "accidentally" neglected and abandoned its own citizens and dedicated more resources and attention to refugees. This also inflicts an unstoppable financial burden on their current and future generations. Traub wrote:

> Ivar Arpi, a columnist at the daily newspaper Svenska Dagbladet said: "People have lost friends over this; families are divided against one another. I've had agonizing discussions with my mother and my little sister". It is very hard to find a middle ground between 'we must' and 'we can't'.

> Diane Jansen, a senior foreign policy advisor to the Moderate Party (which Swedes look as Conservatives) stated: "recent generations of Swedish refugees, including Somalis, had been notably unsuccessful joining the job market."

Traub also added: "People change, cultures change. Society is there to give people the tools to change." Unfortunately, recent generations of refugees with stronger ties to Islamic traditions have failed to integrate. The integration and assimilation efforts by the Swedish government are vastly harder to achieve and are failing profoundly, because refugees seem more and more demanding and disruptive, making the whole process a lot more expensive.

Now, we need to acknowledge that many immigrants are demanding and disruptive, and to make matters worse, the majority discriminates against each other. It is so bad that Yazidis from Mosul (Muslims who practice a syncretic variant of the faith) are considered as heretics who are worse than Christian and Jews by the Islamic State. Traub then wrote that a Muslim person he interviewed told him that 'He could not live with Muslims'. Then Traub asked why and this person answered: "You have the white dog and the black dog, but they are both dogs", referring to discrimination among Muslims themselves and committing atrocities against each other. But being this a fact, would it be fair to ask ourselves the following: Are we supposed to accept both "creeds of Muslims" in our territories and expect they will get along in the future while fully respecting our laws and our values? Are we supposed to be more selective in what kind of Muslims to accept, or we should not "*discriminate*?"

According to Traub, Sweden has never experienced a terrorist attack on its soil, but the day this happens, a drastic negative change in Swedish public opinion is likely to spring up with a social negative force. Already, Swedes fear that they are losing their national identity to multiculturalism. In fact, Tauber also wrote "Paula Bieler of the Sweden Democrats describes herself as a nationalist, who fears that an increasingly multicultural Sweden is in serious danger of losing their national identity they have enjoyed in the past". Traub also quotes Thomas Gur, a critic of Sweden's open-door policy:

> In Sweden, there are more visceral fears, which cannot be raised inside the public opinion corridor. You cannot talk about concepts like marriage, shame, honor. You cannot talk about social trust. The fear is that the recent generations of refugees have become isolated from

Swedish life, as has happened with North Africans in French *banlieues*, the slums that have become incubators for alienation for many North African immigrants. Twenty years ago, Sweden had just 3 residential areas, but that number has substantially increased to 186 areas different from each other. For Swedes that is very troubling. Sweden has finally run out of room, money and patience.

Several questions for Canada arise from this. Should we promote and foster universal brotherhood without restrictions? If we do, how can Canada successfully achieve this when all other countries seem to be failing? Is a one-world approach and universal brotherhood what the younger generation is willing to accept? The world is dynamic and in constant evolution, so perhaps it is time to carefully consider a gentle and harmonious approach, but still a carefully monitored one.

Geographically speaking, in North America (and especially in Canada) we certainly have room for refugees. What we lack is enough money to support them unless the government goes into more debt by printing money or by asking for private donations. But the latter cannot just be a one-time donation. Shouldn't they commit to guarantee that refugees get up and running on their own feet, regardless of how long it takes them before the private donors stop supporting them? Or instead, should we impose a time limit and what would that be?

In the near future, perhaps Canadians will not be able to comfortably talk about social trust, abuse, marriage, shame, honor, or even about "Islamophobia." This word was recently included as a separate category in a definition of racism by PM Trudeau and other politicians, when they supported the anti-Islamophobia motion, separating it from the word of racism which arguably already includes it. In my opinion Ms Erin Mills (Member of Parliament in the House of Commons) fought well for her Muslim community, but she appeared disloyal to the rest of the Canadian people. For more information, please refer to an article published by Anthony Furey (Toronto Sun on March 11, 2017) entitled "Canada's so-called anti-Islamophobia motion is nothing but trouble". Please refer to: torontosun.com/2017/01/28/canadas-so-called-anti-islamophobia-motion-is-nothing-but-trouble).

Unfortunately, this Liberal administration is pushing Canada into an abysm of debt and into a deeper economic stress. The country seems naively proud of PM Trudeau's international trips, big handshakes, friendly smiles and his celebrity status. Unfortunately, he apparently suffers from something I call "superficial talk syndrome." He stutters when he speaks and often lacks concrete and knowledgeable solutions. During his trips to the Philippines, China and India on late 2017 and early 2018, his performance at higher levels fell below expectations. He even offended other dignitaries, such as President Duterte from the Philippines. But most importantly, the main example of lack of professional experience is how the federal budget is heading deeper into deficit with the Liberal party under his command. Joanna Smith wrote an article in the National Post (Mar 3, 2017) that says "Liberals aim to help 'worried' Canadians." In that article, she quotes Finance Minister Morneau admitting that "every day folks who work hard to provide for their families are worried about the future." That is the Canadian reality indeed. It is so alarming that even our respected political commentator Craig Oliver said the following in a CTV News interview with Marcia MacMillan: "without a plan of how to really manage the deficit, I am afraid that the government will lose control as it has done in the past." According to him, if there is no plan, there is no control. This ties in perfectly with how Joanna Smith ends her article:

> The deficit still remains nearly three times the $10 billion limit the Liberals promised in their campaign platform and while the budget's projections show it shrinking over time as the government expects

economic growth to pick up steam, there is still no official word on when they expect to get back to balance.

Now, for those that are either too naïve or extremely positive, I want to bring to their attention the following two examples.

1. "Helping hand or corporate handout?" asked Lisa LaFlamme on the CTV National evening news on Mar 30, 2017. She referred to Bombardier Canada (a Canadian multinational aerospace and transportation company) that asked to be bailed out by the government for the second time with another $1.3 billion loan. This time, PM Trudeau granted them a loan of $372 million instead. But Aaron Wudrick from the Canadian Taxpayers Federation said that nobody knows where that money is going and when it is going to be repaid. Meanwhile, Bombardier sliced 14,500 jobs and increased executive pay by 50 per cent. Yet, according to Trudeau, investing in Bombardier is ensuring long-term Canadian jobs. Many call this "corporate welfare." If the company did not generate jobs in the past, why should we believe it will do so now? In fact, Bombardier is being accused by Boeing of receiving subsidies and creating unfair pricing, which is the reason they "dumped" sales of their CSeries in a deal with Delta Airlines in 2016. On April 27, 2017, Leeham News and Comment published the following: "Boeing claims Bombardier sold the airplanes for about $20m, against a cost to build the airplanes of about $33m." If this is true, how can we keep bailing out a company whose management lacks business acumen, cuts thousands of jobs, drains our economic stability, and dares to increase their own management salaries?

2. Ford Co. Canada had a $10.6 billion profit in 2016, and its forecast for 2017 is $9 billion. If this is true, why did

Trudeau give Ford Canada $100 million grant? According to Wudrick, the grant looks like a corporate bribe to keep Ford Canada from going south of the border. Shouldn't the government be offering companies like Ford tax incentives instead of hard cash grants? Shouldn't these incentives be subject to the company's performance within Canada?

How do Prime Minister Trudeau and his Liberal government expect to reduce the national debt with such so-called investments? Once again, the Mexican saying comes to mind, which goes *"Farol de la calle, oscuridad de la casa."* In this context, it can mean any of the following:

"A great man but an awful father" or "He relates to others but not to his own" or "Friendly with strangers but a stranger with his own" or "Fake façade externally but his true face internally" or "a street light outside but darkness at home."

A Dash Of Hope

Luckily, we have other politicians and intelligent entrepreneurs who actually fully understand what it means to be Canadian and truly care about all Canadians rather than just specific minority groups. There are many good examples, but it is worth bringing just two examples to the table from among the Conservative party, where Andrew Sheers was elected the party leader. These are former Conservative candidates Mr Kevin O'Leary and Ms Kelly Leitch. Contrary to Trump's policy, O'Leary once publicly said he is a "proud, inclusive Canadian" (equal and accepted Canadian). He is committed to "embrace every culture and every religion." CTVnews.ca published this on Jan 14, 2016. It is important to mention that O'Leary's background is Lebanese, a country with strong Muslim traditions. He is a good example of a successful and perfectly integrated and to many, fully assimilated entrepreneur in Canada, regardless of his background. Regarding Kelly Leitch, she is still committed to multiculturalism, tolerance, and diversity, but under the umbrella of accepted Canadian values. In my understanding, inclusiveness for her is not enough, because integration or assimilation is her real end goal. Immigrants with different Western values, will reject integration or assimilation. She worked hard to release her list of these Canadian values, which can be summarized as follows:

- *Equal opportunity* – We must strive to ensure that everyone has as much of an equal opportunity to succeed as possible, especially our youth
- *Hard work* – Everyone must work hard and provide for themselves and their families
- *Helping others* – Once people become prosperous, we all are expected to give back to our communities to help others
- *Generosity* – Canada is a place that shows what is possible when hard work and generosity coincide
- *Freedom and tolerance* – A Canadian identity that is based on freedom and tolerance to allow each of us the chance to pursue our best lives and to become our best selves

Not everybody agrees with her knowledge and vision. Nothing is free in a normal and democratic country. Everybody needs to work hard and make sacrifices for a better future. But many people (immigrants, refugees, asylum seekers, and also Canadian-born) are used to just extending their hands and asking for help. Many immigrants avoid paying taxes, but expect all government services to be provided for them and even improved. If we want to have a strong and free country, we all need to work, pay taxes, and get along with each other, that is, accept and be accepted. It is a two-way street in which government provides adequate services, but we pay our corresponding share of taxes. Period!

Many immigrants and refugees come to Canada expecting a better quality of life, but they bring along with them their shady, under-the-table business practices. These go against our Canadian values, which need to be fully acknowledged and respected. Only by honoring and practicing our Canadian values can we continue being proud of our country, our international image, and our comfortable standard of living. We all have to give with devotion and humbleness to receive with pride!

"As boomers go, newcomers are the answer." This was the title of a cover story done in The Globe and Mail on Feb 18, 2017 and is the real reason Canada has open doors. The truth is that we desperately need new immigrants – carefully selected and properly screened – to help cover the country's economic needs. Why? Because the boomers are retiring and demanding their well-earned pensions. The average Canadian women does not seem to want children; being pregnant and educating their children is apparently too much work for them. They prefer to make money for themselves and be independent. It is so bad, that on February of 2018, Maclean's magazine published an article entitled "I wish I never had a kid. There. I said it." Unfortunately, we need Canadians born in Canada of Canadian parents. Though, let us be honest; we also need immigrants with good skills to help us pay for the past and current mismanagement of government funds, not just to replenish our small population growth. No doubt we need to increase and strengthen our gross national product (GNP) and above all, reduce our internal and external debt.

According to the government, the best way to do this is by having open doors to selected, productive immigrants and a limited, strict, and selective control of those coming as refugees. Personally, I believe that the most important factors to solve our problems are better education, full commitment, change of attitude, hard work, and strong hope and faith. We can achieve economic growth with a stronger and more diversified economy based on productivity, not just with an increase of our population base, unless it is selfishly selective.

Final Words

I cannot say for sure where we are heading or how to handle our growing problems with privacy, freedom, and security. I have exposed specific scenarios about where we come from, where we currently are, and where we are heading but the forecast is blurry and fuzzy, as are the potential solutions: full privacy, security and freedom are just a dream. Putting mathematical science aside, nothing in this world is absolute. That is a given. Artificial intelligence, in my mind, is really what is in our upcoming future.

During World War II, the Jewish people lost all their human rights, the population of India during British colonization also lost all their human rights, and the same thing happened to the native Americans under the Spanish conquistadors. Of course, things have changed since then. Human rights have expanded but with new limitations and conditions. The perfect example happened in Cuba under the US occupation. They gained back their freedom, but only under a different and less visible umbrella of oppression and control under the United States. Situations never go back to what they once were. We change and evolve through time at the rhythm of our new needs and circumstances.

If we were to vote either in favour or against the previous three examples (mentioned in detail in page # 296) regarding the Jews, the British, and the Spanish, we would immediately be shredded into pieces by those who think differently and have totally different interests and values from ours. This proves once more that human rights swing back and forth depending on time and place. They have always done so, and the worst is that they will keep on doing so in the future, like the pendulum of your grandfather's standing clock. We will never, ever please everybody. Not even close. That is the beauty or the curse of our species.

It is sad how humans value things only when they are gone, only value relationships when they have broken down, only value their children after they have left home to start their own lives, only value their parents after they pass away, only appreciate freedom after it is curtailed and privacy after it is robbed from us. In North America, we take our security for granted until it is threatened and learn how to be happy only after it is too late. We do not consciously appreciate and give thanks to the fact that our grocery store shelves are stacked full with an amazing array of brands and products. We take this for granted because we have never had a war or any real scarcity within our territory.

Shouldn't we just accept our surroundings and limitations and perceive our true potential and real possibilities, while learning to live in peace? Shouldn't we control our emotions and change what is within our reach to change, but let go of what is out of our reach? It is easy to get frustrated when we do not achieve what we thought we would or should, even if our goals were based on unrealistic premises. Accepting our destiny can be very valuable for our future development. But aren't we supposed to make our own destiny? We need to acknowledge, respect, and enjoy life and everything that surrounds us before we start our decline to what seems a black hole, which could be extremely dangerous. I humbly encourage all readers to be conscious and grateful for what we have, without indulging ourselves in excess, because times can change with the speed of a light switch. Protecting our environment, saving more, and getting more education (or just learning more) should be everybody's priority. But again, I am just the messenger. Go ahead and change or just keep on doing as you have always done. It is your choice and your "right" to do so.

I have always asked myself and still do: when will we control our emotional intelligence and our ability to acknowledge our own passions and sentiments, and those of others on equal basis? I certainly need to recognize the various feelings of failures and achievements we go through in life, as well as those of others to avoid prejudgment and censorship. We need to guide our understanding, our thinking, and our behavior with controlled emotional intelligence, along with critical and logical thinking. Only then will we have a chance to make positive, long-lasting changes in human affairs. But above all, let us leave passivity and conformism behind. The moment to claim our human rights and our emotional intelligence to "live, love, and laugh" is now, not tomorrow!

APPENDIX 1

The intention of this appendix is to enable the reader to understand the parallelism, with slight but important differences in approach, between "The Death of Common Sense" by Lori Borgman's book and my *Runaway Trilogy* (consisting of *Our Runaway Society*, *Our Runaway Globe*, and *Our Runaway Rights*). Below is Borgman's complete short essay.

Obituary of the Late Mr "Common Sense"

Today we mourn the passing of a beloved old friend, "Common Sense", who has been with us for many years. No one knows for sure how old he was, since his birth records were long ago lost in bureaucratic red tape. He will be remembered as having cultivated such valuable lessons as:

Knowing when to come in out of the rain; Why the early bird gets the worm; Life isn't always fair; and Maybe it was my fault.

"Common Sense" lived by simple, sound financial policies (don't spend more than you can earn) and reliable strategies (adults, not children, are in charge).

His health began to deteriorate rapidly when well-intentioned but overbearing regulations were set in place. Reports of a 6 - year-old boy charged with sexual harassment for kissing a classmate; teens suspended from school for using mouthwash after lunch; and a teacher fired for reprimanding an unruly student, only worsened his condition.

"Common Sense" lost ground when parents attacked teachers for doing the job that they themselves had failed to do in disciplining their unruly children. It declined even further when schools were required to get parental consent to administer Panadol, sun lotion or a band-aid to a student; but could not inform parents when a student became pregnant, and

"Common Sense" lost the will to live as the Ten Commandments became contraband; churches became businesses; and criminals received better treatment than their victims.

"Common Sense" took a beating when you couldn't defend yourself from a burglar in your own home and the burglar could sue you for assault.

"Common Sense" finally gave up the will to live, after a woman failed to realize that a steaming cup of coffee was hot. She spilled a little in her lap, and was promptly awarded a huge settlement.

"Common Sense" was preceded in death by his parents, "Truth", and "Trust"; his wife, "Discretion"; his daughter, "Responsibility"; and his son, "Reason".

He is survived by his 3 stepbrothers; "I Know My Rights", "Someone Else Is To Blame", and "I'm A Victim".

Not many attended his funeral because so few realized he was gone. If you still remember him, pass this on. If not, join the majority and do nothing (loriborgman.com).

APPENDIX 2

(Without Prejudice)

Letter from Lori Ackerman, Mayor of Fort St. John, British Columbia, Canada, published in the Vancouver Sun on Nov 30, 2016. It was published as an "advertisement," but she clearly means every word and very probably influenced a lot of readers, which seems to have been the intention of the article. For clarity, I have used the Times New Roman font and italicized her words below, with my comments in a larger and Helvetica style font after each of Ackerman's quoted section.

"USA Stops Importing Canadian Oil and Gas"

Dear British Columbia Citizens, that is not a current headline, but it could be. What would happen to our economy if it was?

Her headline is biased and based on a kind of Astroturf marketing (artificial creation of a grassroots buzz to promote a political viewpoint, product, or service). If the United States really stopped importing Canadian oil, we would just call "Lady Necessity." That is, we would turn to the creative and resourceful instincts that are part of our DNA but are currently kept dormant by the pure exploitation of our natural resources, regardless of the impact on our environment.

Ackerman: I would like to talk to you about energy, pipelines and our natural resources. I am a mum and a grandma and I have lived in the north all my life. I am also the Mayor of Fort St. John – right smack in the middle of one of the world's largest supplies of oil and gas. I live in a region surrounded by pipelines, wells, hydraulic fracturing (fracking) sites and canola and wheat fields. I have eaten the food we grow here and I drink our water. I understand what it takes to extract our natural resources and what it takes to protect our environment. I live it. I don't want to try to convince you of anything but I would like to share with you what I know to be true. I strongly encourage you to do some of your own research. Learn more than what you read in a tweet or a Facebook post. I have added some links to reliable resources below for you. Where does the petroleum we all use every day come from?

Her information all comes from pro-fossil fuel industry sources, suggesting that this "letter" is either a piece of paid-for advertising or a political stunt to boost the city's economy. All her sources are biased in favour of the oil industry. As corporations, institutions, or associations, they are almost all heavily involved, directly or indirectly, in the exploitation and commercialization of fossil fuels. They depend on this natural resource to survive and grow, and many, at the expense of our environment. How reliable are Mayor Ackerman's sources when their goal is to continue exploiting and exporting more and more crude oil and placing the critical balance of our environment and ecosystem last? Now, please do not take my word for this. Just Google a few of my sources listed below and be "*an informed citizen*," as Mayor Ackerman puts it.

1. What will feed the oil pipeline? It would obviously be Alberta's reservoirs known as The Tar Sands. Kindly Google "aerial view of the damage of the tar sands." Any image you see will be worth a thousand words, and here I rest my case.

2. "The tar sands are "the largest industrial project in human history and likely also the most destructive." The tar sands mining processes release "at least three times the CO_2 emissions as regular oil production" and the tar sands project is set "to become the single largest industrial contributor in North America to Climate Change" (oilsandstruth.org).

3. The Globe and Mail published an article by John Cotter on Feb 3, 2014 entitled "Environmental health risks of Alberta oil sands likely underestimated: study." The University of Toronto environment chemistry research group did the study, which is as alarming the headline suggests. I invite you to Google it yourselves and get informed.

4. Mapleleafweb.com states: Northern Alberta's oil sands are increasingly becoming a source of political conflict, both domestically and globally, as scrutiny of the world's second-largest known oil reserve intensifies. While recent production

in the oil sands has driven rapid economic growth in Alberta, there is increasing concern that this growth is causing unprecedented ecological harm. Major environmental non-government organizations (ENGOs), such as Greenpeace and the Pembina Institute, and local First Nations have begun to call for a moratorium on new oil sands projects until associated environmental destruction can be mitigated." Please visit this site to learn more shocking facts.

5. The Natural Resource Defense Council (NRDC) states the following in "The Dirty Fight Over Canadian Tar Sands Oil - Dredging up oil from under Canada's boreal forest and piping it through the United States is a lose-lose proposition":

Ackerman: Canada has some of the largest petroleum resources in the world and yet Canada imports 634,000 barrels of crude oil from foreign countries every single day. That is $26 BILLION of oil imports every year that we could have supplied to ourselves. That product arrives in tankers and is transported to where it needs to go by truck and train right through our communities. And yet we don't want our own product to flow in pipelines to our communities for our own use or to our ports so we can export it? That just makes no sense at all to me.

The Canadian National Energy Board confirms that eastern Canada does import crude oil from abroad because there is almost no infrastructure connecting western oil suppliers to eastern Canadian consumers. Apparently, Ackerman's true goal is not to provide eastern Canada with oil but to export it, even though we know very well that we should focus on cleaner, renewable energy while reducing Canada's internal demand for fossil fuels and not even contemplating their "export potential" due to its damaging environmental effects. Kindly visit: neb-one.gc.ca/nrg/ntgrtd/mrkt/snpsht/2014/11-01Imprt-eng.html

Ackerman: So let's talk about pipelines. I know pipelines are a safe, cost-efficient means of oil and natural gas transportation and emit fewer greenhouse gases than alternate transportation methods. Canada has

830,000 kilometers of pipelines. Three million barrels of crude oil is transported safely every single day. B.C. has over 43,000 kilometers of pipelines. If we took that oil out of the pipelines, we would need 4,200 rail cars to move it. How many of those cars would you like rolling through your community? Between 2002 and 2015, 99.9995% of liquid was transported through our pipelines SAFELY. You probably spill more when you fill up at the gas station. I understand you don't want tankers floating down our beautiful B.C. coast. But did you know the USA has been shipping up to 600,000 barrels a day of crude from Alaska to the Puget Sound through the Salish Sea for the last 20 years? Did you know that B.C. has a Tanker Exclusion Zone that has been respected for years? That zone stipulates that full tankers must travel on the west side of the zone but those that are not transporting goods can stay inside the protective zone. Other than one natural gas pipeline, Vancouver Island receives all of their petroleum by barge every day. I don't remember ever hearing anyone complain about that. According to Transport Canada over 197,000 vessels arrived or departed from west coast ports in 2015 - 1487 of them were tankers. 400,000 barrels of crude oil is safely transported off the B.C. coast every single day. Sooo.... I think we are OK there.

According to *CBC News*, the pipeline "safety incident" rate doubled in Canada in the past decade. Albert Hildebrandt wrote on Nov 8, 2013, that "according to figures from a National Energy Board (NEB) data set obtained under access-to-information by CBC, the rate of overall pipeline incidents has doubled since 2000." I wonder what the situation is three years later. Hildebrandt added:

"In the meantime, should we agree to save about $8 billion dollars of crude oil imports with this pipeline, which makes sense only while our country adapts to renewable and cleaner energy sources like other European countries are doing very successfully?"

Huffington Post Canada reported the following on Oct 28, 2013: "But while pipeline incidents may be less frequent, evidence suggests they spill more oil. A report this spring from the International Energy Agency said that pipelines spill three times as much oil per kilometer of transport distance, as rail."

A good example of this problem was Nexen pipeline spill in Alberta. Largest oil spill in Canada's history. Other nasty spills have included: Red Earth Creek in Nov 2014 (60,000 litres), Elk Point in June 2012 (230,000 litres), Red River in June 2012 (461,000 litres), Slave Lake in April 2014 (70,000 litres), and Little Buffalo in April 2011 (4.5 million litres). Regarding tankers transporting crude oil, we all remember the Exxon Valdez spill, which was extremely damaging to marine and wildlife, our oceans and air, with irreversible impact in our ecosystem. Mayor Ackerman does not seem to understand that just a few other disasters of this type could wipe out our pristine shores and all the marine and wildlife they sustain.

Ackerman: Emissions? 80% of the emissions associated with fossil fuels are generated in their combustion – not their extraction and transportation. If you want to do something about our reliance on fossil fuels then address the demand for them not the transportation of them. Change starts with consumers not industry. A large part of the demand for fossil fuels in B.C. is transportation. 33% of our fossil fuels are used to operate cars, trucks, planes, trains and ferries. If we switched all of that over to electricity we would need not just one Site C dam but 15 of them. Which communities do you want to flood to provide the energy for your electric cars? Remember I live 7 km from Site C dam so I have a pretty good understanding of them.

The above statement is simply and blatantly untrue. Please refer to sciencealert.com, where David Neil noted on May 12, 2016, that "95% of Germany's energy was provided by renewables last Sunday." If Germany can do it, so can everyone, Neil states. He adds: "As John Fitzgerald Weaver reports for Electrek, a sunny day and strong winds helped contribute to the record-breaking high. Energy consumption in Germany at the time came in at 57.8 gigawatts - solar power met 45.2 % of that total, wind power 36 %, biomass power 8.9 %, and hydropower plants 4.8 %."

Germany has steadily been increasing its use of renewable energy since 1990, while reducing consumption of oil, natural gas, nuclear power, and coal. Their renewable fuel sources in order of importance are: wind (36%), solar (21%), hydropower (5%), and other renewables (38%). Why can't we do the same in Canada instead of just exploiting our resources and damaging the environment in the process? Source: US Energy Information Administration – Independent Statistics and Analysis (eia.gov). Bloomberg.com published an article by Jessica Shankelman on May 16, 2016, in bloomberg.com where she confirms that: "clean power supplied almost all of Germany's power demand for the first time on Sunday, marking a milestone for Chancellor Angela Merkel's *Energiewende* policy to boost renewables while phasing out nuclear and fossil fuels."

In my personal opinion, Ackerman's statement is also unethical. By promoting the export of oil to other countries, she is encouraging what she acknowledges to be the main cause of CO2 emissions, the burning of fossil fuels, mainly for transportation. Now, *The Globe and Mail* published an article on Nov 25, 2016, entitled "Blue Fuel Energy: Liquid renewable electricity driving low carbon mobility." According to this article "[using] electricity produced from renewable forms like hydro and wind, Blue Fuel Energy's innovative and scalable technology transforms natural gas into a variety of low carbon fuels, including methanol, Sulphur-free gasoline and dimethyl ether – a diesel substitute." In other words, we do not need to exploit fossil fuels as much as we do for our transportation fuel needs, as Mayor Ackerman seems to want to do. We have the technology for Blue Fuel Energy. Let's focus on that instead.

Ackerman: I love this quote from Blair King an Environmental Scientist and Writer: He is telling us to look outside our province and see the impact we can have on GHG on our planet. Our LNG is cleaner than the stuff already on the market because our regulations are tougher and we emit far less GHG in our production than in other countries. Our natural gas industry is committed to continuous improvement. I understand that you are concerned about safety. I am too. In Canada, we have some of the strictest safety requirements in the world. Canada's oil and gas producers are continuously improving the safety of their operations and transportation of their products. Emergency Response Plans are customized for each community, covering key areas such as public safety, protection of community infrastructure, and a clear plan of action with local emergency responders. And we have the B.C. Oil and Gas Commission to oversee B.C. projects and the National Energy Board oversees the larger multi-jurisdictional projects. The Oil and Gas Commission is our provincial agency responsible for regulating oil and gas activities in British Columbia, including exploration, development, pipeline transportation and reclamation. Core responsibilities include reviewing and assessing applications for proposed industry activities, engaging with First Nations, cooperating with partner agencies, and ensuring industry complies with provincial legislation and all regulatory requirements. International delegations come to B.C., as world leaders, to learn how we have partnered environmental protection with resource extraction. I think the Oil and Gas Commission does a good job of protecting the interests of citizens.

Mayor Ackerman is strangely confident about the reliability of high-tech innovations, yet new safety technologies have constantly proved inadequate in the past. BP used to say that Deep Water Horizon was accident-proof – until the accident happened in 2010. The coastline in that area is still filthy, ocean life is still far from recovering, and many jobs (tourism and fisheries, etc.) have not recovered either.

Ackerman: Many of you have concerns about the rights of our Indigenous Peoples. I will not speak for them but I will provide you with a quote from Stephen Buffalo, President and CEO of the Indian Resource Council: "I think industry is now willing to be a partner (with First Nations). They want to come with the First Nations together. We are depending on these pipelines for the success of the Canadian economy." Here is the link to the full article: http:// business.financialpost.com/news/energy/ pro-oil-first-nations-seek-end-to-pipelinegridlock?__lsa=f499-1f26 So let's talk about the economy. B.C.'s energy sector offers some of the largest provincial economic opportunities in a generation.

Natives' rights on their remaining lands are constantly under threat from greed and so-called growth and development. In the US, for example, the federal government in Dec 2016, acknowledging the environmental damage potential to Indian reserve land and the violation of federal laws by the companies involved, halted the North Dakota Access pipeline.

The government's order came immediately after a judge had rejected a petition from the Standing Rock Sioux to stop the $3.8 billion construction of the pipeline that was planned to go through four states. As *AP-The Big Story* (bigstory.ap.org) reported: "The tribe, whose cause has drawn thousands to join their protest, has challenged the Army Corps of Engineers' decision to grant permits for the pipeline at more than 200 water crossings. Tribal leaders allege that the project violates several federal laws and will harm water supplies. Ancient sites have been disturbed during construction."

I will stop here and leave this point for the natives to defend, as they have been doing with devotion and high spirit for decades in the United States and in Canada. I take my hat off to them! I hope President Trump will not allow the pipeline to go through. Let's wait and see what happens.

Ackerman: It is estimated that, in 2010, 11.2% of the provincial exports came from the natural resource sector. That was over $21 billion worth. Canada's oil and natural gas sector contributes $1.5 billion to the provincial government but it is estimated that it could go as high as $2.4 billion per year. This is money for health care, education and infrastructure. The resource sector is the foundational stone upon which the B.C. economy was built, and it is as important today as ever. 440,000 Canadians are employed because of the oil and gas sector. A recent study by Philip Cross, former chief economic analyst at Statistics Canada, shows the huge economic value of the natural resource industry in B.C., and in particular the Lower Mainland. Cross' report demonstrates that over 55 percent of resource-related jobs and income (direct, indirect and induced) flow to the Lower Mainland. This means those workers contribute to our economy by renting or buying homes, buying groceries, enjoying a quality life and shopping their local businesses. Let's lead the world in resource extraction, continuous improvements and long term planning. Let's be leaders in reliable and renewable energy development. Let's support Canadian industry and stop buying foreign oil. Let's grow our economy by meeting our domestic needs and exporting our abundant resources. Let's live well now and in the future. Thank you for taking the time to be an informed citizen. Sincerely, Lori Ackerman, Mayor - City of Fort St. John.

We re-import our own natural resources (previously exported

raw) in the form of billions of dollars of finished goods from other countries that lack our resources. This is why our international trade deficit persists. What we really need in Canada is not "billions of dollars" from oil export revenues but effective policies and leadership from the government in cooperation with private companies willing to invest in the clean energy solutions that already exist and have been developed in Canada. A good example is the array of clean energy solutions the University of British Columbia has developed, including carbon capture (absorption) and water treatment technologies. This research, if put to use, will eliminate megatons of carbon emissions and save millions of barrels of fresh water. Unfortunately, we need Canadian investors (for example, oil companies wanting to diversify) in these technologies. The provincial and federal governments should provide proper support to any companies willing to invest, helping them by picking up the difference between the winding down of older technologies and the implementation of the new ones. For more information, please refer to: globeandmail.com/adv/clean50

I respectfully encourage Canadians and every North American not to fall victim to advertisements of the type quoted here from Mayor Ackerman. In my personal opinion, this type of propaganda is not just a betrayal of our duty to protect our planet, but promotes the elitist economic monopoly of a few international companies. Oil companies are fatally damaging our planet and putting people's futures at risk. When humans started extracting fossil fuels thousands of years ago, it made sense to do so. We needed to get out of the dark ages, and there weren't many of us. The earliest oil wells were about 250 feet deep and were drilled in China and Japan around 350 CE. But with recent technological advances and the population explosion forecast for the next 50 to 100 years, if we do not tighten our belts and control the enormous greed of these corporations and the few mega rich individuals behind them, not even their children will enjoy their billions of dollars.

APPENDIX 3

Australian Message to Immigrants

It is a fact of life how Muslims are immigrating heavily to many European countries as well as other places around the world. People in general can live with that fact, but what they cannot live with are two important aspects:

1. The radical Muslims that tag along with groups of regular and normal Muslims and or immigrants, and

2. The refusal by some immigrants to adapt and their continued attitude of supremacy, demanding we fit them into our society while bending our rules in their favour. When we hesitate, they complain and accuse us of being racists.

I want to quote in full what Australia's prime minister said several years ago and which has been published by CNBnews.net (October 17, 2007) and many other sources.

IMMIGRANTS, NOT AUSTRALIANS, MUST ADAPT. Take It or Leave It. I am tired of this nation worrying about whether we are offending some individual or their culture. Since the terrorist attacks on Bali, we have experienced a surge in patriotism by the majority of Australians.

However, the dust from the attacks had barely settled when the "politically correct" crowd began complaining about the possibility that our patriotism was offending others. I am not against immigration, nor do I hold a grudge against anyone who is seeking a better life by coming to Australia. However, there are a few things that those who have recently come to our country, and apparently, some born here, need to understand. This idea of Australia being a multi-cultural community has served only to dilute our sovereignty and our national identity and as Australians, we have our own culture, our own society, our own language and our own lifestyle.

This culture has been developed over two centuries of struggles, trials and victories by millions of men and women who have sought freedom. We speak mainly ENGLISH, not Spanish, Lebanese, Arabic, Chinese, Japanese, Russian, or any other language. Therefore, if you wish to become part of our society learn the language!

Most Australians believe in God. This is not some Christian, right wing, political push, but a fact, because Christian men and women, on Christian principles, founded this nation, and this is clearly documented. It is certainly appropriate to display it on the walls of our schools. If God offends you, then I suggest you consider another part of the world as your new home, because God is part of our culture.

We will accept your beliefs, and will not question why. All we ask is that you accept ours, and live in harmony and peaceful enjoyment with us. If the Southern Cross offends you, or you don't like A Fair Go, then you should seriously consider a move to another part of this planet.

We are happy with our culture and have no desire to change, and we really don't care how you did things where you came from. By all means, keep your culture, but do not force it on others.
This is OUR COUNTRY, OUR LAND, and OUR LIFESTYLE, and we will allow you every opportunity to

enjoy all this. But once you are done complaining, whining, and griping about Our Flag, Our Pledge, Our Christian beliefs, or Our Way of Life, I highly encourage you take advantage of one other great Australian freedom, "THE RIGHT TO LEAVE."

If you aren't happy here then LEAVE. We didn't force you to come here. You asked to be here. So accept the country that accepted YOU."

See more at: fix website) or at:
http://www.gloucestercitynews.net/clearysnotebook/2007/10/prime-minister-.html#sthash.TnTZXVYX.dpuf

It is my personal opinion that the quote above should apply to every immigrant entering a new country, regardless of the country of the immigrant's background and cultural values. As tough as it might sound, we cannot try to please everyone and go through life without offending a soul. The route to success does not require us to try pleasing everybody, or we will certainly fail profoundly. That is guaranteed!

NOTE:

To add a bit of humour, I want to remind the reader that there is a worldwide phenomenon known as "Vulcan Logic" (from the *Star Trek* movies and TV series) that states the basic principle societies should follow: The Needs of the Many Outweigh the Needs of the Few.

So, if you do not agree with me, then just follow what Mr Spock told Captain Kirk (who also completely agreed with him! … LOL … :-)

French Message to Terrorists

You Will Not Have My Hatred

By Antoine Leiris

(English Version: November 16, 2015)

On Friday night, you stole the life of an exceptional being, the love of my life, the mother of my son, but you won't have my hatred. I don't know who you are and I don't want to know – you are dead souls. If this God for which you kill indiscriminately made us in his own image, every bullet in the body of my wife will have been a wound in his heart.

So no, I don't give you the gift of hating you. You are asking for it but responding to hatred with anger would be giving in to the same ignorance that made you what you are. You want me to be afraid, to view my fellow countrymen with mistrust, to sacrifice my freedom for security. You have lost. I saw her this morning. Finally, after many nights and days of waiting. She was just as beautiful as when she left on Friday night, just as beautiful as when I fell hopelessly in love over 12 years ago.

Of course, I'm devastated with grief, I admit this small victory, but it will be short-lived. I know she will accompany us every day and that we will find ourselves in this paradise of free souls to which you'll never have access.

We are two, my son and I, but we are stronger than all the armies of the world. I don't have any more time to devote to you, I have to join Melvil who is waking up from his nap. He is barely 17-months-old. He will eat his meals as usual, and then we are going to play as usual, and for his whole life this little boy will threaten you by being happy and free. Because no, you will not have his hatred either.

Original French Version:

Vous N'aurez Pas Ma Haine

Vendredi soir vous avez volé la vie d'un être d'exception, l'amour de ma vie, la mère de mon fils mais vous n'aurez pas ma haine. Je ne sais pas qui vous êtes et je ne veux pas le savoir, vous êtes des âmes mortes. Si ce Dieu pour lequel vous tuez aveuglément nous a fait à son image, chaque balle dans le corps de ma femme aura été une blessure dans son coeur. Alors non je ne vous ferai pas ce cadeau de vous haïr. Vous l'avez bien cherché pourtant mais répondre à la haine par la colère ce serait céder à la même ignorance qui a fait de vous ce que vous êtes. Vous voulez que j'ai peur, que je regarde mes concitoyens avec un oeil méfiant, que je sacrifie ma liberté pour la sécurité. Perdu. Même joueur joue encore.

Je l'ai vue ce matin. Enfin, après des nuits et des jours d'attente. Elle était aussi belle que lorsqu'elle est partie ce vendredi soir, aussi belle que lorsque j'en suis tombé éperdument amoureux il y a plus de 12 ans. Bien sûr je suis dévasté par le chagrin, je vous concède cette petite victoire, mais elle sera de courte durée. Je sais qu'elle nous accompagnera chaque jour et que nous nous retrouverons dans ce paradis des âmes libres auquel vous n'aurez jamais accès.

Nous sommes deux, mon fils et moi, mais nous sommes plus fort que toutes les armées du monde. Je n'ai d'ailleurs pas plus de temps à vous consacrer, je dois rejoindre Melvil qui se réveille de sa sieste. Il a 17 mois à peine, il va manger son goûter comme tous les jours, puis nous allons jouer comme tous les jours et toute sa vie ce petit garçon vous fera l'affront d'être heureux et libre. Car non, vous n'aurez pas sa haine non-plus.

APPENDIX 4

O CANADA
CANADIAN NATIONAL ANTHEM (English version)
O Canada!
Our home and native land!
True patriot love in all thy sons command. .... (**See NOTE Below**)
With glowing hearts, we see thee rise,
The True North strong and free!
From far and wide
O Canada, we stand on guard for thee.
God keep our land glorious and free!
O Canada, we stand on guard for thee.
O Canada, we stand on guard for thee.

O CANADA
CANADIAN NATIONAL ANTHEM (Bilingual version)
O Canada!
Our home and native land!
True patriot love in all thy sons command.
Car ton bras sait porter l'épée,
Il sait porter la croix!
Ton histoire est une épopée
Des plus brillants exploits.
God keep our land glorious and free!
O Canada, we stand on guard for thee.
O Canada, we stand on guard for thee.

NOTE: Proposed Gender-Neutral Change in the Canadian National Anthem

"True patriot's love in all of us command"

APPENDIX 5

Brief Biography of the Author

Born and raised in Mexico City (D.F.) from 1958 to 1987. He studied his undergraduate degree in Economics (Mexico City) followed by a Master of Business Administration (MBA) in a joint programme between Notre Dame University (USA) and the London Graduate School of Business (England).

His professional career started as a professor and researcher in economics and finance in the Mexican banking system. He immigrated to Canada in 1987 where he concentrated on the creation and promotion of businesses under the 'turn-key-operation' concept. He assisted the Ministry of Economic Development at that time and created a database for businesses in the service industry for the provincial government.

In conjunction with government and banking programs, he worked to assist foreign business investors and local entrepreneurs establish and run a successful business. He assisted his various clients throughout their business start-up stage in trying to achieve their break-even point in the shortest and most efficient time possible, while trying to minimize their risks and expand their potential.

Carreras has acquired extensive professional experience in North America (Mexico, United States and Canada) and has travelled considerably for business and research throughout Europe, Asia and the American continent. As a researcher and writer, he is detailed and always tries to apply a logical and critical thinking to his overall framework and presentation.

As an Author:

His passion for writing is fueled by the desire to open people's eyes to what is happening around them. He trusts this will improve their life style and bring harmony to their lives. Throughout his "Runaway Trilogy", an important goal is to bring awareness regarding the delicate situation Planet Earth is going through. He wants to share his experience and points of view for others to learn and benefit from the way he perceives this world and its progressive changes. As an author, he does not try to change people's views. Backed by real life experience and scientific evidence, his main goal is to create awareness of the real situation our societies and surroundings are going through. It is up to the readers to make an informed decision and act wisely. Always motivated by trust and hard work, the author hopes his readers see their reality in a different light, and perhaps, motivate them to protect their society, environment, and ecosystem above and beyond the search for money and power.

Carreras does his best to experience life from a realistic, responsible, and pragmatic perspective. This trilogy has been written with a down-to-earth and rational approach for anyone to understand and apply to improve their lifestyle if they choose to do so. All his groundwork, structure and conclusions are based on existing research platforms of well-known authors, scientists, book and magazine publications, newspapers, and the web. All this is backed by extensive travel experience and systematic evaluation. He is observant and detailed-oriented, trying always to uncover the truth, with a humble and respectful approach in spirit and to the best of his abilities.

INDEX

www.ingramcontent.com/pod-product-compliance
Lightning Source LLC
Chambersburg PA
CBHW061956280526
45787CB00005B/1890